D1474566

spanish
conversation
DeMYSTiFieD

Demystified Series

Accounting Demystified
Advanced Calculus Demystified
Advanced Physics Demystified
Advanced Statistics Demystified
Algebra Demystified
Alternative Energy Demystified
American Sign Language Demystified
Anatomy Demystified
Astronomy Demystified
Audio Demystified
Biochemistry Demystified
Biology Demystified
Biotechnology Demystified
Business Calculus Demystified
Business Math Demystified
Business Statistics Demystified
C++ Demystified
Calculus Demystified
Chemistry Demystified
Circuit Analysis Demystified
College Algebra Demystified
Corporate Finance Demystified
Databases Demystified
Diabetes Demystified
Differential Equations Demystified
Digital Electronics Demystified
Earth Science Demystified
Electricity Demystified
Electronics Demystified
Engineering Statistics Demystified
English Grammar Demystified
Environmental Science Demystified
Everyday Math Demystified

Fertility Demystified
Financial Planning Demystified
Forensics Demystified
French Demystified
Genetics Demystified
Geometry Demystified
German Demystified
German Conversation Demystified
Global Warming and Climate Change Demystified
Hedge Funds Demystified
Investing Demystified
Italian Demystified
Java Demystified
JavaScript Demystified
Lean Six Sigma Demystified
Linear Algebra Demystified
Macroeconomics Demystified
Management Accounting Demystified
Math Proofs Demystified
Math Word Problems Demystified
MATLAB ® Demystified
Medical Billing and Coding Demystified
Medical-Surgical Nursing Demystified
Medical Terminology Demystified
Meteorology Demystified
Microbiology Demystified
Microeconomics Demystified
Nanotechnology Demystified
Nurse Management Demystified
OOP Demystified

Options Demystified
Organic Chemistry Demystified
Pharmacology Demystified
Physics Demystified
Physiology Demystified
Pre-Algebra Demystified
Precalculus Demystified
Probability Demystified
Project Management Demystified
Psychology Demystified
Public Speaking and Presentations Demystified
Quantum Field Theory Demystified
Quantum Mechanics Demystified
Real Estate Math Demystified
Relativity Demystified
Robotics Demystified
Sales Management Demystified
Signals and Systems Demystified
Six Sigma Demystified
Spanish Demystified
Spanish Conversation Demystified
sql Demystified
Statics and Dynamics Demystified
Statistics Demystified
Technical Analysis Demystified
Technical Math Demystified
Trigonometry Demystified
Vitamins and Minerals Demystified

spanish conversation
DeMYSTiFieD

Jenny Petrow and Saskia Gorospe Rombouts

New York Chicago San Francisco Lisbon London Madrid Mexico City
Milan New Delhi San Juan Seoul Singapore Sydney Toronto

The McGraw·Hill Companies

Copyright © 2010 by The McGraw-Hill Companies, Inc. All rights reserved. Printed in the United States of America. Except as permitted under the United States Copyright Act of 1976, no part of this publication may be reproduced or distributed in any form or by any means, or stored in a database or retrieval system, without the prior written permission of the publisher.

1   2   3   4   5   6   7   8   9   10 11 12 13 14 15 16 17 18   WFR/WFR   0   9

ISBN 978-0-07-162707-8 (book and CD)
MHID   0-07-162707-3 (book and CD)

ISBN 978-0-07-162704-7 (book alone)
MHID   0-07-162704-9 (book alone)

Library of Congress Control Number 2009925527

McGraw-Hill books are available at special quantity discounts to use as premiums and sales promotions or for use in corporate training programs. To contact a representative, please e-mail us at bulksales@mcgraw-hill.com.

CONTENTS

Acknowledgments   vii
Introduction   ix

PART ONE   **BASIC COMMUNICATION SKILLS**

CHAPTER 1   **Introduction to the Spanish Language**   **3**
The Spanish You Know   4
Pronouncing and Spelling Spanish   9
Spanish Grammar Basics   17
QUIZ   26

CHAPTER 2   **Meeting People**   **29**
Making Friends   29
Introducing People   35
Making Small Talk   40
QUIZ   46

CHAPTER 3   **Talking About Who Is Who**   **49**
Describing People   50
Talking About Different People   60
QUIZ   69

CHAPTER 4   **Getting Around Town**   **71**
Asking for Assistance   72
Asking for and Giving Directions   83
QUIZ   93

CHAPTER 5   **Daily Life**   **95**
             Talking About Time and Date   95
             Navigating a Schedule   104
             QUIZ   115

PART TWO **INTERMEDIATE COMMUNICATION SKILLS**

CHAPTER 6   **Talking About People**   **119**
             Talking About Occupations   119
             Gossiping   128
             QUIZ   137

CHAPTER 7   **Getting in Touch with People**   **139**
             Gathering Information   140
             Asking People to Do Things   151
             QUIZ   157

CHAPTER 8   **Planning a Trip**   **159**
             Asking for and Giving Advice   159
             Making Future Plans   166
             QUIZ   175

CHAPTER 9   **Arriving in a New Country**   **179**
             Sharing Experiences   180
             Asking and Offering Politely   191
             QUIZ   202

CHAPTER 10   **Out on the Town**   **205**
             Talking About the Past   205
             Talking the Talk   214
             QUIZ   221

             FINAL EXAM   223
             Answer Key   237
             Index   255

ACKNOWLEDGMENTS

This book is dedicated to all of my Spanish teachers, both official and unofficial. You opened me up to new worlds. Special thanks to Douglas Morgenstern, who showed me that learning a language didn't have to be a chore. And to Adam: thank you for your loving support.

—*Jenny Petrow*

Este libro está dedicado a todas las personas que emprenden la aventura de aprender un idioma nuevo, y en especial a mi cuñada, Angela Heller, que hasta viaja con su libro de español *Spanish Demystified*. También está dedicado a mi hijo Itxaso, que pronto le enseñará más español a su tía, y a Darryl, por apoyarme en todo sin condiciones.

—*Saskia Gorospe Rombouts*

INTRODUCTION

Welcome to *Spanish Conversation Demystified*. If you've picked up this book, you may have already read *Spanish Demystified* and want to hone your Spanish conversation skills. Or maybe you are looking to complement a Spanish class you're taking or planning a trip to a Spanish-speaking country. Whatever your final objective, *Spanish Conversation Demystified* will help you feel comfortable speaking and understanding Spanish.

One of the hardest aspects of learning a new language is producing it. Passive language skills, like listening and reading, are sometimes less intimidating than active skills, like speaking and writing. Often, language learners find speaking to be one of the biggest challenges, as they rarely have the opportunity to practice with native speakers, they feel shy about using the language, or they are not pushed to produce language in the classroom. Many students of Spanish can go through an entire beginner class without being able to utter a complete sentence. In *Spanish Conversation Demystified*, we have written a book that is entertaining, interactive, and designed to make you talk—the next best thing to language immersion.

How to Use This Book

Spanish Conversation Demystified presents a straightforward approach to Spanish conversation, providing clear explanations of new material, a variety of examples to illustrate that material, and copious opportunities to practice what you learn. It focuses primarily on speaking skills, such as *asking politely*, or *giving directions*, and supplements these skills with grammar explanations and vocabulary. The *Grammar Demystified*, *Vocabulary Demystified*, and *Culture Demystified* boxes will give you extra insight into Spanish language and Latin American and Spanish culture.

This book tries to present something that in actuality may not exist: "standard" Latin American Spanish. Spoken in over twenty countries and across four continents, Spanish has an endless number of variations. We've done our best to introduce language that will be widely understood, and to point out when it may not be. In addition, we have noted some important aspects of Iberian Spanish, and have presented the Spanish *vosotros* form for all verbs, although you will not be "tested" on it.

Spanish Conversation Demystified is sequential, following a loose narrative from beginning to end. So it makes sense to start with Chapter 1 and work your way through. Of course, if you want to focus on specific skills, use the table of contents to help you find the language you'd like to practice, and concentrate on those sections. Keep in mind, however, that the book recycles learned language as it goes along; so if you jump right in to a later chapter it may have concepts you haven't yet learned.

Spanish Conversation Demystified is divided into two parts of five chapters each, for a total of ten chapters. With the exception of the first two, each chapter is divided into two sections. Each section is introduced with a conversation, which presents new language and offers an opportunity to practice your listening skills while hearing native speakers interact. The conversations follow a few months in the life of Pablo Torres, a young man from a Puerto Rican family living in the United States, as you meet his friends, family, and acquaintances.

There are written and oral exercises throughout. Most oral exercises have audio tracks that refer to tracks on the companion CDs. They test speaking as well as listening skills, and may ask you to: listen to a question and speak the answers, listen to and fill in a conversation as you listen, listen to short dialogues and answer comprehension questions, form sentences with new language, or translate from English to Spanish. Some oral exercises do not have audio tracks, but you are expected you to speak your answers out loud. Even though written exercises do not have audio, we encourage you to speak the answers to your written practice out loud as much as possible. Language from audio tracks that does not appear on the page can be found in the answer key in the back of the book.

Each chapter ends with a Chapter Practice section, which tests your comprehension by bringing together everything you learned in the chapter in short audio passages. After each Chapter Practice, a ten-question Quiz reviews the concepts you learned in that chapter. This quiz is *open-book*, but does not include English translations of the questions. You should try to achieve a score of eighty percent on the quiz before moving on to the next chapter.

Each part features a bonus online twenty-five-question test, found on the McGraw-Hill website at http://mhprofessional.com/product.php?isbn=0071627073. The tests cover everything from the previous part, but will also build on knowledge you have learned up to that point. These are *closed-book* tests, and you should try to get seventy-five percent of the questions correct before moving on to the next part. The book ends with a Final Exam. The Final Exam consists of one hundred questions and covers everything you learned in the book. It is a *closed-book* test. A good score is seventy-five percent or higher on the final exam.

These quizzes and tests are meant to help you evaluate your progress and manage your own learning. You will find the answers to the quizzes and tests in the answer key in the back of the book.

Audio passages appear primarily in the opening dialogues and oral practice exercises, and they present new language when appropriate, especially in sections where pronunciation is key. One audio track may present a number of items in an exercise, or a number of examples in a chapter. Pause between each excerpt to answer the questions, repeat the phrases, or do whatever else the directions ask of you. For instance:

 TRACK 15

For each name and time of day indicated below, say hello to that person with the appropriate greeting for the time of day. Listen to check your answers.

1. 9:00 A.M./Susana
2. 10:00 P.M./Pablo
3. 2:30 P.M./Sr. Moreno

In the above example, you would: a) say your answer out loud for question 1, b) press "play" on the CD, c) listen to the correct answer, d) press "pause," e) move on to question 2, and so on. We urge you to repeat the language on the CD after hearing each correct answer in order to fix your pronunciation and speak even more!

In the explanatory text, Spanish words are represented in **bold**. English translations appear in *italics*. For example:

Finally, **buenas noches** can also be used to bid *good night*.

In tables and examples, Spanish words appear in Roman print and English words in italics. For example:

Me llamo Julián Torres.	*My name is Julián Torres.*
¿Y tú? ¿Cómo te llamas?	*And you? What's your name?*

And:

el banco	*bank*	la calle	*street*
el baño	*restroom*	la plaza	*square*
el barrio	*neighborhood*	la tienda	*store*

To get the most out of this book, try to work with it two to three times a week. Any less than two hours per week and you probably won't remember what you learned the week before. When you're not studying, sing along with Spanish music to practice your pronunciation, or listen to Spanish radio while you're in the shower. Even if you don't understand the majority of what you hear, being able to pick out words and phrases is pretty rewarding, and before long you'll be able to carry on a conversation without even thinking about it. Good luck and enjoy!

PART ONE

BASIC COMMUNICATION SKILLS

CHAPTER 1

Introduction to the Spanish Language

In this chapter you will learn:

Basic phrases to get started
Borrowed words and cognates
Spanish spelling and alphabet
Pronunciation basics
Spanish grammar basics

The Spanish You Know

Throughout this book you will run into Pablo Torres. Pablo is of Puerto Rican descent, but was born in the United States. Although he speaks Spanish, he is always eager to learn more. You will hear from Pablo as he uses his Spanish in a variety of situations.

Listen to the following dialogue between Pablo and his friend Sandra, who is from Colombia. What does Pablo want to know?

 TRACK 1

PABLO: Sandra ¿cómo se dice «parcha» en Colombia?	*Sandra, how do you say "parcha" in Colombia?*
SANDRA: ¿«Parcha»? ¿Qué es «parcha»?	*"Parcha"? What's "parcha"?*
PABLO: Es una fruta. ¿Fruta de la pasión?	*It's a fruit . . . Passion fruit?*
SANDRA: Ah, sí. Se dice «maracuyá».	*Oh, yeah. You say "maracuyá."*
PABLO: ¿«Maracuyá»? ¿Y cómo se escribe?	*"Maracuyá"? And how do you spell it?*
SANDRA: Se escribe «m-a-r-a-c-u-y-á» con tilde en la «a».	*You spell it "m-a-r-a-c-u-y-á" with an accent on the "a."*
PABLO: Ah bien. Gracias.	*Oh, O.K. Thanks.*

Pablo asks Sandra how to say **parcha**, or *passion fruit*, in Colombia. The direct translation is **fruta de la pasión**. Easy, right? However, in Puerto Rico, passion fruit is **parcha**. In Colombia, it's **maracuyá**. In the Dominican Republic, it's **chinola**, and in Venezuela, it's **parchita**. You probably get the picture. Spanish is a varied and rich language that can change if you get in the car and drive an hour away. This book will try to teach the most "common" or "acceptable" usage, but be aware that as you start speaking to friends and acquaintances, or travel in Latin America and Spain, you will begin to hear many variations.

This book focuses on speaking and understanding Spanish. If this is your first introduction to Spanish, chances are you probably already have a few vocabulary words under your belt, as well as a basic idea of Spanish pronunciation. Spanish is the primary language spoken in about twenty countries and Puerto Rico and is commonly used in many more. It has become a second *lingua franca* in the United States and has crept into many aspects of U.S. culture. Although some people complain about having to "press one" for English, students of Spanish now have a multitude of opportunities to learn Spanish in their own backyard. Increased migration, globalization, and the Internet also give us access to Spanish language media, music, sports, arts, and Latin American and Spanish culture from around the world. Watching Spanish language TV and listening to Spanish language radio will get your ear accustomed to the sounds of Spanish and can improve your pronunciation and comprehension.

All this exposure means you probably know more Spanish than you think you do. This chapter will review words that English borrows from Spanish as well as cognates that are similar in Spanish and English.

BASIC PHRASES TO GET STARTED

Before we dive into the Spanish you know, here are some basic phrases you can use when conversing in Spanish. This book is about speaking and understanding Spanish, which means you'll have to have some tools on hand for when you start conversing with native Spanish speakers and don't quite understand everything. Listen and repeat the following helpful phrases:

 TRACK 2

To ask how to say something in Spanish, say: **¿Cómo se dice** (word) **en español?**

¿Cómo se dice «thank you» en español?	*How do you say "thank you" in Spanish?*
Se dice «gracias».	*You say "gracias."*

To ask what something means, say: **¿Qué quiere decir** (*word*)**?**

¿Qué quiere decir «nieta»?	*What does "nieta" mean? (It means "granddaughter.")*

To ask someone to speak more slowly, say: **Hable más despacio, por favor.**

Hable más despacio, por favor.	*Speak more slowly, please.*

To ask someone to repeat a word or phrase, say: **¿Puede repetirlo, por favor?**

¿Puede repetirlo, por favor?	*Can you repeat it, please?*

To ask how to write or spell a word or phrase, say: **¿Cómo se escribe** (*word*)**?**

¿Cómo se escribe «nieta»?　　　　*How do you write "nieta"?*

Se escribe n-i-e-t-a.　　　　　　*You write it n-i-e-t-a.*

To ask how to pronounce a word in Spanish, say: **¿Cómo se pronuncia esta palabra?**

¿Cómo se pronuncia esta palabra?　*How do you pronounce this word?*

Se pronuncia «nieta».　　　　　　*You pronounce it "nieta."*

Written Practice 1-1

Read the following questions, and circle the statement that best describes each one.

1. ¿Cómo se dice «thanks» en español?

   The speaker wants to know how to _____ a word in Spanish.

   (a) say

   (b) pronounce

   (c) write

2. ¿Qué quiere decir «nada»?

   The speaker wants to know the _____ of a word in Spanish.

   (a) spelling

   (b) pronunciation

   (c) meaning

3. ¿Cómo se escribe «Enrique» en español?

   The speaker wants to know how to _____ a word in Spanish.

   (a) say

   (b) pronounce

   (c) write

4. ¿Cómo se pronuncia esta palabra?

The speaker wants to know the ＿＿＿＿＿＿＿ of a word in Spanish.
   (a) spelling
   (b) pronunciation
   (c) meaning

5. ¿Cómo se dice «end» en español?

The speaker wants to know how to ＿＿＿＿＿＿＿ a word in Spanish.
   (a) say
   (b) pronounce
   (c) write

BORROWED WORDS

English already uses a variety of Spanish words. You've probably ordered **tacos** and **tortillas**, or eaten **cilantro**, listened to **salsa** or **merengue,** or maybe you've petted a **Chihuahua** or an **iguana**. If you've traveled to **San Diego** or **Colorado**, then you've spoken Spanish just by saying those place names. Finally, if you've taken a **siesta**, sipped **sangría** or whacked a **piñata**, then you're already putting your Spanish to use.

English also has a variety of words that have their roots in Spanish, but which have been slightly changed as they have become anglicized. For instance, the English word *canyon* comes from the Spanish **cañón**; *hammock* comes from **hamaca**, and *ranch* comes from **rancho**.

In the United States, especially the Southwest and California, many place names come from Spanish. For instance, towns and cities that begin with **San** or **Santa** (*saint*) such as **Santa Barbara** and **San Luis Obispo**; places that begin with **El, La, Las,** or **Los** (the four forms of *the*), like **Los Angeles** (*the Angels*), **Las Vegas** (*the meadows*), and **El Paso** (*the passage*), and geographic features, like **arroyos** and **mesas** (literally: *tables*) come from Spanish.

COGNATES

Spanish and English share a number of cognates, or words with the same linguistic root. Cognates are similar in spelling and meaning and therefore are easy to figure out. Some cognates in English and Spanish are exactly the same, while others are so similar they're unmistakable. You should be able to tell the meaning of a cognate just by looking at it. Here are some examples of cognates. Can you guess what they mean?

Adjectives	Nouns	Verbs
arrogante	el accidente	admirar
especial	el actor	adoptar
flexible	el adulto	calcular
horrible	el chocolate	celebrar
ideal	la computadora	continuar
importante	el doctor	decidir
interesante	el error	describir
liberal	el honor	evacuar
natural	la idea	facilitar
normal	el mapa	imaginar
popular	la persona	limitar
radical	el presidente	organizar
sensual	la radio	usar
terrible	el restaurante	utilizar

THE SPANISH YOU THINK YOU KNOW . . . BUT MAY NOT

Much to their embarrassment, many English speakers have learned the hard way about false cognates. False cognates are words that are written similarly in English and in Spanish but do not share a similar meaning. One of the most famous in Spanish is the word **embarazada**. It does not mean *embarrassed,* but rather *pregnant.* Here are some false cognates to be aware of:

Spanish Word	Meaning
actual	*current*
asistir	*to attend*
la carpeta	*folder (for documents)*
comer	*to eat*
el compromiso	*commitment*
constipado	*congested (as in having a head cold)*
la librería	*bookstore*
sensible	*sensitive*

The English Influence on Spanish

You've already learned how much the Spanish language influences the English spoken in the United States. English also influences Spanish, especially that spoken by immigrants and their children living in the U.S. Because of the prevalence of *Spanglish* you may hear some of the false cognates above used as their cognate "alter egos." For instance, in the U.S., Spanish speakers may use **carpeta** to say *carpet* instead of *folder*, or **groserías** to say *groceries* instead of *swear words*. Furthermore, some Spanish speakers actually invent Spanish words from English ones, especially if a simple Spanish equivalent doesn't exist, such as, **vacumear** to say *to vacuum* (the traditional expression is **pasar la aspiradora**). So don't be surprised if you hear someone talking about **vacumear la carpeta**. You'll know they're probably not vacuuming their files!

Pronouncing and Spelling Spanish

At work, Pablo meets Señor Aitor Unzueta, a colleague visiting from Spain. Pablo asks him how to pronounce his name. Listen carefully to catch the pronunciation of the **z**.

TRACK 3

PABLO: Hola, soy Pablo Torres.   *Hi, I'm Pablo Torres.*

SR. UNZUETA: Hola, soy Aitor Unzueta.   *Hi, I'm Aitor Unzueta.*

PABLO: ¿Perdón? ¿Cómo se pronuncia su apellido?   *Excuse me? How do you pronounce your last name?*

SR. UNZUETA: (*Slowly*) Unzueta. En España la zeta la pronunciamos «z».   *In Spain we pronounce the zeta as "z."*

PABLO: ¿Y cómo se escribe?   *And how do you write/spell it?*

SR. UNZUETA: Se escribe «u-n-z-u-e-t-a».   *You write/spell it "u-n-z-u-e-t-a."*

When Mr. Unzueta spells his name, he tells Pablo how the letter **z** is pronounced in Spain.

Spanish pronunciation is relatively easy. Unlike English, Spanish sounds as it is written and is written as it sounds. New learners may get tripped up by the different pronunciation of Spanish letters like the **j** or the **g**, the silent **h**, the rolled **r** or the **ñ**, but once you learn the rules, sounding out Spanish words is **facilísimo** (*a piece of cake*)! If you do get stuck remember you can always ask, **¿Cómo se pronuncia?** as Pablo did.

SPELLING AND THE ALPHABET

Below you will find the most complete form of the Spanish alphabet. In older dictionaries, **ch** and **ll** are treated as distinct letters, but these have been integrated alphabetically into modern dictionaries. Although **w** and **k** are often not considered true Spanish letters they are often used to refer to foreign words or words "borrowed" from other languages, so they have been included in this list.

Listen to the letters of the alphabet and repeat each letter after you hear it. Keep listening and repeating until you can say the alphabet all the way through.

🔘 TRACK 4

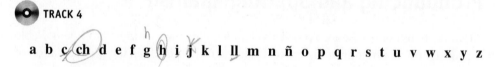

a b c ch d e f g h i j k l ll m n ñ o p q r s t u v w x y z

When spelling in Spanish, **ll** (**elle**) is used as a letter. For instance, to spell **llave** (*key*) you would say **ll-a-v-e**. However, **c** and **h** of **ch** are used separately. To spell **parcha** you would say **p-a-r-c-h-a**. When the letter **r** is doubled, which occurs often in Spanish, it is often "spelled" as **doble r** (**doble erre**) (*double r*). Finally, when a letter has an accent mark on it (´), you should say **con tilde**, as the first dialogue in this chapter shows. For example, **é** would be **e con tilde** or **con tilde en la e**.

Oral Practice 1-1

🔘 TRACK 5

Listen to the question, and pause the recording. Then reply to the question by spelling the word the speaker asks about. Hit play again to listen to the correct answer. Repeat the process for each question.

PRONUNCIATION DEMYSTIFIED

Regional Variations in Pronunciation

You may have heard it said that people in Spain speak differently from those in Latin America. You saw this when Sr. Unzueta spelled his name in the short dialogue. The truth is, Spanish pronunciation and usage varies widely not only by country, but by regions of the same country, states, provinces, even neighborhoods. One thing that makes Castilian (Spanish from Spain) pronunciation unique is the sound that most Spaniards (but not all!) give to the **z** or **zeta**. In most of Spain (with the exception of some Southern provinces), the **zeta (z)** sounds like the hard *th* sound in English. The "soft" **c** (when followed by **i** or **e**) also takes the hard *th* sound, while **s** always sounds like **s**. The sound of the **y** or **ll** may vary as well. In Argentina and Uruguay these letters sound more like the English *sh* than they do the *y*. Finally, if you travel to the Caribbean, to places such as the Dominican Republic, Cuba, or the Colombian and Venezuelan coasts, you may find that people are not pronouncing many letters at all! Both Caribbean people and natives of Southern Spain and the Canary Islands are famous for **comerse las eses** (*eating their esses*), leaving the **s** sound off in the middle and end of words.

1. ¿Cómo se escribe «girasol»?
2. ¿Cómo se escribe «otoño»?
3. ¿Cómo se escribe «lluvia»?
4. ¿Cómo se escribe «chancleta»?
5. ¿Cómo se escribe «Hernández»?
6. ¿Cómo se escribe «terremoto»?

PRONUNCIATION NOTES

Now that you have learned the letters, you will learn how to pronounce them in words. Here are some special tips to help you master Spanish pronunciation. Listen to each set of examples and repeat them.

TRACK 6

- Vowels: The key to pronouncing Spanish well and not sounding like a **gringo** is to get the vowels right. There are only five sounds and they are almost always consistent in their pronunciation.

A	E	I	O	U
Amanda	elefante	iris	otoño	Úrsula

- The letters **b** and **v** are both pronounced similarly to the English *b*. They have a harder sound at the beginning of a word or after **m** or **n** and a softer sound in the middle of a word. Note that the sounds of **v** and **b** are almost indistinguishable.

Hard:	vida	varón	boca	tumba
Soft:	saber	nube	ave	cava

- The letter **c** has a hard sound (*k*) and a soft sound (*s*) (that follow the same rules as in English). The soft **c** occurs before the vowels **e** and **i**. The hard **c** occurs everywhere else.

Hard:	campo	clave	vacuna	marco
Soft:	cero	circo	acera	enlace

- The letter **g** has a soft sound and a hard sound. The soft **g** occurs before the vowels **e** and **i** and is similar to the English *h*. The hard **g** occurs everywhere else.

Hard:	gota	grado	lago	algo
Soft:	gira	gel	agente	ágil

- The groupings **gue** and **gui**, as well as **que** and **qui**, have a hard sound and a silent **u**.

guerra	queso	guía	Quito

- The exception to the silent **u** in **gue** and **gui** occurs if the **u** has an umlaut (¨) over it. In this case, the **ü** and the following vowel are both pronounced, creating a diphthong. (See more on diphthongs in the next section.)

  vergüenza   pingüino   bilingüe   Argüelles

- The letter **d** also has soft and hard variations. At the beginning of a word or after an **n** or **l** it is like in English.

  Harder **d**:   dormir   tilde   andar

  When it falls between vowels or at the end of a word, the sound is much softer, similar to the *th* in the English word *then,* and said with the tongue between the teeth.

  Softer **d**:   Madrid   nada   adoro

- The Spanish letter **h** is always silent.

  hola   ahora   hielo   huracán

- The Spanish **j** sounds like a throaty *h*, similar to the soft **g** sound. The pronunciation of **j** is the same no matter where it is in a word.

  jugo   joven   ajo   reloj

- The **ll** is like a cross between the English *y* and *j*; however you can get away with pronouncing it like a *y*.

  calle   llave   llorar   millón

- The **ñ** is a letter particular to Spanish and sounds like *ny*.

  año   leña   mañana   ñame

- The letter **qu** combination sounds like *k* and is always followed by *e* or *i*.

  qué   alquiler   pequeño   quinto

- The *qu* sound you are familiar with in English is made by **cu** in Spanish.

  cuando   cual   cualificación   cuota

- The **r** is rolled strongly at the beginning of a word; after the letters **l**, **n**, or **s**; or when it is **rr**.

  rojo   enredo   perro   arriba

  When it appears alone in the middle or end of a word, **r** is only slightly rolled, with a single turn of the tongue. To the English speaker, this may sound closer to the *d* in *ladder* than to the English *r* sound.

  pero   amor   mira   tener

- In Latin America, **s** and **z** are always pronounced like the hard *s* in English.

  casa   caza   sol   zapato   diez

- The letter **x** generally sounds like the *ks* sound in English.

  examen   exacto   excusa   excelente

- The letter **y** can behave like a vowel in diphthongs (see diphthongs below) or like a consonant. Here are some examples of **y** used as a consonant. It's similar to the English *y*.

  yo   ayer   yerno   rayo

DIPHTHONGS

When two vowels appear in a row, like **ea** or **ie**, but are pronounced as one syllable, it is called a diphthong. In a diphthong the two vowels retain their individual sounds but are elided into one syllable. Understanding diphthongs can also help you understand Spanish word stress.

Diphthongs are composed of one weak vowel (**i**, **u**, and sometimes **y**) and one strong vowel (**a**, **e**, or **o**). In diphthongs, the stress falls on the strong vowel, except when two weak vowels occur together, in which case it falls on the second vowel. Listen and repeat these examples:

TRACK 7

bueno   **ai**re   **hoy**   **pau**sa   a**gua**   vi**u**da

Sometimes you will see two strong vowels together. In this case, the stress is placed on the first vowel. These combinations are not considered diphthongs, but rather separate syllables.

feo   tarea   faena   aorta   mareo

Did you notice how **feo** has two syllables (**fe-o**) and **hoy** has only one? That is because **oy** is a diphthong but **eo** is not.

Oral Practice 1-2

TRACK 8

Say each name out loud and then spell it. Then listen to each answer to correct yourself. Repeat what you hear.

1. Juan
2. Marta
3. Laura
4. Pablo
5. Jorge
6. Gilda

7. Roberto
8. Mercedes
9. Señor Herrero
10. Señora Castillo
11. Mauro
12. Leo

WORD STRESS

Word stress is the emphasis given to a certain syllable within a word. For instance, in English, *Spanish* is a two-syllable word with the stress on the first syllable: *SPA-nish*. Word stress in Spanish follows a clear set of rules, which will help you when speaking and reading. Here are the three basic guidelines for word stress. Listen to and repeat the audio examples.

TRACK 9

1. If the word ends in a vowel, **n**, or **s**, the stress is on the *second-to-last* syllable. Most Spanish words fall into this category.

   siesta   ca**mi**nan   doc**to**res   **ca**sa

2. For words that end in a consonant other than **n** or **s,** the stress is on the *last syllable*.

   doc**tor**   fi**nal**   mi**tad**   re**loj**   efi**caz**

3. An accent mark is placed over any stressed syllable that does not follow rules 1 and 2.

   águila   ale**grí**a   **mé**dico   fran**cés**   rea**cción**

Note that foreign words usually do not carry accent marks and may defy the rules above.

It's important to remember your diphthongs when applying pronunciation rules because diphthongs count as one syllable, but may look like two. Listen to the stress for the following words, which all have diphthongs:

farma**cia**   inter**med**io   **rei**na   **hie**rro

When you see an accent mark over a weak vowel, however, that vowel is stressed as a separate syllable:

lote**rí**a   **dí**a   ale**grí**a

Sometimes accents are used not to mark word stress, but rather to distinguish the meanings of words that are spelled identically and sound the same, but have different meanings:

el	*the*		él	*he*
que	*that*		qué	*what*
si	*if*		sí	*yes*
tu	*your*		tú	*you*

Spanish Grammar Basics

 TRACK 10

Pablo talks to his friend Amanda who is learning Spanish. The articles are driving her a little crazy, so she asks Pablo about them.

AMANDA: Pablo, ¿cómo es, «el» accidente o «la» accidente?

Pablo, what is it, "el" accidente or "la" accidente?

PABLO: Es *el* accidente. Con «el».

It's "el" accidente. With "el."

AMANDA: ¿Y cómo es, «el» víctima o «la» víctima?

And what is it, "el" víctima or "la" víctima?

PABLO: Es complicado… En un accidente, es «la» víctima para hombre o mujer.

It's complicated. In an accident, it's "la" víctima, whether it is a man or a woman.

AMANDA: ¡Ay, sí! Los artículos son bastante complicados, por eso en *Spanish Conversation Demystified* vienen los artículos con cada nombre.

Oh, yeah! The articles are pretty complicated, that's why in Spanish Conversation Demystified *each noun comes with the article.*

GENDER AND NUMBER

All Spanish nouns and adjectives have a gender—either masculine or feminine. Gender is easiest to understand when words refer to people. Generally, when talking about women and girls, a noun is feminine; when talking about men and boys it is masculine. Objects (things) are another story, however. Certain spelling rules can help you guess which words are masculine and which are feminine, but of course there are always exceptions. For instance, in the above dialogue, Amanda gets confused because the word **víctima** (*victim*) doesn't follow any of the rules she's learned.

Why is it important to know the gender of a noun, you may ask? Well, if you know a noun's gender, you will also know which form of the article or adjective to use. This is called agreement.

Many nouns describing people end in **-o** for masculine and **-a** for feminine:

Masculine		Feminine	
el hermano	*brother*	la hermana	*sister*
el hijo	*son*	la hija	*daughter*

For others you add an **-a** to make the masculine form feminine:

Masculine		Feminine	
el director	*male director*	la directora	*female director*
el profesor	*male teacher*	la profesora	*female teacher*

For some nouns, only the article changes depending on whether you're talking about a man or a woman (you will learn more about articles below):

el estudiante	*male student*	la estudiante	*female student*
el periodista	*male journalist*	la periodista	*female journalist*

And, as always, there are exceptions:

el actor	*actor*	la actriz	*actress*
el hombre	*man*	la mujer	*woman*

Nouns referring to things are not as easy to learn and must be memorized. However, as with people, many nouns ending in **-o** are masculine, and many nouns ending in **-a** are feminine:

la casa	*house*	la silla	*chair*
la mesa	*table*	el teléfono	*telephone*
el plato	*plate*	el vaso	*cup*
la puerta	*door*	el zapato	*shoe*

Of course, there are some exceptions to the **-o/-a** rule. Some common ones are: **la mano** (*hand*), **el tema** (*theme*), **el día** (*day*), and **el mapa** (*map*).

Certain suffixes let you know a word is (probably) feminine. It's easier to remember these if you put them into groups:

-tad, **-dad**, **-tud** (la mitad, *half*; la ciudad, *city*; la gratitud, *gratitude*)

-sión, **-ción**, **-gión** (la televisión; la nación; la religión)

-ez (la validez, *validity*; la vejez, *old age*)

-umbre (la costumbre, *habit*; la incertidumbre, *uncertainty*)

When in doubt, you can always do what Amanda did and ask someone **¿Cómo es, «el... » o «la... »?**

¿Cómo es, «el» o «la» decisión?	*What is it, "el" or "la" decisión?*
¿Cómo es, «el» teléfono o «la» teléfono?	*What is it, "el" or "la" teléfono?*

PLURAL FORMS OF NOUNS

When talking about more than one of something, use the plural form of the noun. Usually this means adding an **-s** if the word ends in a vowel (**a**, **e**, **o**, or **u**), or **-es** if the word ends in a consonant (including **y**). Note that when you're speaking, adding **-es** also adds another syllable.

hija → hija**s**	zapato → zapato**s**
actor → actor**es**	mujer → mujer**es**

There are some exceptions. For nouns ending in **-z**, the plural is made by changing the **z** to a **c** and then adding **-es**. For nouns ending in vowels with a **tilde** (accent mark) on the final vowel, **-es** is added. Note also that when you make **-ión** words plural, you leave off the tilde, and **ó** becomes **o**.

vez → ve**ces**	*time(s)*
colibrí → colibrí**es**	*hummingbird(s)*
intención → inten**ciones**	*intention(s)*

While these rules will help guide you, they are not foolproof. Practice, memorization, and a good dictionary are your best friends when learning the gender of nouns! You should also know how to ask clarifying questions, such as: **¿Cuál es el plural de... ?**

¿Cuál es el plural de «el error»?	*What is the plural of "el error"?*

ARTICLES

Articles are used before a noun to say *a*, *the*, or *some*. Articles in Spanish should match a noun's gender (masculine or feminine), number (singular or plural), and determine if the noun is specific (definite *the*) or general (indefinite *a*).

The definite articles are **el**, **la**, **los**, and **las**. **La** is used before feminine nouns and **el** before masculine nouns to say *the*. **Las** is used before plural feminine nouns and **los** before plural masculine nouns to say *the*.

Definite Articles

	Masculine	Feminine
Singular	el	la
Plural	los	las

For example:

el actor, los actores	*the actor, the actors*
la hija, las hijas	*the daughter, the daughters*

The indefinite articles are **un**, **una**, **unos**, and **unas**. **Un** is used before masculine nouns and **una** before feminine nouns to say *a*. **Unos** is used before plural masculine nouns and **unas** before plural feminine nouns to say *some*.

Indefinite Articles

	Masculine	Feminine
Singular	un	una
Plural	unos	unas

For example:

un restaurante, unos restaurantes	*a restaurant, some restaurants*
una idea, unas ideas	*an idea, some ideas*

Written Practice 1-2

Write the correct definite article before each word: **el**, **la**, **los**, or **las**.

1. _____ vacación (*vacation*)
2. _____ vaca (*cow*)

3. _____ perros (*dogs*)

4. _____ dedo (*finger*)

5. _____ mesas (*tables*)

6. _____ profesor (*teacher*)

Write the correct indefinite article before each word: **un**, **una**, **unos**, or **unas**.

7. _____ abuelo (*grandfather*)

8. _____ novias (*girlfriends*)

9. _____ decisión (*decision*)

10. _____ ventana (*window*)

11. _____ gato (*cat*)

12. _____ mitad (*half*)

ADJECTIVES

An adjective is a word that describes a noun—for example: *happy*, *strange*, *sticky*, or *scary*. You've already learned some adjectives that are cognates in the list in this chapter, such as **normal** and **popular**.

In Spanish, an adjective has to agree with the noun it modifies. In other words, if the noun is masculine, the adjective is masculine. If the noun is plural feminine, the adjective is plural feminine. The spelling of an adjective generally changes to reflect this; it *agrees* with the noun. For example:

el niño alt**o**   *the tall boy*   la niñ**a** alt**a**   *the tall girl*

You already learned that many masculine nouns end in **-o** and many feminine nouns end in **-a**. The same is true for many adjectives. Here are some examples of masculine adjectives:

barato	*cheap*	frío	*cold*
bueno	*good*	gordo	*fat*
caro	*expensive*	malo	*bad*
flaco	*thin*	rico	*rich; tasty*

To make an **-o** adjective feminine, change the **-o** to **-a**. To make either plural, add **-s**. Here are the four forms of the adjective **malo** (*bad*):

malo   mal**a**   mal**os**   mal**as**

And here they are agreeing with a noun:

el libro malo	*the bad book*	los libros malos	*the bad books*
la película mala	*the bad film*	las películas malas	*the bad films*

As with nouns, there are plenty of adjectives that do not end in **-o** or **-a**. Luckily, the spelling of some adjectives stays the same whether the noun is masculine or feminine. Adjectives ending in **-e** or **-a** take only two forms: singular and plural. For example:

alegre	*happy*
fuerte	*strong*
idealista	*idealistic*
optimista	*optimistic*
pesimista	*pessimistic*
pobre	*poor*
realista	*realistic*
triste	*sad*
el hombre optimista	*the optimistic man*
la mujer optimista	*the optimistic woman*

To make the plural, simply add an **-s**:

alegre → alegre**s**   optimista → optimista**s**

Adjectives ending in a consonant (**l**, **n**, or **r**,) have the same spelling for masculine and feminine. To make these adjectives plural, add **-es**, or if it ends in **-z**, change the **z** to a **c** and add **-es**:

popular → popular**es**   feliz → feli**ces**

VOCABULARY DEMYSTIFIED

Cyber Spanish

In the cyber age, socially conscious Spanish speakers will often use the @ symbol when talking about mixed groups, to avoid using masculine pronouns to describe both men and women. This is because the @ symbol looks like an **a** and an **o**. For example:

Nosotr@s   Hola chic@s   Vamos tod@s

This is an exclusively written form that you will often see in e-mails and on websites and blogs.

SUBJECT PRONOUNS

When learning to speak and listen to Spanish, probably the most common topic of conversation will be people: you, your friends, the person you are talking to. Therefore it is important to quickly recognize the *subject pronouns* (*he, she, we, they, etc.*). Here are the subject pronouns in Spanish:

yo	*I*	nosotros, nosotras	*we*
tú	*you (singular, informal)*	vosotros, vosotras	*you (plural, informal)*
él	*he*	ellos	*they (masculine)*
ella	*she*	ellas	*they (feminine)*
usted	*you (singular, formal)*	ustedes	*you (plural, formal)*

Note that **nosotros** and **vosotros** have the feminine forms **nosotras** and **vosotras**. When a mixed group of men and women is the subject, the masculine form is used.

Oral Practice 1-3

 TRACK 11

Read and listen to each question. Pause and respond out loud. Then hit play again to check your answer.

1. ¿Cómo se dice «I» en español?
2. ¿Qué quiere decir «profesora» en inglés?
3. ¿Cuál es el plural de «el hijo»?
4. ¿Qué quiere decir «actores» en inglés?
5. ¿Cómo se dice «we» en español?
6. ¿Qué quiere decir «el hombre» en inglés?
7. ¿Cuál es el plural de «la mujer»?
8. ¿Cómo es, «el» o «la» mesa?
9. ¿Cómo se dice «the good movie» en español?
10. ¿Cómo es, «el» o «la» comunicación?

YOU AND *YOU* AND *YOU* IN SPANISH

Note that Spanish has numerous ways to say *you*. When you start speaking Spanish, it is important to understand the differences between these different *you* forms, because each has its own social and grammatical implications.

- Use **tú** in informal situations to address one person. **Tú** is used throughout Spain and Latin America, although it is used more often in Spain where informal usage is more accepted.

- Social customs in some Latin American countries are extremely formal, and the **usted** form is customary. You can use **usted** to address a person you want to show a degree of respect to, such as someone older than you, a boss, a taxi driver, an official, a police officer, etc. In some Latin American cultures people even use **usted** with friends and family.

- A third form, **vos**, is used widely in certain regions, including Central America, Argentina, Uruguay, Paraguay, and the Andes. In some regions it is used in addition to **tú**, and in other regions it is used instead of **tú**. Either way, **vos** is a very familiar form that should be reserved for intimate acquaintances. **Vos** will not be taught in this book, but you should be aware of its existence.

- **Ustedes**, the plural of **usted**, is most common in Latin America where it is used exclusively to address two or more people, in both formal and informal situations.

- **Vosotros** and **vosotras** are used informally to address two or more people only in Spain. You will see **vosotros/-as** occasionally in this book, but you will not hear it in recordings or be expected to use it.

VERBS

Verbs are words that describe actions, such as eating, sleeping, or thinking. There several ways that Spanish verbs differ from English verbs.

First, the infinitive (not conjugated) form of a verb in English is made up of two words, signaled by the word *to*: *to eat*, *to sleep*, *to think*, etc. The Spanish verb is one word made up of two parts: the root, or stem, and the ending. The infinitive of a verb is signaled by its ending: **-ar**, **-er**, or **-ir**. For example:

pens**ar**	*to think*
com**er**	*to eat*
dorm**ir**	*to sleep*

Second, in English we always use the subject pronouns (*I, you, she, we, they*) with a verb. In Spanish, this subject pronoun can be omitted. For example:

Como.	*I eat.*
Duerme.	*He sleeps.*
Piensan.	*They think.*

The reason the subject pronoun can be left out in Spanish is that, as you conjugate verbs in Spanish, you change the verb's ending to show: a) who is doing the action, and b) what the verb tense is. Unlike in English, which has very few conjugations and often uses auxiliary "helping verbs" to form different tenses (*he will think, they will think, we will think*), Spanish indicates the tense or mood (future, past, conditional, etc.) by changing the verb ending. Look at these examples with the verb **pensar** (*to think*) and **comer** (*to eat*):

pensar**á**	*he will think*	comer**án**	*they will eat*
pens**ó**	*he thought*	comi**ó**	*she ate*
pensar**ía**	*he would think*	comer**íamos**	*we would eat*

Now you've learned the basics of Spanish grammar, and you're ready to start communicating. But first, take this chapter quiz.

QUIZ

Circle the letter of the word or phrase that best answers each question.

1. ¿Cómo se dice «*he*» en español?
   - (a) él
   - (b) ella
   - (c) yo

2. ¿Cómo se dice «the female student» en español?
   - (a) el estudiante
   - (b) la estudiante
   - (c) los estudiantes

3. ¿Cómo se dice «the male students» en español?
   - (a) el estudiante
   - (b) las estudiantes
   - (c) los estudiantes

4. ¿Cómo se dice «an attractive woman» en español?
   - (a) las mujeres atractivas
   - (b) la mujer atractiva
   - (c) una mujer atractiva

5. ¿Cómo se dice «some good restaurants» en español?
   - (a) unos restaurantes buenos
   - (b) los restaurantes buenos
   - (c) los buenos

TRACK 12

Now listen to the recording to hear a phrase or question. What is the person saying? Press pause, and choose your answer: a, b, or c. Then go to the next question, and repeat the process.

6. (a) *Can you spell it?*

   (b) *Which is it, "el favor" or "la favor"?*

   (c) *Can you repeat it, please?*

7. (a) *How do you pronounce it?*

   (b) *Speak more slowly, please.*

   (c) *How do you say it in Spanish?*

8. (a) *What does "CD" mean?*

   (b) *How do you write "CD"?*

   (c) *Which is it, "el CD" or "la CD"?*

9. (a) *How do you spell "Eugenia"?*

   (b) *What is the plural of "Eugenia"?*

   (c) *How do you say "Eugenia" in Spanish?*

10. (a) *What does this word mean?*

    (b) *How do you pronounce this word?*

    (c) *How do you spell this word?*

CHAPTER 2

Meeting People

In this chapter you will learn:

Hellos and good-byes

How to introduce yourself and others

How to make small talk

How to ask people how they are

How to talk about your feelings

The verbs ser *and* estar

Making Friends

In the following dialogue, a woman named Susana introduces herself to Pablo at a party. Listen to the dialogue. Susana introduces a third person. Who is he? What is his name?

SUSANA: Hola, soy Susana.	*Hi, I'm Susana.*
PABLO: Hola, mucho gusto. Soy Pablo.	*Hi, pleasure to meet you. I'm Pablo.*
SUSANA: Éste es Luis.	*This is Luis.*
LUIS: Hola, soy Luis Guzmán.	*Hi, I'm Luis Guzmán.*
PABLO: Encantado.	*Pleasure to meet you.*
(Luis ve a un amigo y se va.)	*(Luis sees a friend and leaves.)*
PABLO: ¿Es tu novio?	*Is he your boyfriend?*
SUSANA: No, es mi hermano. Bueno, nos vemos.	*No, he's my brother. O.K., We'll be seeing each other.*
PABLO: Chau.	*Ciao.*
SUSANA: Adiós.	*Good-bye.*

Susana introduces her brother. His name is Luis Guzmán. If you didn't get this the first time, try listening again. Use the translations to help you.

In the next dialogue, Pablo is at work. He greets Señora Santos, who introduces him to her assistant, Señor Herrero. Listen to the dialogue. How does Pablo introduce himself?

SEÑORA SANTOS: Buenos días.	*Good morning.*
PABLO: Buenos días, Señora Santos. ¿Cómo está?	*Good morning, Ms./Mrs. Santos. How are you?*
SEÑORA SANTOS: Muy bien gracias. Éste es mi colega, el Señor Herrero.	*Very well, thank you. This is my colleague, Mr. Herrero.*
SEÑOR HERRERO: Hola, encantado.	*Hello, nice to meet you.*

PABLO: Hola, es un placer. Soy el   *Hello, pleasure to meet you. I am*
    Señor Torres.   *Mr. Torres.*

SEÑOR HERRERO: Mucho gusto   *It is a pleasure to meet you.*
    en conocerlo.

Because it is a formal situation, Pablo introduces himself as **Señor Torres**. If you didn't catch this the first time, try listening again. Use the translation to help you.

In formal situations, **Señora** (*Mrs./Ms.*) and **Señor** (*Mr.*) are often used. The abbreviation for **Señora** is **Sra.** and the abbreviation for **Señor** is **Sr.** You can use **Señorita** (**Srta.**) for young or unmarried women to say *Miss*.

In this section you will learn how to greet people, how to introduce yourself and your friends, and how to say good-bye.

SAYING HELLO AND GOOD-BYE

In the dialogues above, people used two ways of saying "hello." Listen again. Can you hear them?

They are **hola** and **buenos días**. Now look at the following list of common greetings:

Hola.	*Hi./Hello.*
Buenos días.	*Good morning.*
Buenas tardes.	*Good afternoon/evening.*
Buenas noches.	*Good evening/night.*

Spanish greetings may vary according to the time of day. You can say **hola** at any time of day to say *hello*. **Buenos días** is usually used before 12:00 noon; after 12:00 noon, **buenas tardes** is used. Both are better for formal situations than **hola**. The time of day you say **buenas noches** will vary according to the country you are in; a good rule of thumb is to use this expression when it is dark out. Finally, **buenas noches** can also be used to bid *good night* when you're taking your leave.

Oral Practice 2-1

TRACK 15

For each name and time of day indicated below, say hello to that person with the appropriate greeting for the time of day. Listen to check your answers.

1. 9:00 A.M./Susana
2. 10:00 P.M./Pablo
3. 2:30 P.M./Sr. Moreno
4. Any time of day/David

In the opening dialogue, you heard Pablo and Luis use **chau** and **adiós** to say *good-bye*. Here are some common ways to say good-bye:

Adiós.	*Good-bye.*
Chau.	*Bye./Ciao.*
Hasta luego.	*See you later. (lit.: Until later.)*
Hasta mañana.	*See you tomorrow. (lit.: Until tomorrow.)*
Hasta pronto.	*See you soon. (lit.: Until soon.)*
Hasta el lunes.	*See you Monday. (lit.: Until Monday.)*
Nos vemos.	*We'll be seeing each other.*

VOCABULARY DEMYSTIFIED

Sound Like a Native

Have you ever started a conversation and reached an awkward pause? Or been unable to get past **hola**? If you're having a conversation and need to leave, it can sound rude to suddenly say **adiós**. If you want to end the conversation and don't know how, just preface your farewell with **bueno...** (*good/O.K.*) or **pues...** (*so/well*). Listen again to the opening dialogue in this chapter. Susana does this when she says, **Bueno, nos vemos** to Pablo.

You can use **hasta** (*until*) + any day of the week to say *See you...* Note that days of the week always carry the article **el** and begin with a lower-case letter. The Spanish calendar begins on Monday.

Days of the Week

lunes	*Monday*
martes	*Tuesday*
miércoles	*Wednesday*
jueves	*Thursday*
viernes	*Friday*
sábado	*Saturday*
domingo	*Sunday*

Once you've mastered the basic expressions, try these more advanced greetings and farewells:

Qué alegría verte.	*I'm so happy to see you. (informal)*
¡Cuánto tiempo!	*It's been a long time!*
¡Hace siglos!	*Lit.: It's been centuries!*
Que pase un buen día.	*Have a nice day.*
Que te vaya bien.	*Have a nice day. (lit.: May things go well for you.) (informal)*
Que le vaya bien.	*Have a nice day. (formal)*
Cuídate.	*Take care. (informal)*

Written Practice 2-1

Choose the word or phrase that works best for each situation.

1. You meet a friend in the morning.
   (a) Buenas tardes.
   (b) Buenos días.
   (c) Buenas noches.

2. You leave a friend you will see later that day.
   (a) Hasta mañana.
   (b) Hasta el jueves.
   (c) Hasta luego.

3. You bump into an acquaintance.
   (a) Hola.
   (b) Adiós.
   (c) Chau.

4. You leave a friend you will see on Sunday.
   (a) Hasta el miércoles.
   (b) Hasta el domingo.
   (c) Hasta el sábado.

5. You say good night to your family.
   (a) Buenas tardes.
   (b) Buenas noches.
   (c) Hasta luego.

Oral Practice 2-2

 TRACK 16

Listen to four conversations in which people use the greetings and good-byes that you have just learned. Write the number of the conversation that matches each situation below. If you need to read along, you can find the text in the Answer Key in the back of the book.

a. _____ Two friends bump into each other after not having seen each other for a while.

b. _____ Two colleagues greet each other at work.

c. _____ Two good friends say good-bye to each other.

d. _____ A boss says good-bye to an employee.

Introducing People

Now that you've learned how to start and end a conversation, you will learn how to introduce yourself and others. One way of introducing yourself is to use the verb **ser** (*to be*). Look again at some examples of introductions from the opening dialogues.

Hola, soy Susana.	*Hi, I'm Susana.*
Es mi hermano.	*He's my brother.*
Soy Pablo.	*I am Pablo.*
Éste es Luis.	*That's Luis.*
Soy el Señor Torres.	*I'm Mr. Torres.*
Éste es mi colega.	*This is my colleague.*

When using **ser** to make an introduction, the subject is the person you are introducing. For example, to introduce yourself, say **yo soy** + (*your name*). To introduce a female friend, say **ella es**. To introduce yourself and another person, say **nosotros somos**, and so on.

Here are some examples of people introducing themselves and others with **ser**:

Hola. Soy Teresa y él es José.	*Hi. I'm Teresa and he is José.*

Ella no es Julia. Yo soy Julia.
    Ella es Pilar.
	She's not Julia. I am Julia.
	    She's Pilar.

In the second example, the subject is used for emphasis, to distinguish one person from another: ***Ella* no es Julia. *Yo* soy Julia.** Otherwise the subject can be omitted.

Ser

Ser (*to be*) is an irregular verb. Here is the conjugation:

yo soy	*I am*	nosotros(as) somos	*we are*
tú eres	*you are (informal)*	vosotros(as) sois	*you are (informal, Spain)*
usted es	*you are (formal)*	ustedes son	*you are (formal)*
él/ella es	*he/she/it is*	**ellos/ellas son**	*they are*

INTRODUCING PEOPLE USING *ÉSTE* AND *ÉSTA*

You have learned to introduce people using the subject pronoun (**yo**, **tú**, etc.) and
ser. You can also introduce people using the pronouns éste, ésta (*this*), éstos, éstas
(*these*) with the verb **ser**.

To introduce someone by name, simply say **éste es** + (*man's name*), **ésta es** +
(*woman's name*).

Éste es Javier.	*This is Javier.*
Ésta es Carolina.	*This is Carolina.*

To introduce two women/girls, say **éstas son** + (*names*). If you're introducing all
men/boys or a mixed group, say **éstos son** + (*names*).

Éstas son Susana y María.	*These are Susana and María.*
Éstos son José, Jorge y Carolina.	*These are José, Jorge, and Carolina.*

Here is a list of the people or pets you might meet or introduce to others:

el amigo, la amiga	*friend (male/female)*
el novio, la novia	*boyfriend, girlfriend*
el compañero, la compañera	*partner, companion (male/female)*

el esposo, la esposa	*husband, wife*
el/la colega	*colleague (male/female)*
el/la representante	*representative (male/female)*
el hermano, la hermana	*brother, sister*
el padre, la madre	*father, mother*
el perro, la perra	*dog (male/female)*
el gato, la gata	*cat (male/female)*

If you want to show your relationship to the person you are introducing, use the possessive pronoun **mi** (*my*) for one person or **mis** (*my*) for more than one person (or pet!).

Ésta es mi hermana Sonia.	*This is my sister Sonia.*
Éstas son mis gatas, Alice y Hazel.	*These are my cats, Alice and Hazel.*
Éstos son mis padres, el Dr. Martínez y la Sra. Núñez.	*These are my parents, Dr. Martínez and Mrs. Núñez.*

Oral Practice 2-3

 TRACK 17

The following sentences are used to introduce people. Read each sentence out loud, completing it with the pronoun **éste**, **ésta**, **éstos**, or **éstas**. Listen to the recording to check your answer. Repeat what you hear.

1. Hola, _____ es mi novia Sonia.
2. _____ es la Señora Hernández.
3. Buenas tardes a todos. _____ es mi amigo Andrés.
4. Hola. _____ son Julia, Oscar y Mateo.
5. Le presento al Señor Ponce y _____ es su colega, la Señora Rosado.
6. Les presento a José y _____ es su compañero Jaime.
7. Hola, _____ son José y Alberto.

8. Buenas tardes, _____ son Elena y Ana María.

9. Hola, _____ es Miguel y _____ es Andrea.

10. Le presento al Señor Postas y _____ son los Señores Jiménez y Álvarez.

OTHER WAYS OF INTRODUCING PEOPLE

Another common way to make introductions is to use the verb **llamarse**. **Llamarse** is a reflexive verb that literally translates as *to call oneself* but is used to mean *my name is*, *his name is*, etc. If you've studied Spanish before, **Me llamo** was probably the first thing you learned. Use **llamarse** + (*name*) to introduce yourself or others.

(yo) me llamo	*my name is*
(tú) te llamas	*your name is (informal)*
(usted, él/ella) se llama	*your name is (formal), his name is, her name is*
(nosotros/as) nos llamamos	*our names are*
(ustedes, ellos/ellas) se llaman	*your names are, their names are*

You can put the question word **¿Cómo... ?** (*How . . . ?*) before any of the verb conjugations above to ask a person's name. For example, to say *What is your name?* use **¿Cómo te llamas?** (informal) or **¿Cómo se llama?** (formal). Careful, because **¿Cómo se llama?** can also mean *What is his/her name?* Here are some more examples using **llamarse**:

Me llamo Julián Torres.	*My name is Julián Torres.*
Yo me llamo Andrea y él se llama Mikel.	*My name is Andrea, and his name is Mikel.*
Nos llamamos Marisol y Juan.	*Our names are Marisol and Juan.*
¿Y tú? ¿Cómo te llamas?	*And you? What's your name?*

Finally, you can also say **mi nombre es** (*my name is*) to give your name: **Mi nombre es Sonia.** (*My name is Sonia.*) Use **su** and **sus** to introduce other people: **su nombre es** (*his, her, your, their name is*); **sus nombres son** (*their names are*).

Oral Practice 2-4

Listen to the dialogues to fill in the missing words. Check your answers in the back of the book. Then listen again and repeat what you hear.

🔘 **TRACK 18**

1. A man introduces himself to a woman.

   HÉCTOR: Hola, soy Héctor. ¿_____ tú?

   ALICIA: _____ Alicia. Alicia Guerrero.

2. A man introduces himself and his friend to a woman.

   CARLOS: Buenas tardes, soy Carlos y _____ José Luis.

   JULIA: Encantada. _____ Julia.

3. A woman introduces herself to a group of three people.

   ELENA: Hola, _____ Elena y él es Héctor.

   FERNANDO: Encantado. _____ Fernando. _____ Luisa y _____ David.

RESPONDING TO AN INTRODUCTION

There are a number of ways to respond when introduced to a new person. Here are a few:

Mucho gusto.	*Nice to meet you.*
Encantado./Encantada.	*Pleasure to meet you.*
Es un placer conocerlo/la/te.	*It's a pleasure to meet you.*

Note that if you are a woman, you say **encantada**, and if you are a man, **encantado**. This is an adjective meaning *enchanted*. Also, note that if you are in an informal situation, you can say **Es un placer conocerte**. However, when meeting someone in a formal situation, say **Es un placer conocerlo** when speaking to a man and **... conocerla** when speaking to a woman.

Oral Practice 2-5

 TRACK 19

Imagine you are Pablo Torres in a number of different situations. Read each of the following situations, and respond out loud. If there's more than one answer, try giving multiple answers to practice all of the language you've learned. Listen to the recording to hear possible answers, and repeat what you hear.

1. You say "hello" to a friend.
2. You say "see you later" to someone.
3. You meet someone at an informal party and ask him his name.
4. You introduce yourself at a party.
5. You just met someone and want to say "nice to meet you."
6. You say good-bye to someone you'll be meeting again on Saturday.
7. You introduce your friend Carlos and specify he is a friend.
8. You are with your friend Sonia and you introduce yourselves to someone, starting with "**Hola...**".
9. You arrive at work at 9:00 A.M. and greet your colleague, Sra. Márquez.
10. It is 11 P.M. and you say good night.

Making Small Talk

Now that you've learned how to meet and greet new people, you will learn how to make small talk.

 TRACK 20

Listen to the following conversation in which Pablo meets his friend Ángel at a coffee shop. They discuss Pablo's date with Susana. How did it go?

ÁNGEL: Hola, Pablo.   *Hi, Pablo.*

PABLO: Hola, ¿qué pasa?   *Hi, what's up?*

ÁNGEL: ¿Qué tal la fiesta anoche?   *How was the party last night?*

PABLO: ¡Bacano! La pasamos muy bien.   *Great! We had a great time.*

ÁNGEL: ¿Y qué tal la cita con Susana?   *And the date with Susana?*

PABLO: Ay, terrible… Fuimos a una   *Ugh, terrible . . . We went to a*
churrascaría y resulta que es   *barbecue place, and it turns out*
vegetariana.   *she's a vegetarian.*

ÁNGEL: Lo siento. ¿Cómo estás?   *I'm sorry. How are you?*

PABLO: Estoy un poco triste…   *I'm a little sad. . . .*

ÁNGEL: Oye, tengo que irme. Adiós.   *Hey, I have to go. Bye.*

PABLO: Adiós. Hasta el lunes.   *Bye. See you Monday.*

Apparently the date didn't go so well, and Pablo feels **triste** (*sad*). If you didn't catch this, try listening again, and use the translations to help you.

ASKING PEOPLE HOW THEY ARE

Usually when you greet people, you also ask how they are. Here are the two most common ways of saying *How are you*?

¿Cómo estás?   *How are you? (informal)*

¿Cómo está?   *How are you? (more formal)*

Both phrases use the question word **¿Cómo?** (*How?*) with the verb **estar** (*to be*). Additionally, you will often hear the following phrases, which are generally used in more informal situations and with friends:

¿Qué pasa?   *What's up?*

¿Qué tal?   *How's it going?/How are you?*

Listen to the opening conversation again. How many of the above phrases do you hear? That's right, you hear: **¿Qué pasa?**, **¿Qué tal... ?**, and **¿Cómo estás?** Practice saying them.

There are several ways to answer when someone asks you *How are you?*

What's Up?

Different countries have different informal ways of saying *How are you?* Here are a few more examples of phrases you might hear:

¿Qué onda? (Mexico, Argentina, Chile)	*What's up?*
¿Qué hubo? (Colombia)	*What's up?*
¿Qué cuentas? (Peru)	*Lit.: What are you telling me?*
¿Qué hay (de nuevo)?	*What's new?*

Saying How You Feel

Bien.	*Well.*	Más o menos.	*So-so.*
Muy bien.	*Very well.*	No muy bien.	*Not so well.*
Fenomenal.	*Great.*	Mal.	*Badly.*
Genial.	*Great.*	Bastante mal.	*Quite badly.*
¡Fantástico!	*Fantastic!*	Terrible./Horrible.	*Terrible./Horrible.*

TALKING ABOUT MOOD WITH *ESTAR*

In order to go beyond a simple **bien** or **mal**, it's important to learn how to express your feelings in Spanish. Use the verb **estar** (*to be*) to talk about your mood (happy, sad, etc.) or state of being.

estar (*to be*)

yo estoy	*I am*	nosotros(as) estamos	*we are*
tú estás	*you are (informal)*	vosotros(as) estáis	*you are (Spain)*
usted está	*you are (formal)*	ustedes están	*you are (formal)*
él/ella está	*he/she/it is*	ellos/ellas están	*they are*

To Be

Spanish has two ways to say *to be*. Earlier in the chapter you learned **ser**. **Ser** is used to talk about more permanent states of being and intrinsic qualities such as color, shape, religion, nationality, and material. Meanwhile, **estar** describes things that are more transitive, like mood, feeling, or location. You will learn more about the different uses of these verbs as you work your way through this book.

In the opening dialogue, Pablo says **estoy un poco triste** (*I'm a little sad*) when he talks about his date with Susana. You can use **estar** + (*adjective*) to talk about many moods and states of mind. Here is a list of adjectives you can use with **estar** to describe mood. Note that some adjectives are the same for men and women. Others end in **-o** for men and **-a** for women.

Adjectives to Describe Mood

ansioso(a)	*anxious*	enojado(a)	*upset*
cansado(a)	*tired*	feliz	*happy*
contento(a)	*glad*	harto(a)	*fed up*
deprimido(a)	*depressed*	nervioso(a)	*nervous*
desilusionado(a)	*disappointed*	orgulloso(a)	*proud*
emocionado(a)	*excited*	sorprendido(a)	*surprised*
enfadado(a)	*angry*	triste	*sad*

Here are examples of sentences using **estar** + (*adjective*) to talk about mood. Remember that when using a plural subject (one or more people or things), the adjective becomes plural by adding an **-s**. The exception is **feliz**, which becomes **felices**.

Luisa está contenta.	*Luisa is glad.*
¿Estás sorprendido?	*Are you surprised? (to male)*
Mi amiga está deprimida.	*My friend is depressed. (female)*
María y yo estamos enojadas.	*Maria and I are upset (female plural)*

You can use **muy** (*very*), **un poco** (*a bit*), and **bastante** (*quite*) to show different degrees of feeling.

Hoy estoy un poco triste.	*Today I am a little sad.*
Jaime está muy enojado con sus colegas.	*Jaime is very upset with his colleagues.*
Estoy muy feliz. Mi amiga Ana está de visita.	*I am very happy. My friend Ana is visiting.*

GRAMMAR DEMYSTIFIED

Negatives and *Yes/No* Questions

You may have already noticed that asking *yes/no* questions and making negative sentences in Spanish is not too difficult. To ask a *yes/no* question, simply raise your voice at the end of the question. When writing a question, begin the sentence with an inverted question mark (¿) and end with a standard question mark (**?**). Compare the following affirmative statement with its question form:

 TRACK 21

Estás cansada.	*You're tired.*	¿Estás cansada?	*Are you tired?*

To make a sentence negative, simply add **no** in front of the verb. Listen and compare the following affirmative statement with its negative form.

Estoy cansada.	*I'm tired.*	No estoy cansada.	*I'm not tired.*

Written Practice 2-2

Use the cues provided to create sentences with **estar** and an adjective to describe people's moods.

1. Yo (*happy*). _____
2. Oscar (*surprised*). _____
3. Isabel y Guillermo (*sad*). _____
4. Mi amiga (*depressed*). _____
5. Ester (*very tired*). _____
6. David (*not glad*). _____
7. Los chicos (*a little fed up*). _____
8. Tu hermana (*nervous*)? _____

Chapter Practice

 TRACK 22

Listen to the following conversations and indicate whether each statement following is **cierto** (*true*) or **falso** (*false*). If you have trouble understanding, follow along with the tapescript in the back of the book.

1. Mauricio asks Julián how he is doing.

   ¿Cierto o falso? Julián no está bien. *Julián is not doing well.* _____

2. Manuel and Rosa talk at the end of a workday.

   ¿Cierto o falso? Rosa está cansada. *Rosa is tired.* _____

   Manuel no está cansado. *Manuel is not tired.* _____

3. Miriam asks Gerardo how he is doing.

   ¿Cierto o falso? Gerardo está enfadado. *Gerardo is angry.* _____

QUIZ

Circle the letter of the word or phrase that best completes each sentence.

1. (*It's 3 P.M.*) _____, Señor Cruz. ¿Cómo está?
   - (a) Buenas noches.
   - (b) Buenas tardes.
   - (c) Buenos días.

2. ¡Adiós! Hasta el _____.
   - (a) mañana
   - (b) señorita
   - (c) jueves

3. Éste es _____ hermano Roberto.
   - (a) mis
   - (b) son
   - (c) mi

4. _____ son Ana y María.
   - (a) Éstos
   - (b) Ésta
   - (c) Éstas

5. Rebeca está _____ nerviosa por el evento.
   - (a) muy
   - (b) es
   - (c) poca

TRACK 23

Now listen to the recording to hear a phrase or question. Press pause, and say your answer: a, b, or c. Listen to the correct answer on the recording, and repeat what you hear. Then go to the next question, and repeat the process.

6. (a) Es la Señorita Castillo.

   (b) Estoy muy bien.

   (c) Me llamo Señora Castillo.

7. (a) Muchas gracias.

   (b) Más o menos.

   (c) Buenas noches.

8. (a) Estoy orgulloso.

   (b) Están nerviosos.

   (c) Estás contenta.

9. (a) Están hartos.

   (b) Está enojado.

   (c) Está triste.

10. (a) Adiós.

   (b) Fenomenal.

   (c) Sorprendida.

CHAPTER 3

Talking About
Who Is Who

In this chapter you will learn:

How to describe people

Nationalities

How to specify who is who

How to compare people and places

How to talk about your family

Describing People

 TRACK 24

After the botched date with Susana, Pablo decides to go out Saturday night on his own. He ends up talking to Delia. Listen to their conversation. Where is Delia from?

PABLO: Hola, soy Pablo.

Hi, I'm Pablo.

DELIA: Hola, soy Delia. ¿De dónde eres, Pablo?

Hi, I'm Delia. Where are you from, Pablo?

PABLO: Soy puertorriqueño, pero vivo en Chicago. ¿Y tú?

I'm Puerto Rican, but I live in Chicago. And you?

DELIA: Yo soy dominicana.

I'm Dominican.

PABLO: ¿De qué parte de la República Dominicana eres?

What part of the Dominican Republic are you from?

DELIA: Soy de Puerto Plata.

I'm from Puerto Plata.

PABLO: Puerto Plata es muy bonito.

Puerto Plata is really beautiful.

DELIA: Tú no pareces puertorriqueño. Eres rubio. Generalmente los puertorriqueños tienen el cabello negro.

You don't look Puerto Rican. You're blond. Usually Puerto Ricans have black hair.

PABLO: Mi mamá es norteamericana. Es alta y rubia. Mi papá es puertorriqueño. Tú sí te ves dominicana. Eres muy linda.

My mother is from the United States. She's tall and blonde. My father is Puerto Rican. You do look Dominican. You're very pretty.

(Viene Diego a hablar con ellos...)

(Diego comes over to talk to them . . .)

DELIA: Éste es mi novio, Diego.

This is my boyfriend, Diego.

PABLO: Hola, encantado. Soy Pablo. ¿Eres de la República Dominicana también?

Hi, nice to meet you. I'm Pablo. Are you from the Dominican Republic as well?

DIEGO: No, yo soy de aquí. Soy
   norteamericano, pero mi familia
   es de Perú.

*No, I'm from here. I'm from the United
States, but my family is from Peru.*

PABLO: ¿De qué parte?

From which part?

DIEGO: De Cuzco.

From Cuzco.

TALKING ABOUT NATIONALITY

Delia is **dominicana** (*Dominican*) from **la República Dominicana** (*the Domini-can Republic*). Delia's boyfriend Diego says he's **norteamericano** (*North American/from the U.S.*), but his family is **de Perú** (*from Peru*). Pablo explains that he is **puertorriqueño** (*Puerto Rican*) but his mother is **norteamericana**. Look at these nationalities from the conversation:

puertorriqueño	*Puerto Rican*
dominicana	*Dominican*
norteamericana	*North American/from the U.S.*

As in English, there are two main ways to say where you are from. Both use the verb **ser** (*to be*) that you learned in Chapter 2: **ser de** + (*country, city*, etc.) (*I'm from* + *country, city*, etc.) or **ser** + (*nationality*) (*I'm* + *nationality*). Note that adjectives and nouns of nationality are not capitalized in Spanish.

Soy de Perú.	*I'm from Peru.*
Soy peruano.	*I'm Peruvian.*

Because nationalities are usually treated as adjectives, they need to agree in number and gender with the word they're describing. Look at the following examples:

Diego es peruano.	*Diego is Peruvian.*
Mónica es mexicana.	*Mónica is Mexican.*
Julia y Paula son chilenas.	*Julia and Paula are Chilean.*

Somos todos americanos

Saying you are from the United States in Spanish is more difficult than you may first imagine. While in English you may say *I'm American*, many Latin Americans might be offended: technically anyone from **las Américas** (*the Americas*) is American. Therefore, Latin Americans often describe people from the United States as **norteamericanos** (*North Americans*). However, this clearly poses a new problem, since anyone from Canada, the U.S., or Mexico is technically North American. Spaniards probably have the best answer to this conundrum. They say **estadounidense** (*"United States-ian"*). Another way to solve this problem is to say **Soy de los Estados Unidos** (*I'm from the United States*). What's important is to be culturally sensitive when talking about nationality, and don't assume that only U.S. citizens are "Americans."

Don't forget that when a group is made up of men and women, the adjective takes the masculine form, even if most of the people are women!

José, Alicia, Ana y Mónica son cubanos.

José, Alicia, Ana, and Mónica are Cuban.

There are dozens of nationalities in the world. Here are just a few. All of them follow the preceding rules. If you don't find what you're looking for, remember that you can always look up words in the dictionary.

Nationalities (Spain and the Americas)

argentino(a)	*Argentinean*	guatemalteco(a)	*Guatemalan*
boliviano(a)	*Bolivian*	mexicano(a)	*Mexican*
canadiense	*Canadian*	norteamericano(a)	*North American*
chileno(a)	*Chilean*	nicaragüense	*Nicaraguan*
colombiano(a)	*Colombian*	panameño	*Panamanian*
costarricense	*Costa Rican*	paraguayo(a)	*Paraguayan*
cubano(a)	*Cuban*	peruano(a)	*Peruvian*

dominicano(a)	*Dominican*	puertorriqueño(a)	*Puerto Rican*
español/española	*Spanish*	uruguayo(a)	*Uruguayan*
estadounidense	*from United States*	venezolano(a)	*Venezuelan*

Nationalities (Other Countries)

alemán/alemana	*German*	irlandés/irlandesa	*Irish*
australiano(a)	*Australian*	israelí	*Israeli*
británico(a)	*British*	italiano(a)	*Italian*
chino(a)	*Chinese*	japonés/japonesa	*Japanese*
francés/francesa	*French*	ruso(a)	*Russian*
inglés/inglesa	*English*	sudafricano(a)	*South African*

Use **¿De dónde... ?** (*From where . . . ?*) or **¿De qué... ?** (*From which . . . ?*) to ask someone about his or her nationality or hometown.

¿De dónde eres?	*Where are you from?* (tú, *informal*)
¿De dónde es usted?	*Where are you from?* (usted, *formal*)
¿De qué parte eres?	*Which part are you from?* (tú, *informal*)
¿De qué ciudad son ustedes?	*Which city are you from?* (ustedes, *plural*)

Here are some more examples of questions and answers about nationality. Remember: To form a *yes/no* question, simply use **¿... ?** and inflect upwards with your voice. To make the negative, add **no** before the verb.

¿De dónde es usted?	*Where are you from?*
Soy de España.	*I am from Spain.*
¿Es usted de Madrid?	*Are you from Madrid?*

No, no soy de Madrid.
    Soy de Barcelona.
	No, I am not from Madrid.
	    I am from Barcelona.

¿Eres de Estados Unidos?	*Are you from the United States?*
No, soy canadiense.	*No, I am Canadian.*

Oral Practice 3-1

 TRACK 25

Listen to the following short conversations between people talking about their national origins. Write the name of the country that correctly completes each sentence: **Argentina**, **Colombia**, **Bolivia**, **Ecuador**, **Chile**, **Venezuela**, or **Canadá**.

1. Rita meets David for the first time.

   Rita y David son de _____. *Rita and David are from . . .*

2. Mónica and Mauricio talk about where they are from.

   Mónica es de _____ y Mauricio es de _____.
   Mónica is from . . . and Mauricio is from . . .

3. Juan and Ester talk about where they are from.

   Juan es de _____ y Ester es de _____. *Juan is from . . . and Ester is from . . .*

4. José wants to find out where Elena is from.

   José es de _____ y Elena es de _____. *José is from . . . and Elena is from . . .*

DESCRIBING SOMEONE'S APPEARANCE

In the dialogue, Pablo comments on Delia's hometown of Puerto Plata. He says **Es muy bonito** (*It's very beautiful*). He also tells Delia (before her boyfriend arrives), **Eres muy linda** (*You're really pretty*). **Bonito** and **linda** both mean *pretty* or *beautiful* and can be used with the verb **ser** to describe people and places. In Chapter 2 you learned some adjectives that take **estar** (*to be*). Here you will learn some adjectives that take **ser** (*to be*).

Ser, when used to describe people, is usually paired with adjectives that describe characteristics that are permanent and generally unchanging, such as physical appearance, personality, nationality, race, or religion.

VOCABULARY DEMYSTIFIED

Employing Euphemism

Use your common sense when describing people's weight, height, physical strength, or other aspects of their physical status. For instance, even though some Spanish-speaking cultures can be forthright when speaking about personal appearance, **gordo** (*fat*) is still not a very nice word to describe someone. Often people will use the diminutive (**-ito** form) to take the sting out of a description, such as **gordito/gordita** (*plump*) or will use a milder word, such as **regordete** (*chubby*) or **rellenito(a)** (*"filled out," "lightly padded"*).

Adjectives That Describe People

Personality		**Physical Appearance**	
aburrido(a)	*boring*	alto(a)	*tall*
divertido(a)	*fun*	atractivo(a)	*attractive*
generoso(a)	*generous*	bajo(a)	*short*
gracioso(a)	*funny*	bonito(a)	*pretty, beautiful*
honesto(a)	*honest*	débil, flojo(a)	*weak*
pesado(a)	*annoying*	delgado	*thin*
simpático(a)	*friendly, nice*	feo(a)	*ugly*
tímido(a)	*shy*	fuerte	*strong*
tranquilo(a)	*calm, laid-back*	gordo(a)	*fat*
		lindo(a)	*pretty, beautiful*
		pelirrojo(a)	*red-headed*
		rubio(a)	*blond(e)*

Adjectives: *ser* or *estar*?

As you start speaking more and more Spanish, you may notice that some adjectives can use both **ser** and **estar** to describe people. Confusing, right? Having two ways to say *to be* means that you can imply a different meaning depending on which *to be* you choose. Remember: **Ser** describes a permanent state and **estar** describes a temporary state. See if you can discern the difference in the following example:

SER: Luis es aburrido.   *Luis is boring.*

ESTAR: Luis está aburrido.   *Luis is bored.*

That one was pretty easy. But how about these?

SER: Gema es nerviosa.   *Gema has a nervous personality.*

ESTAR: Gema está nerviosa hoy.   *Gema is nervous today.*

SER: Santiago es bueno.   *Santiago is a good guy.*

ESTAR: ¡Santiago está bueno!   *Santiago is hot!*

To ask what someone is like (personality) or looks like (appearance), say **¿Cómo es** (*person*)**?** *What is (person) like?*

¿Cómo es tu novio?   *What's your boyfriend like?*

Don't confuse this construction with **¿Cómo está?** which asks how someone feels at the moment.

Don't forget that you can qualify almost any adjective you use by adding adverbs such as **muy** (*very*), **un poco** (*a little bit*), and **bastante** (*quite*). For example:

Tú eres muy gracioso.   *You are very funny.*

Gilberto es un poco pesado.   *Gilberto is a little bit annoying.*

Ellos son bastante atractivos.   *They are quite attractive.*

Ser is also used with adjectives that describe race and ethnicity, since these are generally permanent.

Adjectives Describing Race and Ethnicity

afroamericano(a)	*African-American*	hispano(a)	*Hispanic*
afrodescendiente	*person of African descent*	indígena, pueblo originario	*indigenous, native people*
asiático(a)	*Asian*	latino(a)	*Latino*
blanco(a)	*white*	mestizo(a)	*mixed race*
de dos razas	*bi-racial*	negro(a)	*black*

Here are some example sentences:

Daniel es afroamericano.	*Daniel is African-American.*
Susana es asiática.	*Susana is Asian.*

In the opening conversation, both Pablo and Delia talk about hair and eye color. There are different ways of describing someone's hair color. One way is to say, **Tiene el cabello** + (*color or type*). (Note that in Spain the word **pelo** is used more often to say *hair* than **cabello**, which is a common Latin American term.)

Hair Colors and Types

blanco	*white*	lacio	*straight*	rapado	*cut short, shaven*
calvo	*bald*	largo	*long*	rizado	*curly*
canoso	*grayish*	moreno, negro	*black*	rubio	*blond*
castaño	*brown*	pelirrojo	*red-haired*	trenzado	*braided*
corto	*short*				

Note: In Spain, **moreno(a)** is used to describe a person with black hair, so **Es morena** would mean *She has black hair.* In Latin America, however, **moreno(a)** may be used to refer to someone with dark skin tone. Again, this may depend on how a person identifies him or herself.

Race and Ethnicity in Latin America

Concepts of race and ethnicity in Latin America differ from those in the United States, so it's important to understand a person's culture or personal preference before identifying him or her as one race or ethnicity or another. For instance, the same way that a woman of African descent in the United States might refer to herself as **afroamericana** (*African-American*), a woman of African descent in Colombia might say **afrocolombiana**, in Ecuador **afroecuatoriana**, in Perú **afroperuana**, and so on. She may also say **negra**, but then again, she may not identify as black at all. Similarly, various indigenous groups may choose different terminology to describe themselves, either as distinct ethnic identities such as **Quechua**, **Aymara**, **Maya**, or **Guaraní**, or with terms that identify them as Native Americans, such as **indígena**, **pueblo originario**, or **aborigen**, depending on the country or context. Latin America is a melting pot, and many people have European, African, and Native American heritage. **Mestizo** is a word that is commonly used to describe people of mixed ancestry, especially mixed indigenous and white. In some countries this is referred to as **ladino**. Additionally, there is no consensus among people of Latin American descent living in the United States as to whether they prefer to be called **latino** or **hispano**. Notions of race can also be complicated by Latin America's class structure. So, the best thing is probably to listen to how people describe themselves, and go on from there.

To describe someone's eye color you can say **Tiene los ojos** + (*color*). *He/She has (color) eyes.* Remember that since **ojos** is plural, the color describing them should be plural as well.

Eye Colors

azules	*blue*	negros	*black*
grises	*grey*	verdes	*green*
marrones	*brown*		

So, if you put together all of this information, you can describe people in a number of different ways. Connect your statements with **y** (*and*) to string a number of descriptions together.

Sonia es alta y tiene los ojos verdes.	*Sonia is tall and has green eyes.*
Martín es blanco y tiene el cabello rubio.	*Martin is white and has blond hair.*
Victoria es bajita y delgada y tiene el cabello largo y lacio.	*Victoria is short and thin and has long, straight hair.*

Written Practice 3-1

Use the cues below to write sentences in Spanish that describe people.

1. Mario (*blue eyes*) _____
2. Sofía (*long, curly hair*) _____
3. Mónica (*Afroperuvian*) _____
4. Lola y Marisa (*boring*) _____
5. Luis (*laid-back and honest*) _____
6. Mari Carmen (*generous and a bit shy*) _____
7. Yoko (*Asian and quite tall*) _____
8. Amelia (*red-haired, short hair*) _____
9. Ester y Pedro (*Latino*) _____
10. Vicente (*black eyes, grayish hair*) _____

Oral Practice 3-2

 TRACK 26

Read the following dialogue between Ana and Pedro in which they are talking about their spouses. Complete each sentence using the words below. Listen to the recording to check your answers. Pause after each sentence, and repeat what you hear.

cabello   parte   uruguayo   soy   uruguaya   muy   dónde

ANA: Pedro, ¿de dónde es tu esposa?

PEDRO: Es _____. Es de Montevideo.

ANA: ¿Tú eres _____ también?

PEDRO: No, yo _____ argentino. Soy de Buenos Aires.

ANA: ¿Cómo es tu esposa?

PEDRO: Tiene el _____ largo, lacio y negro. Es bajita y _____ divertida. ¿Y tu esposo? ¿Cómo es?

ANA: Es un poco tímido, pero muy atractivo.

PEDRO: ¿De _____ es?

ANA: Es español.

PEDRO: ¿De qué _____ de España?

ANA: De Madrid.

Talking About Different People

 TRACK 27

Pablo works at the front desk of a library. He's talking to a colleague, Miriam, about the people who come in and out of the library. Miriam knows just about everybody! Listen to their conversation. How many people do they talk about?

PABLO: ¿Quién es ese hombre?   *Who is that man?*

MIRIAM: ¿Qué hombre?   *What man?*

PABLO: Es alto y tiene el cabello canoso.   *He's tall and has grayish hair.*

MIRIAM: Es el Señor Galdós.   *That's Mr. Galdós.*

PABLO: ¿Quién es esa mujer de allí?   *Who's that woman over there?*
Tiene el cabello corto y lacio.   *She has short, straight hair.*

MIRIAM: ¿La mujer bajita y regordeta?   *The short, chubby woman?*

PABLO: No, esa muchacha muy atractiva. Es más alta que el Señor Galdós.

No, that very attractive young woman. She's taller than Mr. Galdós.

MIRIAM: Es Lupe. Es la hermana de Teresa.

That's Lupe. She's Teresa's sister.

PABLO: ¿Es más simpática que Teresa?

Is she nicer than Teresa?

MIRIAM: En mi opinión, es menos simpática que Teresa.

In my opinion, she's less nice than Teresa.

PABLO: Es atractiva.

She's attractive.

MIRIAM: Es verdad.

It's true.

PABLO: Pero no es tan atractiva como tú, Miriam. La más atractiva de todas eres tú.

But not as attractive as you are, Miriam. You're the most attractive of them all!

MIRIAM: ¡Y el más mentiroso eres tú!

And you're the biggest liar!

SPECIFYING WHO IS WHO

Pablo and Miriam talk about three people: Señor Galdós; a nameless, short, chubby woman; and Lupe, Teresa's sister. Every time Pablo asks about someone, he says **¿Quién es ese/esa** + (**mujer, hombre, muchacho, muchacha**, etc.)**?** *Who is that woman, man, guy, girl?* He uses **ese** to refer to masculine nouns and **esa** for feminine. Look at these excerpts from the dialogue:

¿Quién es ese hombre?

Who is that man?

¿Quién es esa mujer de allí?

Who is that woman over there?

Here are some more words to describe people.

el anciano, el señor mayor	*old/elderly man*	la anciana, la señora mayor	*old/elderly woman*
el bebé	*baby boy*	la bebé	*baby girl*
el hombre	*man*	la mujer	*woman*

el muchacho, el chico	*young man*	la muchacha, la chica	*young woman*
el niño	*male child, boy*	la niña	*female child, girl*

A good way to clarify who someone is, is to include a description of him or her in your question, as Miriam does in the dialogue, when she says, **¿La mujer bajita y regordeta?** *The short, chubby woman?* Here are some more examples:

¿La mujer alta?	*The tall woman?*
¿Esa niña?	*That girl?*
¿El muchacho delgado?	*The thin young man?*
¿Tiene el cabello rubio?	*Does he have blond hair?*

Miriam describes Lupe through her familial relationship: **Es la hermana de Teresa** (*She's Teresa's sister.*). To describe how one person is related to another, use **Es el/la... de** (*person's name*).

Es la esposa de Juan.	*She's Juan's wife.*
Es el novio de Sofía.	*He's Sofía's boyfriend.*
Es la amiga de Ana y Teresa.	*She's Ana and Teresa's friend.*

In Chapter 2 you learned the words **el/la esposo(a)** (*husband/wife*), **el/la novio(a)** (*boyfriend/girlfriend*), **el/la compañero(a)** (*companion, partner*), **el/la hermano(a)** (*brother/sister*), **el padre/la madre** (*father/mother*), and **el/la amigo(a)** (*friend*). Here are some more words to describe family members:

Family Members

el/la tío(a)	*uncle, aunt*	el/la primo(a)	*male/female cousin*
el/la hijo(a)	*son, daughter*	el/la sobrino(a)	*nephew, niece*
el/la abuelo(a)	*grandmother, grandfather*	el/la nieto(a)	*male/female grandchild*
el/la cuñado(a)	*brother-in-law, sister-in-law*	el/la suegro(a)	*mother-in-law, father-in-law*

Personal Adjectives

You can also describe relationships using the personal (or possessive) adjectives:

mi	*my*	nuestro(a)	*our*
tu	*your*	vuestro(a)	*your (informal, Spain)*
su	*his, her, your* (usted, formal)	su	*their, your* (ustedes)

Here are some examples. Note that **su** is the same for *his* and *her*.

Esa mujer es mi esposa.	*That woman is my wife.*
El niño es su sobrino.	*The boy is his nephew.*

When referring to plural relatives, add an **-s**: **mis hermanos** (*my brothers*), **nuestros tíos** (*our uncles*), **sus nietos** (*his, her, your, their grandchildren*). Context will generally explain who **su, sus** refers to.

Esos hombres son mis tíos.	*Those men are my uncles.*
Maritza y Gilda son nuestras amigas.	*Maritza and Gilda are our friends.*

el/la prometido(a), el/la novio(a)	*fiancé/fiancée*	el/la yerno(a)	*son-in-law, daughter-in-law*
el padrastro	*stepfather*	la madrastra	*stepmother*
el hermanastro	*stepbrother*	la hermanastra	*stepsister*

Here are some more example sentences that talk about family members:

¿Quién es ese hombre?	*Who is that man?*
Es Daniel. Es el sobrino de Pepita.	*That's Daniel. He's Pepita's nephew.*

Note that when asking or talking about more than one person, **ese** becomes **esos**, and **esa** becomes **esas**. **¿Quién... ?** becomes **¿Quiénes... ?**

| ¿Quiénes son esas muchachas? | *Who are those girls?* |
| ¿Esos son los nietos del Sr. Ruiz? | *Are those Mr. Ruiz's grandchildren?* |

Oral Practice 3-3

 TRACK 28

Use the cues to specify who each person is. Listen to the recording to check your answers, and repeat what you hear.

1. ¿Quién es esa niña? (*María's granddaughter*) Es _____.
2. ¿Quién es esa mujer? (*Arturo's mother-in-law*) Es _____.
3. ¿Quién es ese hombre alto? (*Sonia's uncle*) Es _____.
4. ¿Quién es ese muchacho bajito? (*Estela's fiancé*) _____.
5. ¿Quiénes son esas muchachas afroamericanas? (*Andrea's nieces*) _____.
6. ¿Quién es ese señor mayor? (*Linda's grandfather*) _____.

Written Practice 3-2

Read each description of a family member, and write down whom it is describing. Use the same personal (possessive) adjective (**mi**, **tu**, etc.) as the one given in the cue.

1. Es el hijo de mi hermana. Es _____.
2. Es la madre de nuestra madre. Es _____.
3. Es el hijo de tus padres. _____.
4. Es el nuevo esposo de su madre. _____.
5. Son las hijas de mi hermano. Son _____.
6. Son los hijos de sus tíos. _____.

MAKING COMPARISONS

In the conversation between Pablo and Miriam, they use comparisons to describe people and even to joke around and give each other compliments. Look at these comparisons from the dialogue:

Es más alta que el Señor Galdós.	*She's taller than Señor Galdós.*
¿Es más simpática que Teresa?	*Is she nicer than Teresa?*
En mi opinión, es menos simpática que Teresa.	*In my opinion she's less nice than Teresa.*
No es tan atractiva como tú, Miriam.	*She's not as attractive as you, Miriam.*
¡La más atractiva de todas eres tú!	*You're the most attractive of them all!*
¡Y el más mentiroso eres tú!	*And you're the biggest liar!*

To compare two items (people, things, or places), use **más...** (*adjective*) **que** (*more . . . than*). These types of comparisons are expressed in English as *more . . . than* or *-er: prettier, bigger, more interesting than.*

Mónica es más alta que Lucía.	*Mónica is taller than Lucía.*
Ronaldo es más interesante que Julio.	*Ronaldo is more interesting than Julio.*
Chicago es más grande que San Juan.	*Chicago is bigger than San Juan.*

You can also compare two items with **menos...** (*adjective*) **que** (*less . . . than*).

Julio es menos interesante que Ronaldo.	*Julio is less interesting than Ronaldo.*
San Juan es menos grande que Chicago.	*San Juan is smaller (less big) than Chicago.*

To say that two items are equal, use **tan...** (*adjective*) **como** (*as . . . as*).

Luisito es tan alto como su papá.	*Little Luis is as tall as his dad.*
Andrea es tan delgada como su hermana.	*Andrea is as thin as her sister.*

As is always the case in Spanish, put **no** before the verb (in this case, **ser**) to make the negative.

Andrea no es tan delgada como su hermana.	*Andrea is not as thin as her sister.*

USING SUPERLATIVES

In the dialogue, Pablo jokes that Miriam is **la más atractiva de todas** (*the most attractive of all*) and Miriam tells Pablo **¡Y el más mentiroso eres tú!** (*And the biggest liar is you!*). The grammatical form that uses *most* and *-est* (*biggest, funniest*, etc.) is called the *superlative*.

The Spanish superlative is made with **el/la** + (*noun*) + **más** + (*adjective*)**...** or in the case of the plural, **los/las** + (*plural noun*) + **más** + (*plural adjective*)**...** Usually the superlative is the ultimate of a category, such as **de la clase** (*in the class*), **de mi familia** (*of my family*), **que conozco** (*that I know*), or **de todos/todas** (*of all*). It may look confusing; so let's walk you through it.

adjective	Lupe es **una chica linda**.
comparative	Lupe es **más linda que** Teresa.
superlative	Lupe es **la chica más linda de** todas.

Here are some more examples:

Susana es la niña más alta de la clase.	*Susana is the tallest girl in the class.*
Alberto es el tipo más pesado que conozco.	*Alberto is the most annoying guy I know.*

Another way to express the superlative, which you saw in the dialogue, is to omit the noun (**la chica**, **el tipo**, etc.) altogether. In this case, it's important that you know the gender of the noun you're talking about, so you can choose **el/los** or **la/las**.

Susana **es la más alta** de la clase.	*Susana is the tallest in class.*
El Restaurante Olla **es el más caro**.	*Olla Restaurant is the most expensive.*

Some comparatives and superlatives are irregular.

bueno	*good*	→	mejor	*better*	→	el/la mejor	*the best*
malo	*bad*	→	peor	*worse*	→	el/la peor	*the worst*
joven	*young*	→	menor	*younger*	→	el/la menor	*the youngest*
viejo	*old*	→	mayor	*older*	→	el/la mayor	*the oldest*

The plural forms are **mejores** and **peores**.

Las tortillas aquí son las mejores.   *The tortillas here are the best.*

Written Practice 3-3

Translate the following sentences into Spanish.

1. Olivia is more generous than Jaime. ⸻⸻.
2. Rebeca is more interesting than Laura. ⸻⸻.
3. Samuel is less annoying than Alberto. ⸻⸻.
4. Marta is more laid-back than José. ⸻⸻.
5. Rosita is the shyest girl in the class. ⸻⸻.
6. Your uncle is the funniest! ⸻⸻.
7. *Gladiator* (**Gladiador**) is the best movie. ⸻⸻.
8. My sister is less attractive than my cousin (female). ⸻⸻.
9. Our father is not as strong as our uncle. ⸻⸻.
10. Diana's sister is the most honest young woman I know. ⸻⸻.

Oral Practice 3-4

 TRACK 29

Listen to the dialogues and indicate whether the statements following are **cierto o falso** (*true or false*).

1. Esteban asks Andrea about a girl.

   ¿Cierto o falso? Rebeca es la prima de Andrea. *Rebeca is Andrea's cousin.*

   ⸻

   Rebeca tiene el cabello rubio. *Rebeca's hair is blonde.* ⸻

2. David asks Susana about a man.

   ¿Cierto o falso? El hombre es el abuelo de Susana. *The man is Susana's grandfather.* ⸻

3. Daniela and Jorge compare some friends.

   ¿Cierto o falso? Daniela cree que Renata es muy simpática. *Daniela thinks Renata is very friendly.* _____

4. Roberto asks Antonio about his parents.

   ¿Cierto o falso? El padre de Antonio es más alto que Antonio. *Antonio's father is taller than he is.* _____

Chapter Practice

TRACK 30

Read each situation. Write and say the phrase or phrases that apply. Listen to the recording to hear the answers, and repeat what you hear.

1. You are in a formal situation. You ask a woman where she is from.

   _____

2. You want to know which part of Mexico she is from.

   _____

3. Someone asks you **¿De dónde eres?** You are from the United States.

   _____

4. You want to know who that tall man is.

   _____

5. You want to know who that Hispanic young woman is.

   _____

6. Someone asks **¿Cómo es tu hermana?** Say that your sister is very generous.

   _____

7. Someone asks **¿Cómo es la abuela de Antonio?** Say that his grandmother is quite strong.

   _____

8. Someone asks **¿Cómo es tu tío Miguel?** Say that your uncle Miguel is more fun than your uncle José.

   _____

9. Someone asks **¿Cómo es Fernando?** Say that Fernando is short and has green eyes.

_____

10. Someone asks **¿Cómo es tu prima?** Say that she is Latina and has long hair.

_____

QUIZ

Circle the letter of the word or phrase that best completes each sentence.

1. Isabel Allende es _____.
   (a) argentino
   (b) mayor
   (c) chilena

2. Estados Unidos es _____ grande que Nicaragua.
   (a) tan
   (b) menos
   (c) más

3. Este restaurante es _____ caro como ese.
   (a) tan
   (b) mis
   (c) menos

4. La hija de mi hermano es mi _____.
   (a) tía
   (b) sobrina
   (c) madre

5. Delia tiene los _____ negros.
   (a) cabello
   (b) ojos
   (c) hermano

 TRACK 31

Now listen to the recording to hear a phrase or question. Press pause to select your answer: a, b, or c. Listen to the correct answer on the recording, and repeat what you hear. Then go to the next question, and repeat the process.

6. (a) Muy bien, gracias.

   (b) Soy inglés.

   (c) Son de Australia.

7. (a) Soy de Sydney.

   (b) Soy inglesa.

   (c) Soy de Canadá.

8. (a) Es simpático.

   (b) Es bastante aburrida.

   (c) Son bastante felices.

9. (a) Es el abuelo de Ana.

   (b) Tiene el cabello canoso.

   (c) Es nuestra tía.

10. (a) Es nuestra abuela.

    (b) Es la hermana de José.

    (c) Es mi tío.

CHAPTER 4

Getting Around Town

In this chapter you will learn:

How to get someone's attention
Polite expressions
How to ask about places and things
How to ask for and give directions
How to describe a place
How to talk about what you know

Asking for Assistance

As you study Spanish, take the opportunity to explore restaurants and shops in your area run by Spanish speakers. You'll probably find that people are happy to help you practice your speaking and listening skills, especially if you become a regular.

In this chapter, Pablo decides to go to a Dominican restaurant in a Spanish-speaking community in his city. First he needs to find some cash, so he looks for a bank. Listen to the conversation between Pablo and a local resident. What does Pablo ask her?

TRACK 32

PABLO: Perdone, ¿hay un banco cerca?   *Excuse me. Is there a bank nearby?*

SEÑORA: Sí, hay uno allí mismo. En la calle Santa Ana.   *Yes, that's one over there. On Santa Ana Street.*

PABLO: Ah, sí, gracias.   *Ah, yes. Thanks.*

SEÑORA: De nada.   *You're welcome.*

Pablo asks her **¿Hay un banco cerca?** *Is there a bank nearby?* If you didn't catch this, listen again, or use the translations to help you.

Now listen to the next conversation. Pablo can't find the Dominican restaurant, so he decides to ask someone where it is. What does he find out?

TRACK 33

PABLO: Disculpe. ¿Hay un restaurante dominicano por aquí?   *Excuse me. Is there a Dominican restaurant around here?*

SEÑOR: ¿Por aquí? Lo siento. No hay ninguno. Pero hay un restaurante muy bueno en la calle Aguilar, el restaurante Callao.   *Around here? No, I'm sorry. There aren't any. But there is a very good restaurant on Aguilar Street, Restaurante Callao.*

PABLO: ¿Qué tipo de restaurante es?   *What type of restaurant is it?*

SEÑOR: Es un restaurante cubano.   *It's a Cuban restaurant.*

PABLO: Muchas gracias.   *Thanks a lot.*

SEÑOR: No hay de qué.   *You're welcome.*

USING POLITE EXPRESSIONS

Pablo uses a number of polite expressions in the two conversations. Listen again. Can you identify them?

Pablo approaches two strangers to ask for their assistance. To get their attention politely he says, **perdone** (*pardon me*) and **disculpe** (*excuse me*). He says **muchas gracias**, *thanks a lot*, after the man helps him. Polite expressions are important to know when practicing your Spanish. Here are some examples of polite expressions. Listen and repeat each one.

 TRACK 34

Perdone./Perdón./Disculpe. *(formal)*	*Pardon me./Excuse me./I'm sorry.*
Perdona./Disculpa. *(informal)*	*Pardon me./Excuse me./I'm sorry.*
Con permiso./Permiso.	*Excuse me.*
Lo siento.	*I'm sorry./Sorry.*
Por favor.	*Please.*
Gracias.	*Thank you.*
Muchas gracias.	*Thank you very much.*
De nada.	*You're welcome.*
No hay de qué.	*You're welcome.*

The words **perdón** and **perdone/perdona** are related to the verb **perdonar**. As you saw above, **perdonar** is used to say *pardon me*, *excuse me*, and *sorry*.

Perdón, ¿hay un banco cerca?	*Excuse me, is there a bank nearby?*
Ay, le pisé. Perdón.	*Ah, I stepped on your foot. I'm sorry.*
Perdone. Fue un accidente.	*Sorry. It was an accident.*

Excuse Me

Perdón and **perdona** are most commonly used in Spain when you want to get someone's attention or say *excuse me*. In Latin America, the phrase **con permiso** (*lit.: with permission*) is more common, especially when you need to walk past someone, request permission to enter someone's office, or make similar requests. It is rarely used in Spain. **Disculpe** is used throughout Latin America and Spain as a polite way to get someone's attention or to say *I'm sorry*.

Written Practice 4-1

Read each situation. Choose the polite phrase that is appropriate for the situation.

1. Someone helps you carry your bag up the stairs. You say . . .

    (a) Perdón

    (b) Muchas gracias.

    (c) No hay de qué.

2. Someone just told you "thank you." You say . . .

    (a) Disculpe.

    (b) Gracias.

    (c) De nada.

3. You accidentally bump into someone on the street. You say . . .

    (a) Lo siento.

    (b) Gracias.

    (c) No hay de qué.

4. You ask a friend for a favor. You say . . .

    (a) Lo siento.

    (b) De nada.

    (c) Por favor.

5. You stop a stranger on the street to get directions. You say . . .

    (a) Gracias.

    (b) Disculpe.

    (c) De nada.

6. You want to squeeze by someone on the bus. You say . . .

    (a) Con permiso.

    (b) No hay de qué.

    (c) De nada.

USING *HAY* TO TALK ABOUT PLACES AND THINGS

To talk about or locate specific places, you can use **¿Hay... ?** (*Is there?/Are there?*). Read and say aloud these excerpts from the chapter conversations. Remember, the **h** in **hay** is silent.

¿Hay un banco cerca?	*Is there a bank nearby?*
¿Hay un restaurante dominicano por aquí?	*Is there a Dominican restaurant near here?*

Before learning more about finding places, you need to know how to name them! Here is a list to get you started:

Place Names

el banco	*bank*	el gimnasio	*gym*
el baño	*restroom*	la lavandería	*laundromat*
el bar	*bar*	el mercado	*market*
el barrio	*neighborhood*	el museo	*museum*
la biblioteca	*library*	la oficina de correos	*post office*
la cafetería	*coffee shop*	la parada (de bus, de metro)	*(bus, subway) stop*
la calle	*street*	el parque	*park*
el centro comercial	*mall*	la plaza	*square*

el cine	*movie theater*	el restaurante	*restaurant*
la discoteca	*nightclub, disco*	el supermercado	*supermarket*
la estación (de metro, de tren)	*(subway, train) station*	el teatro	*theater*
el estacionamiento	*parking lot*	la tienda	*store*

Hay is the present conjugation of the verb **haber**. In a statement, **hay** means *there is/there are*. When used in a question, it means *is there . . . ?/are there . . . ?* **Hay** is always the same, whether used with singular or plural nouns.

In questions about whether something *is* or *isn't there*, **hay** is usually accompanied by the indefinite articles **un** or **una**, plus the noun.

VOCABULARY DEMYSTIFIED

Going Shopping

Many stores and businesses end in the suffix **-ería**. For example, a place that sells or repairs **zapatos** (*shoes*) is a **zapatería**. An establishment that sells **pan** (*bread*) is a **panadería**. These words ending in **-ería** are always feminine:

la carnicería	*butcher's, butcher shop* (from the word **carne**, *meat*)
la joyería	*jewelry store* (from the word **joya**, *jewel*)
la juguetería	*toy store* (from the word **juguete**, *toy*)
la librería	*bookstore* (from the word **libro**, *book*)
la panadería	*bread store* or *bakery* (from the word **pan**, *bread*)
la pastelería	*pastry shop* (from the word **pastel**, *cake*)
la peluquería	*hairdresser's* (from the words **pelo**, *hair* or **peluca**, *wig*)

Watch out! To say *library*, it's **la biblioteca**. Una **librería** is a *bookstore*.

¿Hay un baño aquí?	*Is there a restroom here?*
¿Hay una panadería cerca?	*Is there a bakery nearby?*

Adverbs of place are commonly used with **hay** to talk about location. For instance: **cerca** (*near, nearby*), **aquí/acá** (*here*), **por aquí** (*around here*), **allí/allá** (*over there*), **en esta calle** (*on this street*), **en este barrio** (*in this neighborhood*).

¿Hay una librería por aquí?	*Is there a bookstore around here?*
¿Hay un bar cerca?	*Is there a bar nearby?*

When you're making a statement or giving an answer, use **hay** to say if something exists or to describe where something is.

Allí hay un restaurante bueno.	*There is a good restaurant over there.*
En Nueva York hay parques grandes.	*In New York there are large parks.*

Use the negative **no hay** (*there isn't/there aren't*) to say that something does not exist. Look at these examples:

No hay paradas de bus cerca.	*There aren't (any) bus stops nearby.*
No, no hay un parque grande en esta ciudad.	*No, there isn't a large park in this city.*

You can use **en** (*in*) plus the location to ask about or to describe where something is. For instance, **en la calle** (*on the street*), **en el barrio** (*in the neighborhood*), **en Toledo** (*in Toledo* [*the city*]).

¿Hay restaurantes cubanos en tu barrio?	*Are there Cuban restaurants in your neighborhood?*
Hay tres parques en la ciudad.	*There are three parks in the city.*

To talk about *this* street or *this* neighborhood use **este/estos** with masculine nouns:

¿Hay museos en este barrio?	*Are there any museums in this neighborhood?*

Use **esta/estas** with feminine nouns.

¿Hay una estación de tren en esta calle? *Is there a train station on this street?*

Note that when a plural noun follows **hay**, no article is used.

¿Hay discotecas buenas en Lima? *Are there good nightclubs in Lima?*

Hay librerías en el centro de la ciudad. *There are bookstores in the city center.*

Oral Practice 4-1

 TRACK 35

For each situation below, make a question or statement with **hay**. Say each answer out loud, and write it down if you have to. Then listen to the recording to check your answer, and repeat what you hear.

1. You'd like to know if there's a bank nearby. ¿_____ un banco cerca?

2. You are looking for a square around here. ¿_____ por aquí?

3. Ask if there is a train station in this neighborhood. ¿_____ en este barrio?

4. Explain that there are no markets nearby. _____ mercados _____.

5. Say that there is a bookstore on this street. _____ una librería _____.

6. You'd like to know if there is a bar nearby. ¿_____?

7. Tell someone that there is a large park in Chicago. _____.

8. You are looking for a museum on this street. ¿_____?

9. Say that there are no stores nearby. _____.

10. Say that there are supermarkets around here. _____.

GIVING INFORMATION WITH *HAY*

You learned above how to give full answers to questions with **¿Hay?** To make simple *yes* or *no* answers with **hay**, simply say **Sí, hay** or **No, no hay**.

¿Hay un gimnasio en el hotel?	*Is there a gym in the hotel?*
Sí, hay.	*Yes, there is.*
No, no hay.	*No, there isn't.*

Instead of repeating the entire noun phrase, you can also make a short answer by using only the indefinite article (**un**, **una**, etc.) in your answer. For example, **unas tiendas** becomes simply **unas**; **unas tiendas cerca** becomes **unas cerca**. Compare the following long and short answers:

¿Hay una juguetería cerca?	*Is there a toy store nearby?*
Sí, hay una juguetería allí.	*Yes, there is a toy store over there.*
Sí, hay una allí.	*Yes, there's one over there.*

Note that when used alone, **un** becomes **uno**.

| ¿Hay un banco por aquí? | *Is there a bank around here?* |
| Sí, hay uno en la esquina. | *Yes, there is one on the corner.* |

You can use the adjectives **muchos** (*many*), **varios** (*several*), **algunos** (*some, a few*), and **pocos** (*few*) to talk about amounts. These adjectives agree with the nouns they modify and replace the article: **una casa** (*a house*) → **muchas casas** (*many houses*).

| Hay varias tiendas en la plaza. | *There are several stores in the square.* |
| Hay pocos restaurantes en mi barrio. | *There are few restaurants in my neighborhood.* |

As with articles, you can use adjectives like **muchos** (*many*), **varios** (*several*), **algunos** (*some, a few*), and **pocos** (*few*) to make short answers by omitting the noun.

¿Hay muchas peluquerías en Santo Domingo?	*Are there a lot of hair salons in Santo Domingo?*
Sí, hay muchas.	*Yes, there are a lot.*
No, hay pocas.	*No, there are few (not many).*

Double Negatives

Technically, **ninguno** means *none*. Therefore, **no hay ninguno** really means *there aren't none*, but we translate it into English as *there aren't any*. You will see that double negatives come up a lot in Spanish. For instance, **no hay nada** (*lit.: there isn't nothing* or *there isn't anything*) and **no hay nadie** (*lit.: there isn't no one* or *there isn't anyone*). These double negatives are not only acceptable in Spanish, they are correct!

Earlier, you learned how to make negative statements with **no hay**. To say there isn't *any* of something, use **ningún** (masculine) or **ninguna** (feminine), plus the singular noun.

¿Hay una juguetería cerca?	*Is there a toy store nearby?*
No, no hay ninguna juguetería.	*No, there aren't any toy stores.*
No, no hay ninguna.	*No, there aren't any.*

When giving a short answer for masculine nouns, use **ninguno** instead of **ningún**.

¿Hay parques en tu ciudad?	*Are there any parks in your city?*
No, no hay ninguno.	*No, there aren't any.*

Written Practice 4-2

Match the question on the left column with an appropriate short answer on the right column (a, b, c, or d).

1. _____ ¿Hay un parque cerca? (sí)	a. Sí, hay una.
2. _____ ¿Hay un estacionamiento cerca? (no)	b. Sí, hay uno.
3. _____ ¿Hay una panadería cerca? (sí)	c. No, no hay ninguno.
4. _____ ¿Hay un centro comercial cerca? (sí)	d. No, no hay ninguna.

5. _____ ¿Hay un baño cerca? (no)

6. _____ ¿Hay una pastelería cerca? (sí)

7. _____ ¿Hay muchas tiendas cerca? (no)

8. _____ ¿Hay varios gimnasios cerca? (no)

WHAT'S THAT? ASKING ABOUT PLACES AND THINGS

When learning a new language and learning its culture, it's important to be able to ask questions about unfamiliar names and things. Use the question word **¿Qué... ?** (*What . . . ?*) with the verb **ser** (*to be*) (see Chapter 2) to ask basic *What is . . . ?* questions about things.

¿Qué es eso?   *What's that?*

¿Qué es el Prado?   *What is the Prado?*

¿Qué es una «bodega»?   *What is a "bodega"?*

To ask what type or kind of something is, use **¿Qué tipo de** + (*noun*) + **es?**

¿Qué tipo de restaurante es?   *What type of restaurant is it?*

¿Qué tipo de museo es?   *What type of museum is it?*

¿Qué tipo de tienda es?   *What type of store is it?*

Es una tienda de ropa.   *It's a clothing store.*

Written Practice 4-3

Write the question that goes with each answer using **¿Qué tipo de... es... ?**

1. ¿_____ es Old Navy? Es una tienda de ropa.

2. ¿_____ es Él Chalán? Es un restaurante peruano.

3. ¿_____ es McSorley's? Es un bar irlandés.

4. ¿_____ es Aldi? Es un supermercado.

5. ¿_____ es Alicia? Es una persona muy simpática.

VOCABULARY DEMYSTIFIED

De

While in English we often join two nouns together to describe particular places or things (*fruit stand*, *fish market*, *art museum*), Spanish often uses **de** (*of*) + (*noun*) to describe and specify types of things. For instance, to describe various types of markets you can say **el mercado de frutas** (*fruit market*), **el mercado de artesanías** (*craft market*), and **el mercado de pescado** (*fish market*). Here are some more examples:

la estación de metro	*subway station*	la parada de autobús	*bus stop*
la estación de tren	*train station*	la parada de metro	*subway stop*
el museo de arte	*art museum*	la tienda de comida	*food store*
el museo de ciencias	*science museum*	la tienda de ropa	*clothing store*

Oral Practice 4-2

 TRACK 36

Listen to the following dialogues, and indicate what the people are looking for. Say your answer out loud.

1. Dora stops a man on the street.

   Dora busca _____. *Dora is looking for . . .*

2. Teo stops a young man on the street.

   Teo busca _____. *Teo is looking for . . .*

3. Gilda stops a man on the street.

   Gilda busca _____. *Gilda is looking for . . .*

4. Diana stops a man on the street.

   Diana busca _____. *Diana is looking for . . .*

Oral Practice 4-3

 TRACK 37

Read each situation, and say your answer out loud. Then listen to the recording to check your answer, and repeat what you hear.

1. You are on a bus in Mexico, and you'd like to walk past someone.
2. You say, "thank you very much."
3. Someone says **gracias**, you say . . .
4. You want to know if there is a coffee shop around here.
5. You want to know if there is a parking lot on Calle Sol.
6. You want to know what Falabella is.
7. You want to know what type of restaurant Restaurante Callao is.
8. Someone asks you if there is a post office nearby. There aren't any post offices nearby.
9. Someone asks you if there is a subway station around here. There aren't any around here.
10. Someone asks you whether there is a gym nearby. There is one on Calle Central.

Asking for and Giving Directions

Pablo decides he's going to try to find **el restaurante Callao**, the Cuban restaurant the man told him about. Listen to the conversation. Where is the restaurant?

 TRACK 38

PABLO: Por favor, ¿puede ayudarme? ¿Conoce el restaurante Callao?

Excuse me. Can you help me? Do you know Callao Restaurant?

MANUEL: Sí, claro. Es un restaurante cubano. ¡Es muy bueno!

Yes, of course. It's a Cuban restaurant. It's very good!

PABLO: ¿Sabe dónde está?

Do you know where it is?

MANUEL: Sí, está en la Calle Rosales. ¿Sabe dónde queda?	*Yes, it's on Rosales Street. Do you know where that is?*
PABLO: No, no sé. No conozco este barrio. ¿Está lejos de aquí?	*No, I don't know this neighborhood. Is it far from here?*
MANUEL: No muy lejos...	*Not very far . . .*
PABLO: ¿Dónde está exactamente?	*Where is it exactly?*
MANUEL: Está al lado del Museo de Arte. Está a diez minutos en autobús.	*It's next to the Art Museum. It's ten minutes away by bus.*
PABLO: ¿Dónde está la parada de autobús?	*Where is the bus stop?*
MANUEL: Allí, en la Avenida Central. A dos bloques de aquí.	*Over there, at Central Avenue. Two blocks from here.*
PABLO: Muchas gracias.	*Thanks a lot.*
MANUEL: De nada.	*You're welcome.*

Pablo learns that the **restaurante Callao** is on **la Calle Rosales**, near the art museum about ten minutes away by bus. If you didn't catch any or all of this, try listening again, or use the translation to help you.

ASKING ABOUT AND DESCRIBING LOCATION

Above you learned how to ask *what* something is, using **¿Qué es... ?** Now you will learn to ask *where* something is, using **¿Dónde está... ?**

¿Dónde está el cine?	*Where is the movie theater?*
¿Dónde está la Calle Soria?	*Where is Soria Street?*
¿Dónde está Lucía?	*Where is Lucía?*

To ask where more than one thing is, use **¿Dónde están... ?**

¿Dónde están las tiendas?	*Where are the stores?*
¿Dónde están Rosa y Alejandro?	*Where are Rosa and Alejandro?*

You can use the other forms of the verb **estar** (see Chapter 2) to ask where people are, as well.

¿Dónde estás?	*Where are you?*
¿Dónde estamos?	*Where are we?*

¿Dónde queda... ? is another way commonly used to ask where something is located. **¿Dónde quedan... ?** is the plural.

¿Dónde queda el hospital?	*Where is the hospital located?*
¿Dónde quedan los baños?	*Where are the bathrooms located?*

In order to give or understand directions, it's important to know certain prepositions and prepositional phrases. Here is a list to get you started:

Prepositions

en	*in, at*	encima de	*above, on top of*
delante de	*in front of*	debajo de	*below, under*
detrás de	*behind*	dentro (de)	*inside (of)*
al lado de	*next to*	fuera (de)	*outside (of)*
a la izquierda (de)	*to the left (of)*	cerca (de)	*near*
a la derecha (de)	*to the right (of)*	lejos (de)	*far (from)*

Here are some examples of these prepositions used in sentences:

El banco está al lado del supermercado.	*The bank is next to the supermarket.*
La tienda de ropa está a la izquierda de la lavandería.	*The clothing store is to the left of the laundromat.*
El restaurante está encima del bar.	*The restaurant is above the bar.*
Aurora está detrás de Manuel.	*Aurora is behind Manuel.*
El cine está dentro del centro comercial.	*The movie theater is inside the mall.*

To describe how far away something is, use **estar** + **a** + (*distance*). You can refer to the number of **bloques** (*blocks*) or **calles** (*streets*), or you can talk about its distance in **minutos** (*minutes*) or **horas** (*hours*).

El banco está a dos bloques.	*The bank is two blocks away.*
El cine está a cinco minutos.	*The movie theater is five minutes away.*

To specify distance using a certain mode of transportation, follow the above construction with **en** + (*mode of transportation*): **en carro**, **en tren**, **en bus**. Careful! The exception to the rule is **a pie** (*on foot*).

La discoteca está a veinte minutos en carro.	*The disco is twenty minutes away by car.*
El parque está a diez minutos a pie.	*The park is ten minutes away on foot.*

To say how many blocks or minutes away something is, first you will need to know the numbers. Let's start with 1 to 15. You will learn more numbers in the next chapter.

Numbers 1 to 15

1 uno	6 seis	11 once
2 dos	7 siete	12 doce
3 tres	8 ocho	13 trece
4 cuatro	9 nueve	14 catorce
5 cinco	10 diez	15 quince

Oral Practice 4-4

Practice asking for directions to each place using **¿Dónde está(n)... ?**

1. el parque
2. la biblioteca
3. las tiendas baratas
4. la parada de metro
5. Andrés y Sergio
6. los buses
7. el supermercado natural
8. la oficina de correos

Written Practice 4-4

Translate the following sentences into Spanish.

1. The supermarket is next to the parking lot.

   _____

2. The square is to the left of the museum.

   _____

3. The gym is to the right of the clothing store.

   _____

4. The art museum is near Avenida Central.

   _____

5. Bar Sol is far away.

   _____

6. The library is behind the park.

   _____

7. The coffee shop is a five-minute walk away.

   _____

8. The bookstore is ten minutes away by bus.

   _____

GETTING INFORMATION ABOUT LOCATION WITH
SABER AND *CONOCER*

Spanish has two ways of saying *to know*: **saber** and **conocer**. Say these excerpts from the opening conversation out loud:

¿Conoce el restaurante Callao?	*Do you know Callao Restaurant?*
¿Sabe dónde está?	*Do you know where it is?*
No conozco este barrio.	*I don't know this neighborhood.*
No, no sé.	*No, I don't know.*

GRAMMAR DEMYSTIFIED

Saber and conocer

Here are the conjugations for the verbs **saber** and **conocer**:

yo sé	*I know*	yo conozco	*I know*
tú sabes	*you know (informal)*	tú conoces	*you know (informal)*
usted sabe	*you know (formal)*	usted conoce	*you know (formal)*
él/ella sabe	*he/she/it knows*	él/ella conoce	*he/she/it knows*
nosotros(as) sabemos	*we know*	nosotros(as) conocemos	*we know*
vosotros(as) sabéis	*you know (informal, Spain)*	vosotros(as) conocéis	*you know (informal, Spain)*
ustedes saben	*you know (formal)*	ustedes conocen	*you know (formal)*
ellos/ellas saben	*they know*	ellos/ellas conocen	*they know*

Saber means *to know* in the most traditional sense of the word: to have knowledge of. You can use ¿**Saber** + **dónde está...** ? or ¿**Saber** + **dónde hay...** ? to ask if someone knows where a certain place or person is. **Saber** is most often followed by clauses, verbs, and question words.

¿Sabe dónde está la Calle San Miguel?	*Do you know where San Miguel Street is?*
¿Sabes dónde hay una biblioteca?	*Do you know where there is a library?*

People may answer with **No sé** or **No lo sé** (*I don't know*).

Conocer is used in the sense of *to be familiar with*, often with people or places. You would use it to ask if a person has visited a certain country or met a certain person. **Conocer** is often followed by a noun.

¿Conoce usted este barrio?	*Do you know this neighborhood?*
¿Conoce a Carmen?	*Do you know Carmen?*

Conocer is also used to mean *to meet* when meeting someone for the first time.

No, pero la quiero conocer.   *No, but I want to meet her.*

When using **conocer** to talk about people, you must use the personal **a** after the verb: **conocer a**. Note that **a** + **el** → **al**.

¿Conoce a Pablo?   *Do you know Pablo?*

¿Conoces al Señor Hernández?   *Do you know Mr. Hernández?*

To be more specific when asking for directions, you can use some of the adjectives you learned in Chapter 2 to describe people, such as **divertido**, **aburrido**, etc., to describe **lugares** (*places*). Here are some more adjectives:

Adjectives to Describe Places

agradable	*pleasant*	histórico(a)	*historic*
amplio(a)	*spacious*	malo(a)	*bad*
bueno(a)	*good*	romántico(a)	*romantic*
de moda	*in, fashionable, trendy*	turístico(a)	*touristy*

Here are some examples of sentences asking about places:

¿Sabe dónde hay un parque agradable?   *Do you know where there is a pleasant park?*

¿Sabes dónde está la zona histórica?   *Do you know where the historic area is?*

¿Conoces una discoteca de moda?   *Do you know a trendy disco?*

¿Conoces un restaurante romántico?   *Do you know a romantic restaurant?*

Note that **bueno** and **malo** often fall before the noun in the shortened forms **buen** and **mal**.

¿Conoces un buen lugar para comer marisco?   *Do you know a good place to eat seafood?*

Using the "a" personal

Spanish uses the **a personal** (*personal "a"*), as it is known, before the direct object when the direct object is a person (or a pet). The **a personal** is not used with things. Compare these examples:

Vemos **a** Matilde.	*We see Matilde.*
Llamo **a** alguien.	*I call someone.*
El policía persigue **al** ladrón.	*The police officer chases the burglar.*

But . . .

Vemos una película.	*We see a movie.*

The personal **a** is not used with the verb **tener** (*to have*).

Tengo dos hijas.	*I have two daughters.*

Written Practice 4-5

Complete the following sentences with **sabe** or **conoce**.

1. ¿_____ usted dónde hay un restaurante romántico?
2. ¿_____ usted bien este barrio?
3. ¿_____ dónde está la Plaza La Sala?
4. ¿_____ usted a Luisa, la hermana de Andrés?
5. ¿_____ usted Nueva York?
6. ¿_____ dónde hay un bar divertido?

Written Practice 4-6

Translate the following sentences into English.

1. ¿Sabe usted dónde hay un estacionamiento amplio?

   _____

2. ¿Conoce usted el Barrio San Juan?

   _____

3. ¿Sabe usted dónde está la estación Atocha?

   _____

4. ¿Sabe usted dónde hay una parada de metro?

   _____

5. ¿Sabe usted dónde está la Calle Dolores?

   _____

6. ¿Conoces a Ana, la amiga de Eduardo?

   _____

Oral Practice 4-5

Listen to the following dialogues, and indicate whether the statements are **cierto o falso** (*true or false*).

🔘 TRACK 39

1. A woman asks about a bookstore.

   ¿Cierto o falso? La librería Alcón está a la izquierda del restaurante. *The Alcón bookstore is to the left of the restaurant.* _____

2. A man is looking for Restaurante Olla.

   ¿Cierto o falso? El Restaurante Olla está al lado del Bar Copa. *Restaurante Olla is next to the Bar Copa.* _____

3. A man is looking for calle Mayor.

   ¿Cierto o falso? La calle Mayor está muy cerca. *Calle Mayor is nearby.*

   _____

4. A woman is looking for a coffee shop in a mall.

¿Cierto o falso? La cafetería está dentro del centro comercial. *The coffee shop is inside the mall.* _____

Chapter Practice

 TRACK 40

Imagine Pablo stops you in your neighborhood to ask for directions. Listen to what he says, and then write your responses below. You can answer in any way that makes sense, as if it were a real conversation. Then listen to the recording, and practice your conversation with him during the pauses. After you are done, listen to the model dialogue to hear one version of the conversation.

PABLO: Disculpe. ¿Hay un restaurante mexicano cerca?

YOU: Sí, _____ uno en la Calle Mayor.

PABLO: Qué bien. ¿Está lejos la calle Mayor?

YOU: Sí, _____.

PABLO: ¿Hay una parada de metro cerca?

YOU: Sí, _____.

PABLO: Muchas gracias.

YOU: _____

PABLO: Hasta luego.

YOU: _____

QUIZ

Circle the letter of the word or phrase that best completes each sentence.

1. _____ ¿Dónde está la calle Abeto?

    (a) No hay de qué.

    (b) Disculpe.

    (c) De nada.

2. Perdone, ¿_____ un banco cerca?

    (a) aquí

    (b) está

    (c) hay

3. ¿Hay _____ restaurante mexicano en el barrio?

    (a) el

    (b) un

    (c) una

4. El restaurante está _____ la Plaza Aquiles.

    (a) detrás

    (b) en

    (c) izquierda

5. Hay _____ restaurantes buenos en el barrio.

    (a) ningún

    (b) muchas

    (c) varios

TRACK 41

Now listen to the recording to hear a phrase or question. Press pause, and say your answer: a, b, or c. Listen to the correct answer on the recording, and repeat what you hear. Then go to the next question, and repeat the process.

6. (a) Está a la derecha del cine.

    (b) Es una tienda de comida.

    (c) No hay ninguno.

7. (a) Detrás.

    (b) De nada.

    (c) Sí, hay muchas.

8. (a) Está a la derecha.

    (b) Es una tienda de ropa.

    (c) No hay ninguna.

9. (a) No, no hay una.

    (b) No hay de qué.

    (c) No, no sé.

10. (a) Sí.

    (b) A la derecha.

    (c) Fuera.

CHAPTER 5

Daily Life

In this chapter you will learn:

How to talk about time and date

How to talk about habits and schedules

Common regular verbs and the verb ir *(to go)*

How to talk about travel and timetables

Talking About Time and Date

 TRACK 42

Pablo is surprised to hear from Susana after their unfortunate date. Maybe it wasn't so bad after all! Listen to the conversation. Why does Susana have to get off the phone?

TELÉFONO: *¡Rin, rin!*   *Ring, ring!*

PABLO: ¿Aló?   *Hello?*

SUSANA: ¿Está Pablo?   *Is Pablo there?*

PABLO: Sí, soy yo. ¿Quién es?   *Yes, this is he. Who's this?*

SUSANA: Hola, soy Susana.   *Hi, it's Susana.*

PABLO: ¡Hola!   *Hi!*

(Pasan treinta minutos...)   *(Thirty minutes go by . . .)*

SUSANA: Entonces, ¿cuándo es tu cumpleaños?   *So, when is your birthday?*

PABLO: El veintinueve de marzo.   *March twenty-ninth.*

SUSANA: ¡Ah! Eres Aries. ¡Qué interesante!   *Oh, you're an Aries. How interesting!*

PABLO: ¿Y tu cumpleaños? ¿Qué fecha es?   *And your birthday? When is it?*

SUSANA: El dos de diciembre. Soy sagitario.   *December second. I'm a Sagittarius.*

PABLO: ¿De qué año?   *What year?*

SUSANA: ¡Tú quieres saber mi edad! No es muy caballeroso...   *You want to know my age? That's not very gentlemanly of you . . .*

PABLO: Lo siento.   *I'm sorry.*

SUSANA: ¡Era broma! Nací en el año 1975. ¿Y tú?   *It was a joke. I was born in 1975. And you?*

PABLO: Yo también. ¡Qué casualidad! Oye, ¿qué hora es?   *Me, too. What a coincidence! Hey, what time is it?*

SUSANA: Son las diez de la noche. ¡Qué tarde!   *It's ten P.M. So late! . . .*

(Continuará...)   *(To be continued . . .)*

TELLING TIME

Susana and Pablo end the conversation because it has gotten late. **Son las diez de la noche** (*It's ten o'clock at night.*). Look again to see how Pablo asks what time it is and how Susana responds.

¿Qué hora es?	*What time is it?*
Son las diez de la noche.	*It's ten o'clock at night.*

There are a number of ways to ask someone what time it is.

¿Qué hora es?	*What time is it?*
¿Tiene(s) hora?	*Do you have the time?*
¿Sabe(s) qué hora es?	*Do you know what time it is?*

To tell the time, first you will need to know the numbers. You already learned 1 to 15 in Chapter 4. Listen and repeat what you hear.

TRACK 43

1 uno	6 seis	11 once
2 dos	7 siete	12 doce
3 tres	8 ocho	13 trece
4 cuatro	9 nueve	14 catorce
5 cinco	10 diez	15 quince

The numbers 16 through 19 begin with **dieci-**, which comes from **diez** + **y** (*ten and*). Listen and repeat what you hear.

16 dieciséis	17 diecisiete	18 dieciocho	19 diecinueve

Similarly, 21 to 29 begin with **veinti-**, which comes from **veinte** + **y** (*twenty and*). Listen and repeat what you hear.

21 veintiuno	24 veinticuatro	27 veintisiete
22 veintidós	25 veinticinco	28 veintiocho
23 veintitrés	26 veintiséis	29 veintinueve

As long as you are learning the numbers, you might as well go up to 100! Here are the tens, from 20 to 100. Listen and repeat what you hear.

20 veinte	50 cincuenta	80 ochenta
30 treinta	60 sesenta	90 noventa
40 cuarenta	70 setenta	100 cien

Compound numbers after 30 are written as three words: (*tens*) + **y** + (*ones*). Listen and repeat what you hear.

31 treinta y uno	53 cincuenta y tres	78 setenta y ocho
42 cuarenta y dos	66 sesenta y seis	99 noventa y nueve

To answer the question **¿Qué hora es?** (*What time is it?*), you can say: **Es la una**, for *one o'clock* and **Son las** + (*time*) for all other times. Listen and repeat what you hear.

¿Qué hora es?	*What time is it?*
Es la una.	*It's one o'clock.*
Son las dos.	*It's two o'clock.*
Son las once.	*It's eleven o'clock.*

For half past the hour, say the hour plus **y media** (*half past*) or **y treinta** (. . . *thirty*).

Es la una y media.	*It's 1:30.*
Son las cinco y media.	*It's 5:30.*
Son las siete y treinta.	*It's 7:30.*

For a quarter to the hour say (*hour*) + **menos cuarto** (*quarter to*). For a quarter past the hour say (*hour*) + **y cuarto** (*quarter past*). Or you can use the actual number of minutes: **y quince**, **menos quince**, **y cuarenta y cinco**.

Es la una y cuarto./Es la una y quince.	*It's 1:15.*
Son las once menos cuarto./Son las diez y cuarenta y cinco.	*It's 10:45.*
Son las tres y quince./Son las tres y cuarto.	*It's 3:15.*

For all other times use **y** (*and*) + (*number of minutes*) to talk about minutes past the hour and **menos** (*minus*) + (*number of minutes*) to talk about minutes before the hour.

Son las tres y veinte.	*It's 3:20.*
Son las diez y diez.	*It's 10:10.*
Es la una menos cinco./Son las doce y cincuenta y cinco.	*It's 12:55.*
Son las doce menos veinte./Son las once y cuarenta.	*It's 11:40.*

Note that in Spanish you never use **menos** with more than twenty-nine minutes before the hour. However, you can always use **y** with any number of minutes after the hour.

To distinguish between A.M. and P.M., use **de la mañana** (*in the morning*), **de la tarde** (*in the afternoon/evening*), and **de la noche** (*at night*).

Son las diez de la mañana.	*It's 10:00 A.M.*
Son las tres de la tarde.	*It's 3:00 P.M.*
Son las once de la noche.	*It's 11:00 P.M.*

Oral Practice 5-1

 TRACK 44

¿Qué hora es? (*What time is it?*) Answer this question for each of the times listed. Say your answers out loud, and listen to the recording as you go along to check your answers. There may be more than one way to express each time of day.

1. 2:00
2. 3:30
3. 1:10
4. 7:15
5. 7:45

6. 11:13
7. 9:40
8. 5:27 A.M.
9. 4:15 P.M.
10. 12:50

Oral Practice 5-2

 TRACK 45

Listen to the short dialogues of people asking for and telling the time. Circle the correct time according to what you hear.

1. (a) It's 11:00 P.M.
   (b) It's 11:00 A.M.
   (c) It's 11:11 P.M.
2. (a) It's 10:00 P.M.
   (b) It's 10:10 A.M.
   (c) It's 10:00 A.M.
3. (a) It's 1:15 P.M.
   (b) It's 12:45 P.M.
   (c) It's 4:00 P.M.
4. (a) It's 7:40.
   (b) It's 8:20.
   (c) It's 12:08.
5. (a) It's 6:30 A.M.
   (b) It's 6:00 A.M.
   (c) It's 6:30 P.M.
6. (a) It's 2:10 P.M.
   (b) It's 2:25 P.M.
   (c) It's 1:50 P.M.

ASKING AND TELLING THE DATE

In the opening conversation, Pablo and Susana ask each other's birthday. Look at how they express dates in these excerpts:

¿Qué fecha es?	*What's the date?*
El veintinueve de marzo.	*March 29th.*
El dos de diciembre.	*December 2nd.*
Nací en el año 1975 (mil novecientos setenta y cinco).	*I was born in 1975.*

To ask what day it is, simply say **¿Qué fecha es?** (*What is the date?*). To answer this question, you have to know the months of the year. Note that, as with days of the week, the months in Spanish are not capitalized. Listen and repeat what you hear.

 TRACK 46

Months

enero	*January*	julio	*July*
febrero	*February*	agosto	*August*
marzo	*March*	setiembre/septiembre	*September*
abril	*April*	octubre	*October*
mayo	*May*	noviembre	*November*
junio	*June*	diciembre	*December*

To answer the question **¿Qué fecha es?** (*What is the date?*), say **Es el** (*number*) + **de** + (*month*). (Note: The **el** is not obligatory.)

Es el 30 de abril.	*It is April 30th.*
Es el 12 de agosto.	*It's August 12th.*

Although you can use **primero** for the *first* of the month, usually **uno, dos, tres** are used to say the *first, second,* and *third.*

El primero de marzo./El uno de marzo.	*The first of March.*
El dos de julio.	*July second.*
El tres de enero.	*January third.*

If you would like to mention the year, Spanish speakers say the whole number, starting with *one thousand, two thousand,* etc.

1700s: mil setecientos...	*1900s*: mil novecientos...
1800s: mil ochocientos...	*2000s*: dos mil...

For example:

1970: mil novecientos setenta	*2002*: dos mil dos
1926: mil novecientos veintiséis	*2009*: dos mil nueve

So, to give the day, month, and year that something happened, add the year by saying **de/del** + *(year).*

February 20, 2010	el veinte de febrero del dos mil diez
October 13, 1994	el trece de octubre de mil novecientos noventa y cuatro

In Chapter 2 you learned the days of the week. You can use the days of the week after **hoy** *(today)*, **mañana** *(tomorrow)*, and **ayer** *(yesterday)* + **ser** to give the date.

Hoy es martes doce.	*Today is Tuesday the twelfth.*
Mañana es miércoles veintiséis.	*Tomorrow is Wednesday the twenty-sixth.*
Ayer fue lunes trece.	*Yesterday was Monday the thirteenth.*

Written Practice 5-1

Write the following dates in Spanish.

1. November 5 _____
2. July 20 _____
3. February 9 _____
4. May 27 _____
5. June 7 _____
6. September 22, 2011 _____
7. March 13, 1953 _____
8. August 30, 2009 _____
9. January 1, 1996 _____
10. December 25, 2001 _____

Oral Practice 5-3

 TRACK 47

Listen to the following dialogues, and indicate whether the statements are **cierto o falso** (*true or false*).

1. A man stops someone to ask the time.

   ¿Cierto o falso? Son las diez de la mañana. *It's 10:00 A.M.* _____

2. A friend asks for the time.

   ¿Cierto o falso? Son las once menos cuarto. *It's 10:45.* _____

3. During an emergency call, an EMT asks a patient basic questions.

   ¿Cierto o falso? Es el veinte de junio. *It's June 20th.* _____

   Son las once de la noche. *It's 11:00 P.M.* _____

4. At work, two colleagues talk about their birthdays.

   ¿Cierto o falso? Es el tres de abril. *It's April 3rd.* _____

   Son las cinco y media de la tarde. *It's 5:30 P.M.*

Navigating a Schedule

 TRACK 48

Listen as Pablo and Susana continue their conversation.

SUSANA: Son las diez de la noche. ¡Qué tarde!

It's 10:00 P.M. It's so late!

PABLO: ¿A qué hora vas a dormir?

What time do you go to bed?

SUSANA: Generalmente a las diez...

Generally at ten . . .

PABLO: ¿Tan temprano?

So early?

SUSANA: Sí. Trabajo de siete a cinco. ¿A qué hora vas tú a dormir?

Yeah. I work from seven to five. What time do you go to bed?

PABLO: Yo bastante tarde. Generalmente hacia las doce o la una. ¿Cómo vas al trabajo? ¿Manejas?

Me? Pretty late. Usually around twelve or one. How do you go to work? Do you drive?

SUSANA: Voy en autobús.

I go by bus.

PABLO: ¿Y a qué hora sales de casa por la mañana?

What time do you leave in the morning?

SUSANA: Salgo a las seis de la mañana.

I leave at six in the morning.

PABLO: Entonces, buenas noches. Veo que tienes sueño.

Well, good night. I can see you're tired.

SUSANA: Buenas noches, Pablo.

Good night, Pablo.

TALKING ABOUT HABITS AND CALENDAR

In the opening conversation Pablo and Susana use the present tense to talk about habits, or things they do on a regular basis. Look at these examples from the dialogue:

Trabajo de siete a cinco.	*I work from seven to five.*
¿Cómo **vas** al trabajo? ¿**Manejas**?	*How **do you go** to work? **Do you drive**?*
Voy en autobús.	*I go by bus.*
Salgo a las seis de la mañana.	*I leave at six in the morning.*

The present tense is often used to describe something that happens regularly, or that has a definite beginning or end.

El evento comienza a las ocho.	*The event starts at eight.*
Estudio los lunes y viernes.	*I study on Mondays and Fridays.*

To ask at what time something happens in the present, say **¿A qué hora** + (*present tense*)**?** (*What time...?*), and respond with **A las...** + (*time*) (*At . . .*).

¿A qué hora es el evento?	*What time is the event?*
A las ocho de la noche.	*At 8:00 P.M.*

You can use the same structures to ask or talk about someone's routine or calendar. You can ask with **¿A qué hora... ?** (*What time . . . ?*) or with **¿Cuándo... ?** (*When . . . ?*)

¿A qué hora empiezas a trabajar?	*What time do you start work?*
A las ocho de la mañana.	*At 8:00 A.M.*
¿Cuándo almuerza usted?	*When do you eat lunch?*
Generalmente a las doce y media.	*Generally at 12:30.*

You can use time expressions such as **por la mañana**, **por la tarde**, and **por la noche** with the present tense to talk about the time of day that something happens.

Por la mañana, camino al trabajo.	*In the morning, I walk to work.*
Leo un libro por la tarde.	*I read a book in the afternoon.*
Por la noche, miro la televisión.	*At night, I watch TV.*

Some expressions of time also signal that an action is habitual, such as **generalmente** (*generally*), **normalmente** (*normally*), **a menudo** (*often*), **siempre** (*always*), **nunca** (*never*), and **con frecuencia** (*frequently*). You can also use **los** + (*day of the week*) to talk about events that occur regularly on that day (*on Mondays, on Tuesdays*, etc.) To say *on the weekends*, use **los fines de semana**.

Los lunes voy al gimnasio.   *On Mondays I go to the gym.*

Visito a mi abuela a menudo.   *I visit my grandmother often.*

Written Practice 5-2

Ramón is asking Carla about her schedule. Using the translation to help you, write the missing text in the blank. Practice saying the dialogue out loud, completing each sentence with the correct expressions.

1. Ramón: ¿A qué hora empiezas _____ la mañana?
   What time do you start work in the morning?

2. Carla: Empiezo _____ nueve de la mañana.
   I start at 9:00 A.M.

3. Ramón: ¿Y _____ terminas?
   And what time do you finish?

4. Carla: Termino a las seis de la _____ .
   I finish at 6:00 P.M.

5. Ramón: ¿Trabajas _____ fines de semana?
   Do you work on the weekends?

6. Carla: Sí. Normalmente trabajo _____ sábados.
   Yes. Usually I work on Saturdays.

CONJUGATING REGULAR VERBS IN THE PRESENT

In Chapter 1 you learned that the verb is made up of two parts, the root (or stem) and the ending, and that when verbs are conjugated, their endings indicate the verb's tense as well as who is carrying out the action. The majority of verbs are "regular," with predictable patterns. Regular verbs have one of three endings in the infinitive form: **-ar**, **-er**, or **-ir**.

To conjugate regular verbs in the present tense, drop the endings **-ar**, **-er**, or **-ir**, and add the ending specific to the person doing the action. Like this:

hablar (*to speak*) → drop **-ar**: **habl-** → add ending **-o** for **yo** → **yo hablo** (*I speak*)

beber (*to drink*) → drop **-er**: **beb-** → add ending **-es** for **tú** → **tú bebes** (*you drink*)

escribir (*to write*) → drop **-ir**: **escrib-** → add ending **-en** for **ellos/ellas** → **ellos/ellas escriben** (*they write*)

Here are the present tense endings for regular **-ar**, **-er**, and **-ir** verbs:

Ending in -ar: hablar	Ending in -er: beber	Ending in -ir: escribir
yo habl**o**	yo beb**o**	yo escrib**o**
tú habl**as**	tú beb**es**	tú escrib**es**
él/ella, usted habl**a**	él/ella, usted beb**e**	él/ella, usted escrib**e**
nosotros(as) habl**amos**	nosotros(as) beb**emos**	nosotros(as) escrib**imos**
vosotros(as) habl**áis**	vosotros(as) beb**éis**	vosotros(as) escrib**ís**
ellos/ellas, ustedes habl**an**	ellos/ellas, ustedes beb**en**	ellos/ellas, ustedes escrib**en**

Note that the endings for **-er** and **-ir** verbs are the same, with the exception of **nosotros(as)** and **vosotros(as)**.

Many verbs are English cognates and should be easy to understand. You saw some examples of these in Chapter 1. For example: **inventar** (*to invent*), **imaginar** (*to imagine*), **exagerar** (*to exaggerate*), **celebrar** (*to celebrate*), **practicar** (*to practice*), and **preparar** (*to prepare*).

Here are some of the most common **-ar** verbs:

Regular -ar Verbs

bailar	*to dance*	descansar	*to rest*	necesitar	*to need*
besar	*to kiss*	hablar	*to talk*	pronunciar	*to pronounce*
caminar	*to walk*	lavar	*to wash*	trabajar	*to work*
cocinar	*to cook*	limpiar	*to clean*	viajar	*to travel*
comprar	*to buy*				

Here are some example sentences with regular **-ar** verbs in the present tense. Remember that the subject (**yo**, **tú**, etc.) can be omitted in Spanish.

Trabajo de ocho a seis.	*I work from eight to six. (from* **trabajar** *to work)*
Elena siempre camina a la oficina.	*Elena always walks to work. (from* **caminar** *to walk)*
¿Viajas mucho?	*Do you travel a lot? (from* **viajar** *to travel)*

Here are some of the most common **-er** and **-ir** verbs:

-er verbs		**-ir verbs**	
aprender	*to learn*	abrir	*to open*
beber	*to drink*	admitir	*to admit*
comer	*to eat*	discutir	*to argue*
comprender	*to understand*	escribir	*to write*
correr	*to run*	recibir	*to receive*
leer	*to read*	subir	*to climb, to go up*
vender	*to sell*	vivir	*to live*

Here are some example sentences with **-er** and **-ir** verbs:

Gerardo lee muchos libros.	*Gerardo reads a lot of books. (from* **leer** *to read)*
¿Ustedes comprenden mucho español?	*Do you understand a lot of Spanish? (from* **comprender** *to understand)*
Diego es dominicano, pero vive aquí.	*Diego is Dominican, but he lives here. (from* **vivir** *to live)*

Don't forget that you can also use question words with the present tense to ask about habits or things that are generally true.

¿Qué ves?	*What do you see? (from* **ver** *to see)*
¿Quién trabaja aquí?	*Who works here? (from* **trabajar** *to work)*
¿Dónde vive usted?	*Where do you live? (from* **vivir** *to live)*

The Verb *ir*

To talk about how you go from one place to another, you can use the verb **ir** (*to go*). It is an *irregular* verb.

ir (*to go*)

yo voy	*I go*	nosotros(as) vamos	*we go*
tú vas	*you go (informal)*	vosotros(as) vais	*you go (Spain)*
usted va	*you go (formal)*	ustedes van	*you go*
él/ella va	*he, she goes*	ellos/ellas van	*they go*

Here are some example sentences with the verb **ir**:

¿Cómo vas a trabajar?   *How do you go to work?*

Voy a trabajar en metro.   *I go to work by subway.*

¿Ustedes van a clase de español en autobús?   *Do you go to Spanish class by bus?*

Nosotros no vamos a clase de español.   *We don't go to Spanish class.*

Written Practice 5-3

Match the conjugated verbs on the left with their English translations on the right.

1. nosotros aprendemos _____   a. you need

2. ellos bailan _____   b. you dance

3. tú escribes _____   c. they dance

4. ustedes abren _____   d. we don't drink

5. yo no comprendo _____   e. you write

6. usted necesita _____   f. we fix

7. ella vende _____   g. you open

8. arreglamos _____   h. we learn

9. bailas _____
10. no abren_____
11. comprendes_____
12. no bebemos _____

i. I don't understand
j. she sells
k. you understand
l. they don't open

Oral Practice 5-4

Read each sentence out loud, conjugating the verb according to the subject provided. Try to do the exercise without writing your answers first.

1. Yo _____ (aprender) español con este libro.

2. Anabel _____ (correr) el maratón de Boston.

3. Rebeca y Tomás _____ (discutir) todos los días.

4. ¿_____ (comer) ustedes en ese restaurante?

5. Isabel _____ (limpiar) la casa los sábados.

6. ¿Dónde _____ (trabajar) ustedes?

7. Nosotros _____ (comprar) en el supermercado Plas.

8. María _____ (vivir) en Chicago, pero yo _____ (vivir) en Nueva York.

9. ¿_____ (comprender) usted?

10. Tú _____ (pronunciar) muy bien.

GETTING AROUND

In the second half of the conversation between Susana and Pablo, Susana explains how she gets to work. Which of the following forms of transportation does she use?

el metro	*subway*	el autobús; el bus	*bus*
el tren	*train*	el carro	*car*

That's right, she goes by bus: **en autobús.**

Written Practice 5-4

Fill in the blanks with the correct form of the verb **ir**.

1. Ellos _____ en autobús.

2. Yo no _____ en tren.

3. Elena _____ en metro.

4. ¿Ustedes _____ a la fiesta?

5. Nosotras _____ a India de vacaciones.

6. Tú _____ a trabajar en tren, ¿no?

TALKING ABOUT TIMETABLES

To get somewhere on time, you will have to be able to read a timetable: **el horario**.
You'll encounter schedules for the train (**el horario de tren**), the subway (**el horario del metro**), and the bus (**el horario de bus**).

In much of Latin America, timetables use the twenty-four-hour (or "military")
system.

Llega a las veinte horas.	*It arrives at 20:00 (8:00 P.M.).*

When talking about **el horario**, you can use the verbs **salir** (*to leave, go out*) and
llegar (*to arrive*) to refer to departures (**salidas**) and arrivals (**llegadas**). Ask questions about the time with **¿A qué hora?** Note that only the first person (**yo** form) of
salir is irregular: **salgo**. Otherwise it is conjugated like other **-ir** verbs.

¿A qué hora sale el metro?	*What time does the subway leave?*
Sale a las ocho.	*It leaves at 8:00.*
¿A qué hora llega el tren?	*What time does the train arrive?*
Llega a las tres.	*It arrives at 3:00.*

Words like **siguiente** (*next*), **próximo** (*next*), and **último** (*last*) are extremely
useful when asking or talking about timetables.

¿A qué hora sale el siguiente tren?	*What time does the next train leave?*
El último autobús llega a medianoche.	*The last bus arrives at midnight.*

Other verbs commonly used when talking about schedules are **abrir** (*to open*), **cerrar** (*to close*), **empezar** (*to begin*), and **terminar** (*to end*).

¿A qué hora abre el centro comercial?	*What time does the mall open?*
La tienda cierra a las seis de la tarde.	*The store closes at 6:00 P.M.*
¿A qué hora empieza la película?	*What time does the movie start?*
El concierto termina a las diez.	*The concert ends at ten.*

In reading schedules you'll probably end up talking about frequency, using **cada** (*every*) + (*amount of time*): **minutos** (*minutes*), **media hora** (*half hour*), **horas** (*hours*), or **días** (*days*).

GRAMMAR DEMYSTIFIED

More Common Irregular Verbs

Below are some examples of commonly used irregular verbs. **Salir** and **venir** are both irregular; note their similarities in the first person. **Empezar** and **volver** are both stem-changing verbs. Stem-changing verbs follow a regular pattern, but within this pattern the stem changes as well as the endings. There are three types of stem-changing verbs: **o → ue**, **e → ie**, and **e → i**. For each type, the vowel in the stem (either **o** or **e**) changes in the present tense in every form except for **nosotros(as)** and **vosotros(as)**. For example:

volver → yo v**ue**lvo (**o → ue**)   empezar → ella emp**ie**za (**e → ie**)

Finally, note how **venir** (*to come*), even though it is irregular, shares similarities with the stem-changing verb **empezar** (*to begin, start*). Recognizing these types of similarities is a good way to help you memorize verb conjugations.

	salir *to leave*	**empezar (ie)** *to start*	**venir** *to come*	**volver (ue)** *to return*
yo	**salgo**	emp**ie**zo	**vengo**	v**ue**lvo
tú	sales	emp**ie**zas	v**ie**nes	v**ue**lves
usted	sale	emp**ie**za	v**ie**ne	v**ue**lve
él/ella	sale	emp**ie**za	v**ie**ne	v**ue**lve
nosotros(as)	salimos	empezamos	venimos	volvemos
vosotros(as)	salís	empezáis	venís	volvéis
ustedes	salen	emp**ie**zan	v**ie**nen	v**ue**lven
ellos/ellas	salen	emp**ie**zan	v**ie**nen	v**ue**lven

Hay un metro cada diez minutos.	*There is a subway every ten minutes.*
El autobús viene cada veinte minutos.	*The bus comes every twenty minutes.*
El tren sale cada media hora.	*The train leaves every half hour.*

You can also use the irregular verb **salir** (*to leave, go out*) to talk of people's plans.

Yo salgo a trabajar a las siete.	*I leave for work at 7:00.*
¿A qué hora quieres salir?	*What time do you want to go out?*

Written Practice 5-5

Pablo is checking the schedule for buses, subways, and trains. Use the schedules to help you answer the questions below.

Horario de autobús: 8:00 A.M., 8:30 A.M., 9:00 A.M., 9:30 A.M., 10:00 A.M., 10:30 A.M. . . .

Horario de metro: 8:10 A.M., 8:20 A.M., 8:30 A.M., 8:40 A.M., 8:50 A.M., 9:00 A.M., 9:10 A.M. . . .

Horario de tren: 8:08 A.M., 8:32 A.M., 8:48 A.M., 9:14 A.M., 9:54 A.M., 10:12 A.M. . . .

First, indicate whether the following statements are **cierto o falso** (*true or false*).

1. El autobús sale cada quince minutos. _____

2. El metro sale cada media hora. _____

3. Hay un autobús a las diez de la mañana. _____

4. Hay un tren a las nueve y cuarto. _____

5. Hay un autobús a las nueve y media. _____

Then, answer the following questions. Imagine it's 8:45 A.M. now.

6. ¿A qué hora sale el siguiente autobús? _____

7. ¿A qué hora sale el siguiente metro? _____

8. ¿A qué hora sale el siguiente tren? _____

9. ¿Hay un autobús a las ocho y treinta y dos? _____

10. ¿Hay un tren a las nueve de la mañana? _____

Oral Practice 5-5

Listen to the following dialogues, and indicate whether the statements are **cierto o falso** (*true or false*).

 TRACK 49

1. A man asks about a bus schedule.

    ¿Cierto o falso? El autobús sale a las dos y media. *The bus leaves at 2:30.*
    _____

2. A woman asks about a party.

    ¿Cierto o falso? La fiesta es a las nueve de la noche. *The party is at 9:00 P.M.* _____

    El bar cierra a las seis de la tarde. *The bar closes at 6:00 P.M.* _____

3. A man asks about a subway schedule.

    ¿Cierto o falso? El sábado el metro es cada media hora. *On Saturdays the subway runs every half hour.* _____

4. A woman asks about a train schedule.

    ¿Cierto o falso? El tren sale a las quince y cuarenta. *The train leaves at 3:40 P.M.* _____

Chapter Practice

 TRACK 50

Imagine you are chatting with a nosy friend who wants to know all the details about your life. Listen to what he says, and then write your responses below. After you are done, practice your conversation with him by interacting with the recording. Give any answer you want or that applies to you. Continue listening to hear a model dialogue.

FRIEND: Hola. Oye, ¿cuándo es tu   *Hi. Hey, when's your birthday?*
cumpleaños?

YOU: _____

FRIEND: ¿Celebras tu cumpleaños?   *Do you celebrate your birthday?*

YOU: _____

FRIEND: ¿Cómo vas a trabajar?   *How do you get to work?*

YOU: _____

FRIEND: ¿A qué hora vas a trabajar?   *What time do you go to work?*

YOU: _____

FRIEND: ¿Y a qué hora vas a casa?   *And what time do you go home?*

YOU: _____

FRIEND: ¿Qué hora es?   *What time is it?*

YOU: _____

FRIEND: Ay, ¡es tarde! Adiós.   *Oh, it's late! Bye.*

YOU: _____

QUIZ

 TRACK 51

Listen to the recording to hear a question. Press pause, and say your answer: a, b, or c. Listen to the correct answer on the recording, and repeat what you hear. Then go to the next question, and repeat the process.

1. (a) Son las tres y media.
   (b) A las cinco menos veinte.
   (c) Catorce de junio.
2. (a) Por la tarde.
   (b) Dos mil once.
   (c) Sábado.

3. (a) Es la una y cinco.

   (b) El dos mil dos.

   (c) A las diez y doce.

4. (a) Domingo.

   (b) El nueve de marzo.

   (c) Las cinco de la mañana.

5. (a) Luisa no trabaja.

   (b) A las ocho de la mañana.

   (c) Voy en autobús.

6. (a) Vivo en Estados Unidos.

   (b) Viven en Canadá.

   (c) Van a México.

7. (a) No, no viajamos mucho.

   (b) Sí, viaja mucho.

   (c) Sí, viajan mucho.

8. (a) Sí, aprendemos español.

   (b) No aprende usted español.

   (c) Sí, aprendo español.

9. (a) No, no comprendemos.

   (b) Sí, ustedes comprenden.

   (c) No comprendes tú.

10. (a) Camina a las tres.

    (b) Abre a las cinco.

    (c) Sale a las dos y veinte.

PART TWO

INTERMEDIATE COMMUNICATION SKILLS

CHAPTER 6

Talking About People

In this chapter you will learn:

How to talk and ask about occupations

How to talk about what is happening right now

How to ask questions to get details

How to express an opinion

Talking About Occupations

At a party, Pablo walks around the room and mingles. He meets Gerardo for the first time and asks about what he does. Listen to their conversation. What does

Pablo do for a living? What does Gerardo do? If you don't understand, use the translation to help you.

 TRACK 1

PABLO: Hola, soy Pablo.	*Hi, I'm Pablo.*
GERARDO: Hola, encantado. Gerardo Torres.	*Hi, nice to meet you. I'm Gerardo Torres.*
PABLO: ¿Qué haces, Gerardo?	*What do you do, Gerardo?*
GERARDO: Soy consultor. Trabajo en una fábrica.	*I'm a consultant. I work at a factory.*
PABLO: ¿Y qué hacen allí?	*And what do you make there?*
GERARDO: Hacemos carros. ¿Y tú? ¿Qué haces?	*We make cars. And you? What do you do?*
PABLO: Soy estudiante, pero tengo un trabajo de tiempo parcial.	*Pablo: I'm a student, but I have a part-time job.*
GERARDO: ¿Y qué haces en tu trabajo?	*And what do you do at your job?*
PABLO: Doy clases de computadoras en una biblioteca.	*I teach computers at a library.*
GERARDO: ¿Arreglas computadoras también?	*Do you also fix computers?*
PABLO: Sí, arreglo de todo.	*Yes, I fix just about everything.*
GERARDO: Qué bien. Yo tengo un pequeño problema con mi computadora…	*Great. I have a small problem with my computer . . .*
PABLO: ¿Qué tienes, Mac o PC?	*What do you have, a Mac or a PC?*

ASKING ABOUT SOMEONE'S JOB

In the dialogue, Pablo asks Gerardo **¿Qué haces?** *What do you do (for a living)?* It is not as common in Latin America and Europe as it is in the United States to ask

The Verb *hacer*

As you can see from the opening conversation, **hacer** has two meanings: *to do* and *to make*. Therefore, the question **¿Qué haces?** can have a number of meanings, depending on the context in which it is used: *What do you do (for a living)?* and *What do you make?* If you walk in on someone in the middle of something, it can also mean *What are you doing (right now)?*

Hacer is a versatile word used in a number of Spanish expressions. Here is the present-tense conjugation of **hacer**. Note that it is irregular only in the first person.

hacer (*to do; to make*)

yo hago	*I do, make*	nosotros(as) hacemos	*we do, make*
tú haces	*you do, make*	vosotros(as) hacéis	*you do, make (plural informal, Spain)*
usted hace	*you do, make (formal)*	ustedes hacen	*you do, make*
él/ella hace	*he/she does, makes*	ellos/ellas hacen	*they do, make*

people about their work, so Pablo might sound a little pushy when he asks Gerardo this question. However, Gerardo seems happy to talk about his work, so they carry on their conversation.

Review the following excerpts from the dialogue. Notice the different uses of the verb **hacer** (*to do, make*).

¿Qué haces, Gerardo?	*What do you do, Gerardo?*
¿Y qué hacen allí?	*And what do you make there?*
¿Y tú? ¿Qué haces?	*And you, what do you do?*
¿Y qué haces en tu trabajo?	*What do you do at your job?*

To ask a question about someone's job or what they are doing, you can use **qué** (*what*) with **hacer**. For example:

¿Qué haces?	*What do you do? (one person, informal)*
¿Qué hace?	*What does he/she do?/What do you do? (formal)*
¿Qué haces en la calle Trébol?	*What are you doing on Trebol Street?*
¿Qué hacen los domingos?	*What do they do on Sundays?*
¿Qué hace Enrique en el hospital?	*What does Enrique do at the hospital?*

To respond to the question **¿Qué haces?** (*What do you do?*), use **Soy** + (*profession*) *without* the article. For instance: **Soy abogado** (*I'm a lawyer.*). Here is a list of common professions:

Professions

el/la abogado(a)	*lawyer*	el/la estudiante	*student*
el/la artista	*artist*	el/la funcionario(a)	*government employee*
el/la cajero(a)	*cashier*	el/la maestro(a)	*teacher*
el/la camarero(a)	*waiter, waitress, server*	el/la mecánico(a)	*mechanic*
el/la cocinero(a)	*cook*	el/la médico(a)	*doctor*
el/la consultor(a)	*consultant*	el/la periodista	*journalist*
el/la empleado(a) de banco	*bank clerk*	el/la recepcionista	*receptionist*
el/la enfermero(a)	*nurse*	el/la vendedor(a)	*salesperson*
el/la escritor(a)	*writer*		

Here are some example sentences that talk about professions. Listen and repeat what you hear.

TRACK 2

¿Qué haces en Mercedes?	*What do you do at Mercedes? (informal)*
Soy vendedor.	*I am a salesperson. (male)*
¿Qué hace usted?	*What do you do? (formal)*
Soy empleada de banco.	*I am a bank clerk. (female)*

Ser + (*profession*) can be used to describe anyone's job. The name of the profession, as with adjectives, usually matches the gender and number of the person/people it describes. Here are some examples. Listen and repeat what you hear.

Miguel es camarero.	*Miguel is a waiter.*
Dora es consultora.	*Dora is a consultant.*
Elena y Rosa son maestras.	*Elena and Rosa are teachers.*

There are some exceptions, however. The following professions stay the same for men and women. Usually these end in **-ista** or **-ante**. Listen and repeat what you hear.

José Luis es periodista.	*José Luis is a journalist.*
Lucila es estudiante.	*Lucila is a student.*

You can also use **ser** to ask people *yes/no* questions.

¿Es usted abogada?	*Are you a lawyer?*
¿Pedro es cocinero?	*Is Pedro a cook?*

You probably noticed that in the first example above, the subject and verb are inverted. Spanish word order can go either way for *yes/no* questions.

Oral Practice 6-1

 TRACK 3

Imagine you are at a conference, asking people about their jobs. Look at the cues, and say the question you would ask beginning with **¿Qué . . . ?**. Then listen to the recording to check your answers. Repeat what you hear.

1. tú/hacer
2. usted/hacer
3. Héctor y José/hacer
4. ustedes/hacer
5. ellas/hacer
6. Rebeca/hacer

DESCRIBING WHAT YOU DO

In addition to stating a profession, you can talk about what you or others do for a living using the verb **trabajar** + **para** (*for*) or **en** (*in/at*). Some of the workplaces that you have already learned are: **el banco** (*bank*), **el supermercado** (*supermarket*), **el restaurante** (*restaurant*), **la biblioteca** (*library*), **la oficina de correos** (*post office*), and **el centro comercial** (*mall*). Here are some other workplaces:

Workplaces

el aeropuerto	*airport*	el hospital	*hospital*
el despacho de abogados	*law office*	el hotel	*hotel*
la escuela	*school*	la oficina	*office*
la fábrica	*factory*	la universidad	*university*

Or you can specify the type of company:

la compañía de Internet	*Internet company*
la organización sin fines de lucro	*nonprofit organization*
Trabajo en una oficina.	*I work at an office.*
Elena trabaja en un despacho de abogados.	*Elena works at a law firm.*
Esteban y Luz trabajan en una editorial.	*Esteban and Luz work at a publishing house.*

You can also use certain verbs in the present tense to describe what you do. In Chapter 5 you learned how to conjugate regular **-ar**, **-er**, and **-ir** verbs in the present. Here are some regular verbs related to jobs:

arreglar	*to fix*	escribir	*to write*
ayudar	*to help*	organizar	*to organize*
cocinar	*to cook*	trabajar	*to work*
enseñar	*to teach*	vender	*to sell*

Here are some example sentences with these verbs:

Delia y Ana organizan eventos culturales.	*Delia and Ana organize cultural events.*
El mecánico arregla carros.	*The mechanic fixes cars.*
¿Usted ayuda a gente con problemas?	*Do you help people with problems?*
¿Ustedes enseñan en una escuela pública?	*Do you teach at a public school?*

Written Practice 6-1

Read the description of each person's job. Then write a sentence stating what his or her profession is. The first one has been done for you as an example.

1. Gerardo cocina en el restaurante Rumberos. *Gerardo cooks at Rumberos Restaurant.*

   Gerardo es cocinero.

2. David va a clase en la Universidad Pontífica. *David goes to class at the Pontifica University.*

3. Irma y Manuela trabajan con los médicos en el Hospital de la Paz. *Irma and Manuela work with the doctors at La Paz Hospital.*

4. Yo enseño en una escuela. (*female*) *I teach at a school.*

_____

5. Alicia vende ropa en una tienda. *Alicia sells clothing in a store.*

_____

6. Javier escribe para el periódico *El Diario*. *Javier writes for the newspaper El Diario.*

_____

7. Julia y Debora trabajan en el despacho García, Marcos y Jiménez, LLP. *Julia and Debora work at the law firm García, Marcos and Jiménez, LLP.*

_____

The verbs **tener** and **dar** may help you further explain what you do for a living. For instance, you can explain whether you have **un trabajo de jornada completa** (*a full-time job*), or **un trabajo de jornada parcial** (*a part-time job*), **un trabajo fijo** (*a steady job*), **un trabajo temporal** (*temporary work/a temp job*). Note that **trabajo** can mean *job* or *work*. You can also tell someone **Doy masajes** (*I give massages*) or **Doy clases de español** (*I give Spanish classes*).

Tengo un trabajo de tiempo parcial.	*I have a part-time job.*
Tengo un equipo de veinte personas.	*I have a team of twenty people.*
Doy préstamos a gente.	*I give loans to people.*
Doy clases de inglés.	*I give English lessons.*

Written Practice 6-2

Complete the sentences with the correct form of the verb in parentheses. Then translate the sentences into English.

1. Petra _____ (tener) un trabajo temporal.

2. ¿Ustedes _____ (dar) información?

3. Yo _____ (dar) instrucciones a los clientes.

4. ¿Tú _____ (tener) trabajo?

5. Nosotros no _____ (dar) préstamos.

6. Nosotros _____ (tener) mucho trabajo.

GRAMMAR DEMYSTIFIED

The Irregular Verbs *tener* and *dar*

In the opening dialogue, Pablo says **Tengo un trabajo de tiempo parcial** and **Doy clases de computadoras**. **Tengo** and **doy** come from the irregular verbs **tener** (*to have*) and **dar** (*to give*). Here are the present tense conjugations of both verbs. With **tener**, note the irregularities in the first person where the root changes to **teng-** and in the second/third persons where it changes to **tien-**; with **dar**, only the first person **doy** is irregular.

	tener (*to have*)	**dar** (*to give*)
yo	tengo	doy
tú	tienes	das
usted	tiene	da
él/ella	tiene	da
nosotros(as)	tenemos	damos
vosotros(as)	tenéis	dais
ustedes	tienen	dan
ellos/ellas	tienen	dan

Oral Practice 6-2

 TRACK 4

Listen to the following dialogues, and indicate whether the statements are **cierto o falso** (*true or false*).

1. Jerónimo asks someone about Manuel's work.

   ¿Cierto o falso? Manuel es médico. *Manuel is a doctor.* _____

2. Graciela asks Diego about his sisters.

   ¿Cierto o falso? Rocío es consultora. *Rocío is a consultant.* _____

3. Delia asks Ernesto about what he does.

   ¿Cierto o falso? Ernesto es recepcionista. *Ernesto is a receptionist.*

   _____

4. Susana asks Rubén about the type of work he does.

¿Cierto o falso? Rubén tiene un trabajo de jornada completa. *Rubén has a full-time job.* _____

Oral Practice 6-3

 TRACK 5

Read each situation, and say your answer out loud. Then listen to the recording to check your answer, and repeat what you hear.

1. In a formal situation, ask someone what he does for a living.
2. Someone asks you **¿Qué haces?** You are a student.
3. Someone asks you **¿Qué hace tu hermana?** She's a salesperson.
4. Someone asks you **¿Qué hacen tus hermanos?** They are all doctors.
5. You want to ask your friend if she has a job.
6. Say that you have a part-time job.
7. Explain that you teach computers.
8. Explain that you and a friend (we) help other students.
9. Explain that Inés gives Spanish lessons.
10. Explain that Mr. Ruiz has a team of five people.

Gossiping

 TRACK 6

At the same party, a woman catches Pablo's attention. He asks his friend Luis about her. Listen to the conversation. What does he find out?

PABLO: Luis, ¿conoces a esa mujer de allí?   *Luis, do you know that woman over there?*

LUIS: ¿Quién?   *Who?*

PABLO: Esa mujer de pelo castaño y ojos verdes.	*That woman with brown hair and green eyes.*
LUIS: ¿Qué está haciendo ahora?	*What is she doing now?*
PABLO: Está hablando con Lola. Ahora está comiendo.	*She's talking to Lola. Now she's eating.*
LUIS: Es Elena. Es la prima de Lola.	*That's Elena. She's Lola's cousin.*
PABLO: ¿Qué te parece Elena?	*What do you think of Elena?*
LUIS: Me parece simpática.	*I think she's nice.*
PABLO: A mí me parece muy atractiva. ¡Creo que me está mirando!	*I think she's very attractive. I think she's looking at me!*
LUIS: Entonces, ¿qué estás haciendo aquí? Habla con ella.	*Then, what are you doing here? Talk to her.*

Pablo finds out that the woman is Elena, Lola's cousin. He gets up the courage to talk to her and can't think of anything better to say than . . .

PABLO: Hola, ¿qué está haciendo una chica como tú en un lugar como éste?	*Hi, what is a girl like you doing in a place like this?*
ELENA: ¡Qué original!	*How original!*
PABLO: Está bien. Otra vez. Hola, me llamo Pablo.	*O.K. Again. Hi, my name is Pablo.*
ELENA: Hola, soy Elena.	*Hi, I'm Elena.*
PABLO: ¿De dónde eres?	*Where are you from?*
ELENA: Soy venezolana.	*I'm Venezuelan.*
PABLO: ¿Qué estás haciendo en Chicago?	*What are you doing in Chicago?*
ELENA: De momento, estoy trabajando para una compañía de relaciones públicas. Soy consultora.	*For now, I am working for a PR company. I'm a consultant.*
PABLO: Qué interesante. ¿Te gusta?	*How interesting. Do you like it?*

ELENA: Sí. ¿Y tú? ¿Qué haces?

Yes. And you? What do you do?

PABLO: Yo disfruto de la vida. Soy estudiante.

I enjoy life. I'm a student.

GETTING THE JUICY DETAILS WITH THE PRESENT PROGRESSIVE TENSE

El chisme (*gossip*) is an important part of Latin American life, so it's important to be able to know how to dish **en español**. In the dialogue, Luis and Pablo use the present progressive to ask and talk about Elena's every move. Look at the following phrases from the conversation:

¿Qué está haciendo ahora?

What is she doing now?

Está hablando con Lola.

She's talking to Lola.

Ahora está comiendo.

Now she's eating.

The *present progressive*, sometimes called the present continuous, is usually expressed with *to be -ing* in English: *is walking, are eating, is talking*, etc. It usually describes an impermanent action taking place at the moment of speaking. It's very useful for reporting what you see taking place.

The present progressive is formed by using the present tense of the verb **estar** + (*present participle*). You will recognize the Spanish present participle (-*ing* form) because it ends in **-ndo**.

To form the present participle, add **-ando** to the root of **-ar** verbs and **-iendo** to the root of **-er** and **-ir** verbs (Note: There are a couple of exceptions for verbs with irregular spellings.)

Present Participles

-ar verbs			-er and -ir verbs		
dar	→ dando	*giving*	escribir	→ escribiendo	*writing*
hablar	→ hablando	*talking*	hacer	→ haciendo	*doing/making*
mirar	→ mirando	*looking*	tener	→ teniendo	*having*
trabajar	→ trabajando	*working*	vivir	→ viviendo	*living*

Present and Future

In English the present progressive can be used to talk about the near future: *I'm going to New York tomorrow; I'm having lunch with Pedro next week.* In Spanish, this is usually done with the simple present: **Mañana voy a Nueva York**, or in the future construction with the verb **ir**: **Voy a almorzar con Pedro la semana que viene.** Remember that in Spanish the present progressive is only used to talk about situations taking place at the moment of speaking.

Look at some example sentences:

Elena está hablando.	*Elena is talking.*
Andrés está teniendo una crisis.	*Andrés is having a crisis.*
Armando y Ester están escribiendo un libro.	*Armando and Ester are writing a book.*
¿Usted está viviendo en México ahora?	*Are you living in Mexico now?*

Oral Practice 6-4

 TRACK 7

Read the following sentences in the present tense; then say them in the present progressive. Listen to the recording to check your answers, and repeat what you hear.

1. Bernardo come chocolate.
2. Susana habla con su hermana.
3. Ana vive con su novio.
4. Nosotros escribimos emails.
5. Ustedes hablan español.
6. Tú organizas fiestas.

EXPRESSING AN OPINION WITH THE VERB *PARECER*

 TRACK 8

In the dialogue, Pablo asks his friend what he thinks of Elena by asking **¿Qué te parece Elena?** You can use the verb **parecer** to ask someone's opinion. Listen and repeat what you hear.

¿Qué te parece?	*What do you think? (informal)*
¿Qué le parece?	*What do you think? (formal)*

You can also ask someone's opinion about something in particular with **¿Qué te parece** + (*thing*)**?** Listen and repeat what you hear.

¿Qué te parece la fiesta?	*What do you think of the party? (informal)*
¿Qué le parece la música?	*What do you think of the music? (formal)*

Note that **parece** changes to **parecen** when you are referring to more than one person or item.

¿Qué le parecen los actores?	*What do you think of the actors?*
¿Qué te parecen las canciones?	*What do you think of the songs?*

To give your opinion, say **Me parece(n)** + (*adjective*). In Chapter 3, you learned **simpático(a)** *friendly*, **aburrido(a)** *boring*, and **gracioso(a)** *funny*. You know a number of cognates as well: **arrogante**, **interesante**, **atractiva**. Listen to a few more:

Adjectives to Express an Opinion

bueno(a)	*good*	feo(a)	*ugly*
delicioso(a)	*delicious*	genial	*great*
hermoso(a)	*beautiful*	malo(a)	*bad*
horrible	*horrible*	precioso(a)	*gorgeous*

increíble	*incredible*	ridículo(a)	*ridiculous*
interesante	*interesting*	terrible	*terrible*
fenomenal	*great*	triste	*sad*

Remember that you can modify these adjectives with **muy** (*very*), **un poco** (*a bit*), **bastante** (*quite*). The adverbs **bien** (*well, good*) and **mal** (*bad, badly*) can also be used with **Me parece(n)...**

Listen and repeat some more examples with **parecer**:

¿Qué te parece Rosa?	*What do you think of Rosa?*
Me parece un poco aburrida.	*I think she's a bit boring.*
Me parece bastante graciosa.	*I think she's quite funny.*
¿Qué te parecen los actores?	*What do you think of the actors?*
Me parecen muy buenos.	*I think they are very good.*
Me parecen horribles.	*I think they are horrible.*

EXPRESSING AN OPINION WITH THE VERB *GUSTAR*

TRACK 9

In the dialogue, Pablo asks Elena how she feels about her job, using the verb **gustar** (*to like, to be pleasing to*). He asks her, **¿Te gusta?** *Do you like it?*

To ask someone a *yes/no* question about a like, dislike, or opinion, use **¿Te gusta + (*thing*)?** to ask about one thing, and **¿Te gustan + (*things*)?** to ask about more than one thing. The "thing" you ask about can be a noun, a verb, or a phrase. Listen and repeat these examples:

¿Te gusta el chocolate?	*Do you like chocolate?*
¿Te gusta viajar?	*Do you like to travel?*
¿Te gustan los perros?	*Do you like dogs?*

In formal situations use **le** instead of **te**.

¿Le gusta el béisbol?	*Do you like baseball?*
¿Le gustan las albóndigas?	*Do you like meatballs?*

To answer, say **Sí, me gusta(n)** or **No, no me gusta(n)**.

You can also ask about likes or opinions with **¿Qué te gusta?** *What do you like?* (*informal*) or **¿Qué le gusta?** *What do you like?* (*formal*).

To express likes, dislikes, or an opinion, say **Me gusta...** or **No me gusta...** with a single thing and **Me gustan...** or **No me gustan...** for plural things. To say that you like something a lot, use **Me gusta(n) mucho**.

Me gusta David.	*I like David.*
Me gustan los gatos.	*I like cats.*
No me gusta el fútbol.	*I don't like soccer.*
No me gustan los secretos.	*I don't like secrets.*
Me gusta mucho tu casa.	*I really like your house.*

Note that actions (verbs and verb phrases) take the singular form **gusta**.

Me gusta leer.	*I like to read.*
Me gusta probar platos nuevos.	*I like to try new dishes.*

What do you say when you love something? **¡Me encanta!** It works just like **Me gusta**.

Me encantan los perros.	*I love dogs.*
Me encanta bailar.	*I love to dance.*

Oral Practice 6-5

 TRACK 10

Use the cues to say sentences that describe what you like or dislike. Choose from
me gusta(n) (+), **me gusta(n) mucho** (+ +), **me encanta(n)** (+ + +), and **no
me gusta(n)** (−). Then listen to the recording to check your answers, and repeat
what you hear.

1. el chocolate (+ + +)
2. la música clásica (+)
3. viajar en avión (−)
4. visitar a mi familia (+ +)
5. las novelas de misterio (+ + +)
6. las pupusas de queso (−)

Oral Practice 6-6

Use the cues to ask questions to find out how people feel about the following
items. Remember to use **te** for informal and **le** for formal questions.

1. ¿gustar/leer? (*informal*)
2. ¿gustar/la música rock? (*formal*)
3. ¿parecer/la fiesta? (*informal*)
4. ¿parecer/los cuchifritos? (*informal*)
5. ¿parecer/la novela? (*formal*)
6. ¿gustar/comer en restaurantes? (*informal*)
7. ¿gustar/las películas? (*formal*)
8. ¿parecer/el trabajo? (*formal*)
9. ¿parecer/la nueva profesora? (*informal*)
10. ¿parecer/el hermano de Javier? (*informal*)

Oral Practice 6-7

 TRACK 11

Imagine you are hosting a party and **chismeando** (*gossiping*) with friends about everyone there. Read each of the following situations, and respond out loud. Listen to the recording to check your answers, and repeat what you hear.

1. You ask your friend what he thinks of Pablo.
2. A friend asks **¿Qué te parece Ramón?** You think he is attractive.
3. A friend asks **¿Qué te parece Julia?** You think she is interesting.
4. A friend asks **¿Te gusta bailar?** You love dancing!
5. You ask your friend what Luisa is doing.
6. A friend asks you where Luisa is living now. You say she's living in Paris.
7. A friend asks **¿Dónde estás trabajando?** You say you are working at an office.
8. A friend asks **¿Qué está haciendo Roberto?** You say he is speaking Spanish.
9. A friend asks **¿Qué estás haciendo?** You are making tamales.
10. A friend asks you and a friend **¿Qué están haciendo?** Both of you are eating tamales.

Chapter Practice

 TRACK 12

Listen to the following dialogues, and indicate whether the statements are **cierto o falso** (*true or false*).

1. Mario and Ester are talking about what they do.

   ¿Cierto o falso? Ester es camarera. *Ester is a waitress.* _____

2. Luis and Ángela talk about Pablo.

   ¿Cierto o falso? Ángela cree que Pablo es atractivo. *Ángela thinks Pablo is attractive.* _____

3. Marta and Gerardo gossip about Rosa's new boyfriend.

   ¿Cierto o falso? El novio nuevo de Rosa, Miguel, es maestro de español. *Miguel, Rosa's new boyfriend, is a Spanish teacher.* _____

4. Alberto and Elena talk about Ariana.

   ¿Cierto o falso? Ariana está viviendo y trabajando en Lima. *Ariana is living and working in Lima.* _____

QUIZ

 TRACK 13

Listen to the recording to hear a phrase or question. Press pause, and say your answer: a, b, or c. Listen to the correct answer on the recording, and repeat what you hear. Then go to the next question, and repeat the process.

1. (a) Me parece interesante.

   (b) Luis es profesor.

   (c) ¡Me encanta!

2. (a) Son camareros.

   (b) Es periodista.

   (c) Son vendedoras.

3. (a) Trabaja en un hospital.

   (b) Enseña español.

   (c) Es abogado.

4. (a) Es una organización de fines sin lucro.

   (b) Edita libros.

   (c) Arregla carros.

5. (a) Tiene un trabajo fijo.

   (b) Tenemos un equipo de diez personas.

   (c) Dan instrucciones.

6. (a) Me encanta hablar español.

   (b) Estamos dando clases de español.

   (c) Está aprendiendo español.

7. (a) Sí, me gusta mucho.

   (b) Ella viaja mucho.

   (c) Están viajando ahora.

8. (a) Están hablando por teléfono.

   (b) Estoy escribiendo un email.

   (c) Estamos bailando.

9. (a) Me parecen bastante graciosas.

   (b) Me parece muy buena.

   (c) Me parece aburrido.

10. (a) Me parece mala.

   (b) Me parecen muy buenos.

   (c) ¡Me encanta!

CHAPTER 7

Getting in Touch with People

In this chapter you will learn:

How to gather information
How to make polite requests
How to talk on the phone
How to ask about the weather
How to ask people to do things
How to give commands

Gathering Information

 TRACK 14

Pablo decides it's time to travel to Puerto Rico. He hasn't been there since he was a kid. He calls his relatives in Puerto Rico to ask for information so he can plan his trip. First, he calls his cousin Juan Soto at work. Listen to the conversation. Does Pablo reach his cousin?

SEÑORA JIMÉNEZ: ¿Aló?   *Hello?*

PABLO: Buenos días. Quisiera hablar con el Señor Soto.   *Good morning. I'd like to speak to Mr. Soto.*

SEÑORA JIMÉNEZ: El Señor Soto no está disponible en este momento. ¿Quiere dejar un mensaje?   *Mr. Soto is not available at the moment. Do you want to leave a message?*

PABLO: Sí, por favor. Dígale que llamó su primo.   *Yes, please. Tell him that his cousin called.*

SEÑORA JIMÉNEZ: ¿Su nombre, por favor?   *Your name, please?*

PABLO: Pablo. Pablo Torres.   *Pablo, Pablo Torres.*

SEÑORA JIMÉNEZ: De acuerdo. Le daré el recado.   *O.K. I'll give him the message.*

PABLO: Muchas gracias. Adiós.   *Thank you very much. Bye.*

Pablo didn't reach Juan at work, so he calls him later at home.

LUISA: ¿Aló?   *Hello?*

PABLO: ¿Está Juan, por favor?   *Is Juan there, please?*

LUISA: ¿De parte de quién?   *Who's calling?*

PABLO: Soy su primo Pablo. Quiero hablar con él sobre Puerto Rico.   *I'm his cousin, Pablo. I wanted to speak to him about Puerto Rico.*

LUISA: Hola, Pablo. ¡Cuánto tiempo! Un momentito, por favor.   *Hi, Pablo. It's been a long time! One moment, please.*

JUAN: ¿Sí?   *Yes?*

PABLO: Hola Juan. Soy Pablo, tu primo de Chicago.	*Hi, Juan, this is Pablo, your cousin from Chicago.*
JUAN: Hola, Pablo. ¿Cómo andas? ¿Qué tal?	*Hey, Pablo. How's it going? How are you?*
PABLO: Bien, gracias. Te llamaba porque quiero ir a Puerto Rico y quisiera información sobre San Juan.	*Fine. I was calling because I want to go to Puerto Rico, and I'd like information about San Juan.*
JUAN: Pues, ¿cuándo quieres venir?	*When do you want to come?*
PABLO: Me gustaría ir en verano. ¿Qué tiempo hace en julio allí?	*I'd like to go in the summer. What's the weather like there in July?*
JUAN: Hace calor. También llueve, pero en general hace buen tiempo.	*It's hot. It also rains, but generally the weather is good.*
PABLO: ¿Y ahora? ¿Qué tiempo hace?	*And now? What's the weather like?*
JUAN: Ahora también hace calor. Hoy está despejado. ¿Y allí?	*Now it's hot, too. Today it's clear. And there?*
PABLO: Aquí está nevando.	*Here it's snowing.*

MAKING POLITE REQUESTS

In the opening conversations, Pablo makes a number of requests. He asks to speak to his cousin, and he asks for information about the weather in San Juan. Whether you are talking on the phone, talking to a friend, or at a hotel counter, there are different ways of requesting information.

Look at the following excerpts from the dialogue in which Pablo requests information:

Quisiera hablar con...	*I'd like to speak with . . .*
Quisiera información sobre...	*I'd like information about . . .*
Quiero hablar con...	*I want to speak with . . .*

As you can see, Pablo uses two main ways of making a request: with **quisiera** (more polite) and with **quiero** (less polite).

Quisiera (*I'd like*) is a form of the verb **querer** (*to like*). You can use **quisiera** followed by a verb or noun to make requests.

Quisiera información sobre...	*I'd like information about . . .*
Quisiera un folleto sobre...	*I'd like a brochure about . . .*
Quisiera hacer una reservación.	*I'd like to make a reservation.*
Quisiera hablar con...	*I'd like to speak to . . .*

Quiero (*I want*) is a more direct way to ask for something. It is used to make requests in less formal situations, to make more assertive requests, or to express what you want or want to do. **Quiero** is the present tense of the verb **querer** (*to want*), which is a stem-changing verb. You can use **querer** followed by a noun or a verb when making requests. Remember that adding **por favor** (*please*) to any request always makes it more polite!

Here are some examples of sentences with **querer** in the present:

Queremos detalles sobre la fiesta.	*We want details about the party.*
¿Quieren comer tamales?	*Do you want to eat tamales?*
No quiero hablar con Marta.	*I don't want to speak with Marta.*
¿Quieres información sobre San Juan?	*Do you want information about San Juan?*

GRAMMAR DEMYSTIFIED

The Verb *querer* (present tense)

yo quiero	*I want*	nosotros(as) queremos	*we want*
tú quieres	*you want*	vosotros(as) queréis	*you want (plural, Spain)*
él/ella, usted quiere	*he, she wants you want (formal)*	ellos/ellas, ustedes quieren	*they, you want (plural)*

Oral Practice 7-1

 TRACK 15

Say the following sentences in Spanish. Then listen to the recording to check your answers. Repeat what you hear.

1. I'd like information about Puerto Plata.
2. We want a brochure about Brazil.
3. I'd like to speak with Roberto.
4. I want to speak Spanish.
5. I'd like to make a reservation.
6. He doesn't want to go to Argentina.
7. I want information about Portugal.
8. Do you (*plural*) want to speak with a doctor?

TALKING ON THE TELEPHONE

In the dialogue, Pablo makes two phone calls. Look at these excerpts of telephone language from the conversations:

¿Aló?	*Hello?*
¿Quiere dejar un mensaje?	*Would you like to leave a message?*
Dígale que llamó Pablo.	*Tell him that Pablo called.*
Un momento, por favor.	*One moment, please.*
¿Sí?	*Hello? (lit.: Yes?)*
¿Está Juan, por favor?	*Is Juan there, please?*

Here is some more useful telephone language. Use **Quisiera hablar con...** (*I'd like to speak with . . .*) and **¿Me puede comunicar con... ?** (*Can you connect me with . . . ?*) to ask to speak with someone in formal situations. **Con** is a preposition that means *with*. Listen and repeat what you hear.

🔘 TRACK 16

Quisiera hablar con la Señora Nuñez.	*I'd like to talk with Ms. Nuñez.*
¿Me puede comunicar con el Señor Cruz?	*Can you connect me with Mr. Cruz?*

A less formal, but extremely common way to ask for someone is to say **¿Está +** (*name*)**?** For instance, Pablo says, **¿Está Juan?** This sometimes sounds strange to English speakers who are accustomed to saying *Is Juan **there**?* But in Spanish, simply using **Está** does the trick.

¿Está Marina?	*Is Marina in?*
¿Está Roberto, por favor?	*Is Roberto there, please?*

Identifying yourself is similarly straightforward. Say **Soy** + (*your name*).

Soy Pablo.	*This is Pablo.*
Soy Edith.	*This is Edith.*

VOCABULARY DEMYSTIFIED

Hello?

In the dialogues you heard, there were two ways of answering the phone: **¿Aló?** and **¿Sí?** **¿Aló?** is the most common way of answering the phone in Latin America. Other common expressions include:

¿Aló? (*most of Latin America*)	Diga./Dígame. (*Spain*)
¿Sí? (*informal*)	Bueno. (*Mexico*)
¿Hola? (*Argentina*)	

If you want to say someone isn't at home or is unavailable, you say:

No está disponible.	*He/She is not available.*
No está.	*He/She is not in.*

To say that someone is otherwise occupied:

Lo siento, está ocupado/a.	*I'm sorry. He/She is busy.*
Lo siento, está en una reunión.	*I'm sorry. He's/She's at a meeting.*

To ask who's calling:

¿De parte de quién?	*Who's calling?*
¿Con quién hablo?	*Who(m) am I talking to?*
¿Quién le llama, por favor?	*Who's calling, please?*

To ask if the caller would like to leave a message:

¿Quiere(s) dejar un mensaje?	*Would you like to leave a message?*

To ask the caller to hold:

Un momento, por favor.	*One moment, please.*
¿Puede esperar al teléfono?	*Can you hold the line?*

To leave a message:

¿Puede(s) decirle que llamó... ?	*Could you tell him/her that . . . called?*
¿Podría dejar un mensaje?	*Could I leave a message?*

To say you'll call back:

Llamaré más tarde.	*I'll call back later.*
Llamaré otra vez a las ocho.	*I will call again at 8:00.*

Oral Practice 7-2

 TRACK 17

Read each dialogue, and use the context to figure out the missing words. Say the completed dialogues out loud. Listen to the recording to check your answers, and repeat what you hear.

1. Miguel calls his friend Andrea.

   ANDREA: ¿Aló? *Hello?*

   MIGUEL: Hola, ¿_____ Andrea, por favor? *Hi, is Andrea there please?*

   ANDREA: Sí, soy yo. *Yes, this is she.*

   MIGUEL: Hola, _____ Miguel. ¿Cómo estás? *Hi, this is Miguel. How are you?*

   ANDREA: Muy bien, gracias. *Very well, thanks.*

2. Rosa calls to speak to her friend Isabel.

   PEDRO: Bueno. *Hello?*

   ROSA: Hola. ¿_____, por favor? *Is Isabel there, please?*

   PEDRO: No, no está. ¿Quiere dejar _____? *No, she's not in. Do you want to leave a message?*

   ROSA: Sí, ¿Puede decirle _____? *Yes. Can you tell her that Rosa called?*

   PEDRO: Sí, muy bien. *Yes, O.K.*

   ROSA: _____ a las ocho. *I'll call back at eight.*

   PEDRO: De acuerdo. Adiós. *O.K., bye.*

   ROSA: Adiós, gracias. *Good-bye, thanks.*

3. Ester Ponce calls Señor Román at his workplace.

   RECEPCIONISTA: Empresas Soles. ¿Dígame? *Soles Company. Hello?*

   ESTER: Buenos días. _____ hablar con el Señor Román, por favor. *Good morning. I'd like to speak to Mr. Román, please.*

   RECEPCIONISTA: ¿De parte _____? *Who's calling?*

   ESTER: _____ la Señora Ponce. Ester Ponce. *This is Mrs. Ponce. Ester Ponce.*

RECEPCIONISTA: _____ , por favor. ¿Puede esperar al teléfono?
One moment, please. Can you hold the line?

ESTER: Sí, claro. *Yes, of course.*

RECEPCIONISTA: Lo siento, el Señor Román no está _____ .
¿Quiere dejar _____? *I'm sorry, Mr. Román isn't available.*
Do you want to leave a message?

ESTER: No, llamaré más tarde. *No, I'll call back later.*

RECEPCIONISTA: De acuerdo. *O.K.*

ESTER: Gracias, adiós. *Thanks, good-bye.*

ASKING ABOUT THE WEATHER

When you're deciding where to go on vacation, the weather is usually an important factor. To find out what the weather is like, you can go to **el pronóstico del tiempo**, *the weather forecast*, on TV, in the newspaper, or online. Or, you can ask someone. In the opening dialogue, Pablo asks **¿Qué tiempo hace... ?** (*What is the weather like . . . ?*). To ask about weather in a certain season, you can add **en invierno** (*in winter*), **en verano** (*in summer*), **en primavera** (*in spring*), or **en otoño** (*in the fall*), or during a particular month: **en enero** (*in January*), **en febrero** (*in February*), etc. Listen and repeat these examples:

TRACK 18

¿Qué tiempo hace en verano?	*What's the weather like in summer?*
¿Qué tiempo hace en julio?	*What's the weather like in July?*

Pablo's cousin answers **hace calor** (*it's hot*). To describe the weather, use **Hace...** followed by the type of weather. Listen to some of the most common ways to describe the weather:

Hace buen tiempo.	*The weather is nice.*	Hace mal tiempo.	*The weather is bad.*
Hace frío.	*It's cold.*	Hace calor.	*It's hot.*
Hace sol.	*It's sunny.*	Hace viento.	*It's windy.*

Talking about temperature is similar. To ask what the temperature is, say, **¿Qué temperatura hace?** (*What's the temperature?*) To give the temperature, say **Hace... grados**. Don't forget that Spanish-speaking countries may use the Celsius system.

¿Que temperatura hace hoy?	*What's the temperature today?*
Hace quince grados.	*It's fifteen degrees.*
Hace setenta y siete grados Fahrenheit.	*It's seventy-seven degrees Fahrenheit.*
Hace aproximadamente veinte grados.	*It's approximately twenty degrees.*

Other expressions use **Está** followed by an adjective to describe the weather. For instance:

Está nublado.	*It's cloudy.*
Está despejado.	*It's clear.*

However, note that in Spanish you should not use the verb **estar** to say *It is hot*, but rather **Hace calor**. (**Está caliente** is something different entirely!)

You can also use the present tense or the present progressive of certain verbs to describe the weather: **llover** (*to rain*), **nevar** (*to snow*), **granizar** (*to hail*).

Está lloviendo.	*It's raining.*	or	Llueve.	*It rains.*
Está nevando.	*It's snowing.*	or	Nieva.	*It snows.*
Está granizando.	*It's hailing.*	or	Graniza.	*It hails.*

Remember that the present progressive is used to talk about what's happening **ahora** (*now*) or **ahora mismo** (*right now*), while the present tense is used for something that happens **normalmente** or at a particular time, such as during a season or month.

Ahora mismo está lloviendo.	*It is raining right now.*
En invierno nieva mucho.	*It snows a lot in the winter.*

Written Practice 7-1

Choose the word or phrase that works best for each situation, and say it out loud.

1. You want to know what the weather is like.

    (a) ¿Qué hora es?

    (b) ¿Qué tiempo hace?

    (c) ¿Cómo está?

2. Someone asks you **¿Qué tiempo hace?** It's cold.

    (a) Está nevando.

    (b) Hace calor.

    (c) Hace frío.

3. Someone asks you **¿Qué tiempo hace?** The weather is bad.

    (a) Hace mal tiempo.

    (b) Hace buen tiempo.

    (c) Hace viento.

4. Someone asks you **¿Qué tiempo hace?** It's clear.

    (a) Está nublado.

    (b) Está lloviendo.

    (c) Está despejado.

5. Someone asks you **¿Qué temperatura hace?** It's thirty degrees.

    (a) Hace frío.

    (b) Hace quince grados.

    (c) Hace treinta grados.

6. Someone asks you **¿Qué tiempo hace ahora?** It's snowing.

    (a) Está nevando.

    (b) Está granizando.

    (c) Está lloviendo.

7. Someone asks you **¿Qué tiempo hace en Chicago en invierno?** You say it snows a lot.

   (a) Llueve mucho.

   (b) Nieva mucho.

   (c) Hace calor.

8. Someone asks you **¿Qué tiempo hace?** It's sunny.

   (a) Hace sol.

   (b) Llueve.

   (c) Hace calor.

Oral Practice 7-3

 TRACK 19

Listen to the phone conversations on the recording. Then circle the statement that best describes what happened.

1. Rosa calls asking for Ernesto.

   (a) Ernesto answers the phone.

   (b) Ernesto is not in.

   (c) Ernesto does not answer the phone, but he is in.

2. Ana calls Pedro, and they talk about the weather.

   (a) It's raining at Pedro's.

   (b) It's cold at Ana's.

   (c) It's snowing at Pedro's.

3. Fernando calls the Puerto Rican Tourism office.

   (a) Fernando requests a brochure.

   (b) Fernando asks to speak to Mr. Rico.

   (c) Fernando reserves a hotel room.

4. Alicia calls her friend Rubén to request some information.

   (a) Rubén answers the phone and gives Alicia the information.

   (b) Rubén is not in, and Alicia says she'll call back later.

   (c) Rubén is not in, and Alicia leaves a message.

Asking People to Do Things

 TRACK 20

Pablo tries to gather as much information about Puerto Rico as he can from different sources. He calls the Tourism Office in San Juan and requests some materials about El Yunque National Forest. He asks for a number of things using **quisiera** and some other expressions. Listen to the conversation. How else does Pablo ask for things?

REPRESENTANTE: Oficina de Turismo de San Juan. ¿En qué le puedo servir?	*San Juan Tourism Office. How may I help you?*
PABLO: Buenas tardes. ¿Tienen ustedes información sobre El Yunque?	*Good afternoon. Do you have information about El Yunque?*
REPRESENTANTE: Sí, claro. Tenemos libros y folletos. Podemos mandarlos por correo electrónico, si lo desea.	*Yes, of course. We have books and brochures. We can send them via e-mail, if you'd like.*
PABLO: Sí, por favor. Mándeme un libro sobre el parque.	*Yes, please. Send me a book about the park.*
REPRESENTANTE: ¿Quiere también un DVD?	*Would you also like a DVD?*
PABLO: No, no me mande el DVD. El reproductor de DVD está estropeado.	*No, don't send me a DVD. The DVD player is broken.*
REPRESENTANTE: Dígame su email. Tenemos el libro en formato PDF. Imprímalo y lo tiene en cinco minutos.	*Tell me your e-mail address. We have the book in PDF format. Print it, and you'll have it in five minutes.*
PABLO: De acuerdo. Es pablotorres, arroba, email.com.	*O.K. It's pablotorres@email.com.*
REPRESENTANTE: Repita otra vez, por favor.	*Repeat it, please.*
PABLO: pablotorres, arroba, email.com. ¿Otra vez?	*pablotorres@email.com. Again?*
REPRESENTANTE: No, no lo repita. Ya lo tengo. Gracias.	*No, don't repeat it. I have it. Thanks.*
PABLO: Gracias a usted.	*Thank you.*

GIVING FORMAL COMMANDS

Both Pablo and the tourism representative use commands to ask each other to do things. Here are some examples from the conversation:

Mándeme un libro sobre el parque.	*Send me a book about the park.*
No, no me mande el DVD.	*No, don't send me the DVD.*
Dígame su email.	*Tell me your e-mail.*
Imprímalo.	*Print it.*
Repita otra vez.	*Repeat it again.*
No, no lo repita.	*No, don't repeat it.*

When you are in a formal situation, use formal commands (the imperative with **usted**) to ask or tell someone to do something. You might have noticed in the examples above that when giving commands, the personal (subject) pronoun is usually dropped. However, to sound more formal, **usted** or **ustedes** can be used after the imperative.

When making formal commands, with most verbs, **-ar** verbs that usually end in **-a** in the present will end in **-e** in the imperative. Verbs ending in **-er** or **-ir** that usually end in **-e** in the present will end in **-a** in the imperative. Just remember: **ar → e** and **er/ir → a**. To make the negative, put **no** before the verb. Here are some examples:

-ar verbs: → -e

esperar	*to wait*	→	espere	*wait*	no espere	*don't wait*
hablar	*to speak*	→	hable	*speak*	no hable	*don't speak*
llamar	*to call*	→	llame	*call*	no llame	*don't call*
mandar	*to send*	→	mande	*send*	no mande	*don't send*

-er and -ir verbs: → -a

comer	*to eat*	→	coma	*eat*	no coma	*don't eat*
escribir	*to write*	→	escriba	*write*	no escriba	*don't write*
leer	*to read*	→	lea	*read*	no lea	*don't read*
repetir	*to repeat*	→	repita	*repeat*	no repita	*don't repeat*

Some verbs are *irregular* in the imperative:

decir	*to say*	→	diga	*say*	no diga	*don't say*
hacer	*to make, do*	→	haga	*make, do*	no haga	*don't make, don't do*
ir	*to go*	→	vaya	*go*	no vaya	*don't go*
tener	*to have*	→	tenga	*have*	no tenga	*don't have*

Here are some example sentences with irregular verbs:

Tenga paciencia.	*Have patience.*
Haga la maleta.	*Pack your bag.*
Diga su nombre, por favor.	*Say your name, please.*

When addressing more than one person (**ustedes**), add an **-n** to the end of the imperative.

Manden información.	*Send information.*
Lean las instruccciones.	*Read the instructions.*
Tengan paciencia.	*Have patience.*

In the opening conversation you heard **Mándeme un libro...** and **Dígame su email...** The **me** in both of these phrases is an *indirect object pronoun*: *Send **me** a book; Tell **me** your e-mail.* You will learn more about indirect object pronouns in Chapter 9.

Oral Practice 7-4

Use the words below to make formal singular and plural commands. Practice speaking the answer out loud.

1. hablar/en español (usted)
2. repetir/su nombre/por favor (usted)
3. escribir/un email (ustedes)
4. leer/el libro (ustedes)
5. comer/una empanadilla (usted)
6. no hacer/ruido (ustedes)

7. no mandar/el paquete por correo (usted)

8. decir/la verdad (usted)

9. esperar/un minuto/por favor (usted)

10. no decir/su nombre (ustedes)

GIVING INFORMAL COMMANDS

In informal situations, like when you're talking to a friend (or bossing someone around), you may want to use informal commands. For **-ar** verbs, the informal imperative is the same as the third person (it ends in **-a**). The negative informal imperative switches to an **-e**. A similar pattern is followed for **-er** and **-ir** verbs. Look at these examples of informal commands to a single person:

Informal Commands (tú)

-ar verbs	→	-a, no -es	-er and -ir verbs	→	-e, no -as
esperar	→	espera; no esperes	comer	→	come; no comas
hablar	→	habla; no hables	escribir	→	escribe; no escribas
llamar	→	llama; no llames	leer	→	lee; no leas
mandar	→	manda; no mandes	repetir	→	repite; no repitas

VOCABULARY DEMYSTIFIED

Computer Spanish

Today, it is as important to be able to talk about computers and the Internet as it is to be able to talk on the phone. Here's some common language related to computers, the Web, and the Internet in Spanish.

la arroba	*at (@)*	el guión	*hyphen (-)*
copiar y pegar	*copy and paste*	el enlace	*link*
el punto	*dot (.)*	la contraseña	*password*
bajar	*download*	la barra	*slash (/)*
bajar el archivo	*download the file*	la línea de subrayo	*underscore (_)*
el correo electrónico, el email	*e-mail*	el sitio web	*website*
el archivo	*file*		

Here are some example sentences with informal commands (said to one person):

Manda un email todos los días.	*Send an e-mail every day.*
Llama a tu novio.	*Call your boyfriend.*
Lee este artículo.	*Read this article.*
No comas tan rápido.	*Don't eat so fast.*

Here are the irregular informal commands:

decir	→	di; no digas
hacer	→	haz; no hagas
ir	→	ve; no vayas
tener	→	ten; no tengas

When talking to more than one person, the formal plural command is used, with the exception of Spain, where the **vosotros(as)** form (which you will not learn in this book) is used.

Oral Practice 7-5

 TRACK 21

Luisa likes telling people what to do, especially her best friend Rubén. Say the following dialogue out loud, making informal commands with the verbs in parentheses. Listen to the recording to check your answers. Repeat what you hear.

RUBÉN: Quisiera comer un burrito de pollo.

LUISA: No _____ (comer) un burrito de pollo. _____ (comer) uno de vegetales.

RUBÉN: Quiero beber una soda.

LUISA: No _____ (beber) soda. _____ (beber) agua. La soda no es saludable.

RUBÉN: Quiero ir a México.

LUISA: No _____ (ir). _____ (ir) a Brasil. Es muy divertido. Y _____ (hacer) la reservación por Internet.

RUBÉN: No tengo computadora.

LUISA: Entonces _____ (comprar) una computadora y _____ (aprender) a usarla.

RUBÉN: Luisa, no _____ (hablar) tanto...

Oral Practice 7-6

 TRACK 22

Listen to the phone conversation between Eva and Daniel. Then indicate whether the following statements are **cierto o falso** (*true or false*).

1. Eva and Daniel are good friends. _____

2. Daniel is traveling to Spain and wants Eva's opinion. _____

3. Daniel asks about the weather in Spain. _____

4. Eva says it's freezing in Sevilla in winter. _____

5. Eva offers tips about bars. _____

6. Eva tells Daniel to write down her friend's number. _____

Chapter Practice

TRACK 23

Say the phrase that works best for each situation. Listen to the recording to hear the correct answer, and repeat what you hear.

1. You'd like information about Costa Rica.

2. You want to know what the weather is like in Costa Rica.

3. Someone asks you **¿Qué tiempo hace?** It's cold.

4. Someone asks you **¿Qué temperatura hace?** It's eighty degrees.

5. You ask someone you don't know well to speak **más despacio**, slower please.

6. You tell a friend to speak Spanish.

7. You tell a friend not to go to Restaurante Cortés.

8. You tell two people to say their names.

QUIZ

Circle the letter of the word or phrase that best completes each sentence.

1. _____ información sobre Nueva York, por favor.

   (a) Hace

   (b) Quisiera

   (c) Escriben

2. _____ hacer una reservación, por favor.

   (a) Queremos.

   (b) Enseña

   (c) Está

3. Señora Díaz, _____ su nombre, por favor.

   (a) lee

   (b) decir

   (c) escriba

4. Antonio y Rosita, _____ las instrucciones.

   (a) lean

   (b) lee

   (c) leas

5. Pedro, _____ paciencia.

   (a) tener

   (b) dan

   (c) ten

Now listen to the recording to hear a phrase or question. Press pause, and say your answer: a, b, or c. Listen to the correct answer on the recording, and repeat what you hear. Then go to the next question, and repeat the process.

6. (a) Hace viento.

   (b) ¿Quiere dejar un mensaje?

   (c) Lo siento, está ocupado.

7. (a) Hace bastante calor.

   (b) Está nevando.

   (c) Está lloviendo.

8. (a) Hace frío.

   (b) Hace veinte grados.

   (c) Está despejado.

9. (a) Dígale que llamó Ana.

   (b) Hace calor.

   (c) Lo siento, no está.

10. (a) Llamaré más tarde.

    (b) Sí, un momento, por favor.

    (c) ¿Aló?

CHAPTER 8

Planning a Trip

In this chapter you will learn:

How to ask for and give advice

How to discuss needs

How to make and talk about future plans

Asking for and Giving Advice

 TRACK 25

Pablo is getting excited about his upcoming trip to Puerto Rico and decides to get advice from as many people as possible. He talks to his friend Ana, who has visited Puerto Rico several times. Listen to the following conversation between Ana and Pablo. Which place in Puerto Rico does Ana feel particularly passionate about?

PABLO: Voy a ir a Puerto Rico. En tu opinión, ¿qué debería hacer allí?	*I'm going to go to Puerto Rico. What do you think I should do there?*
ANA: Deberías visitar San Juan, la capital.	*You should visit San Juan, the capital.*
PABLO: Sí, tengo familia allí. ¿Y qué debería hacer en San Juan?	*Yes, I have family there. And what should I do in San Juan?*
ANA: Deberías visitar El Morro y el Viejo San Juan.	*You should visit El Morro and Old San Juan.*
PABLO: ¿Y qué más?	*And what else?*
ANA: Si vas a Puerto Rico, ¡tienes que ir al Yunque! A mí me encanta.	*If you go to Puerto Rico, you have to go to El Yunque! I love it.*
PABLO: ¡Sí! Ya pedí información sobre "El Yunque." ¿Qué necesito si voy al Yunque?	*I know! I already asked for information about "El Yunque." What do I need if I go to El Yunque?*
ANA: Es un bosque lluvioso tropical. Llueve mucho allí, así que necesitas ropa impermeable.	*It's a tropical rainforest. It rains a lot there, so you need waterproof clothing.*
PABLO: ¿Qué más tengo que llevar?	*What else do I need to take?*
ANA: Lleva unas buenas botas de caminar.	*Take some good walking boots.*
PABLO: Si voy al Yunque, te mandaré una postal.	*If I go to El Yunque, I'll send you a postcard.*
ANA: ¡Excelente!	*Excellent!*

Ana seems to be particularly fond of the El Yunque National Park. Read on to learn about different ways to ask for and give advice.

ASKING FOR ADVICE

In the opening conversation, Pablo asks Ana for advice in a number of different ways. Read the following excerpts from the dialogue out loud.

¿Qué debería hacer allí?	*What should I do there?*
¿Qué necesito si voy al Yunque?	*What do I need if I go to El Yunque?*
¿Qué más tengo que llevar?	*What else do I have to take?*

One of the most common ways to ask for advice is to use the structure (*question word*) + **debería** +(*verb*). For example: **¿Qué debería hacer?** (*What should I do?*) Here are some more examples:

¿Qué debería llevar?	*What should I take?*
¿Qué debería decir?	*What should I say?*
¿Dónde debería ir?	*Where should I go?*
¿Cuánto debería comprar?	*How much should I buy?*

Before you practice using **debería**, here is a quick review of the question words:

¿Cómo... ?	*How . . . ?*
¿Cuánto... ?	*How much . . . ?*
¿Dónde... ?	*Where . . . ?*
¿Por qué... ?	*Why . . . ?*
¿Qué... ?	*What . . . ?*
¿Quién... ?	*Who . . . ?*

Oral Practice 8-1

 TRACK 26

Imagine you are taking a trip soon. Use the cues to ask for advice about your travels. After each question, listen to the recording to check your answers, and repeat what you hear.

1. where/go (**ir**) ? ¿Dónde _____ ?
2. what/take (**llevar**) ? ¿Qué _____ ?
3. what/visit (**visitar**) ? ¿_____ ?

4. where/eat (**comer**) ? ¿_____?

5. what/buy (**comprar**) ? ¿_____?

6. how much/pay (**pagar**) ? ¿_____?

7. why/go (**ir**) ? ¿_____?

8. how/travel (**viajar**) ? ¿_____?

GIVING ADVICE

There are different ways to give advice, depending on how strongly you feel about your recommendation. In the opening dialogue, Ana says **deberías** (*you should*) to recommend San Juan, but **tienes que** (*you have to*) to recommend El Yunque, her favorite part of the island. Here are some more examples of giving advice:

Deberías viajar en avión.	*You should travel by plane.*
Tienes que ir a Costa Rica. Es bellísimo.	*You have to go to Costa Rica. It's beautiful.*

You can give advice in formal situations using the **usted** forms **debería** and **tiene que**.

Debería conocer a la Señora Ruiz.	*You should meet Ms. Ruiz.*
Tiene que ir a la conferencia.	*You have to go to the conference.*

Note that the construction **tener que** is also used to talk about what you *must* do out of obligation—when you don't have a choice either way.

Usted tiene que viajar en tren. No hay autobús.	*You have to travel by train. There is no bus.*
Tienes que hacer una reservación o no tendrás mesa.	*You have to make a reservation, or you won't get a table.*

To recommend what someone *shouldn't* do, use **no debería(s)**.

No deberías llevar dólares. Allí usan pesos.	*You shouldn't bring dollars. They use pesos there.*
No debería beber el agua. Está contaminada.	*You shouldn't drink the water. It's polluted.*

The structure **no + tener que** talks about lack of obligation, something you *don't have to* do.

No tienes que llevar dinero. Hay cajeros allí.	*You don't have to bring cash. There are ATMs there.*
No tiene que hacer una reserva. No es necesario.	*You don't have to make a reservation. It's not necessary.*

GIVING CONDITIONAL ADVICE

At times, the kind of advice you give will depend on the situation. In this case, you can use a conditional **si** (*if*) clause before imparting your wisdom. For instance, Ana tells Pablo, **Si vas a Puerto Rico, ¡tienes que ir al Yunque!** (*If you go to Puerto Rico you have to go to El Yunque!*). The construction is: **Si + (*present tense*), ... debería(s)** or **tiene(s) que...** Look at these examples:

Si vas a Perú, deberías hacer el camino Inca.	*If you go to Peru, you should do the Inca Trail.*
Si vas a Costa Rica, ¡tienes que ir a Tortuguero!	*If you go to Costa Rica, you have to go to Tortuguero!*
Si quieres viajar en tren, deberías hacer una reservación.	*If you want to travel by train, you should make a reservation.*

For formal situations, make sure you use the **usted** form of both verbs.

Si va a la República Dominicana, debería ir a Puerto Plata.	*If you go to the Dominican Republic, you should go to Puerto Plata.*
Si quiere vivir en México, tiene que aprender español.	*If you want to live in Mexico, you have to learn Spanish.*

You can also use this structure to tell people what to do under certain conditions using the commands you learned in Chapter 7: **si** + (*present tense*) ... (*command*) ...

Si tienes el dinero, contrata a un guía.   *If you have the money, hire a guide.*

Si van a San Juan, visiten la catedral.   *If you (plural) go to San Juan, visit the cathedral.*

Oral Practice 8-2

 TRACK 27

Imagine a friend is taking a trip and asks you for advice. Use the cues provided to give her advice with **deberías**. Then listen to the recording to check your answers. Repeat what you hear.

1. (*go to Mexico/take pesos*)
   Si vas a _____ _____ pesos.

2. (*go to Costa Rica/go to Poás Volcano*)
   Si _____ _____ al Volcán Poás.

3. (*go to Colombia/go to Cartagena*)
   _____ _____ .

4. (*go to Argentina/don't travel by train*)
   _____ _____ .

5. (*go to Chile/call Marta*)
   _____ _____ .

Now imagine a friend of a friend is asking you for advice. You don't know him well, so you give him advice using **debería**. Here are some vocabulary words you might need as well.

las artesanías	*crafts*	regatear	*to bargain*
necesitar	*to need*	repetir	*to repeat*

6. (*go to Mexico/take pesos*)   Si va a _____ ,
   _____ .

7. (*go to Restaurante Cuzco/make a reservation*)   Si _____ ,
   _____ .

8. (*buy crafts at the market/bargain*) _____ en el
   mercado, _____ .

9. (*need information/don't send an e-mail*) _____ ,
   _____ .

10. (*make a reservation/repeat your name*) _____ ,
    _____ .

EXPRESSING NEEDS

In the dialogue, Ana tells Pablo that he needs to take **ropa impermeable** (*water-proof clothing*) to El Yunque. She uses the verb **necesitar** (*to need*), which is a regular verb and also a cognate. Here are some example sentences with the verb **necesitar**:

Claudia necesita ayuda.	*Claudia needs help.*
¿Necesitas algo?	*Do you need anything?*
¿Necesitan ustedes un mapa?	*Do you need a map?*
No necesitamos un mapa. El carro tiene GPS.	*We don't need a map. The car has a GPS.*

Written Practice 8-1

Imagine you are traveling to the rainforest with a group. Read each cue, and decide whether it's an item you would need in the rainforest or not. Then write a sentence using the correct form of the verb **necesitar** in the negative or affirmative, depending on whether the item is necessary or not. Here is some vocabulary to help you:

unas botas de caminar	*walking boots*	una gorra	*hat, cap*
una corbata	*necktie*	una guía turística	*guidebook*

1. yo/unas botas de caminar _____

2. nosotros/unas gorras _____

3. ustedes/una guía turística del bosque tropical _____

4. tú/una computadora _____

5. ellas/un mapa del bosque _____

6. usted/una corbata _____

Oral Practice 8-3

 TRACK 28

Listen to the following conversations between people asking for and giving each other advice. Indicate whether each sentence is **cierto** (*true*) or **falso** (*false*) according to what you hear. If you have trouble understanding, follow along with the tapescript in the answer key in the back of the book, or use the translation to help you.

1. Marta asks José advice about traveling to Peru.

   ¿Cierto o falso? José sugiere que Marta debería ir a Cuzco. *José suggests that Marta go to Cuzco.* _____

2. Aurora gives Gilberto advice about eating at a restaurant.

   ¿Cierto o falso? Gilberto no necesita hacer una reservación. *Gilberto doesn't need to make a reservation.* _____

3. Mónica wants to buy something at the arts and crafts market. Ramón gives her advice.

   ¿Cierto o falso? Mónica puede pagar con dólares. *Mónica can pay with dollars.* _____

4. Rocío and Julio are talking about renting a car.

   ¿Cierto o falso? Rocío necesita un mapa. *Rocío needs a map.* _____

Making Future Plans

 TRACK 29

Pablo is almost ready for his trip. He's made his reservations and prepared his itinerary. He fills in his grandmother Rosa on the details. She's a bit nervous that her grandson is traveling alone, and wants him to keep in touch. In their conversation,

Pablo and Rosa use two ways to describe future actions. Listen to their conversation. Can you tell what they are?

PABLO: Voy a salir el veinticinco de junio.

I'm going to leave on June 25th.

ROSA: ¿Cómo vas a viajar?

How are you going to travel?

PABLO: Voy a viajar en avión. Te mandaré los detalles en un email.

I'm going to travel by plane. I'll send you the details in an e-mail.

ROSA: Sí, manda toda la información del viaje. Quiero saber dónde estarás.

Yes, send all the information about the trip. I want to know where you'll be.

PABLO: El veinticinco de junio voy a estar en San Juan.

On June 25th I'll be in San Juan.

ROSA: ¿Qué vas a hacer en San Juan?

What are you going to do in San Juan?

PABLO: Estaré en casa del primo Juan. Visitaré la ciudad con él.

I'll be at cousin Juan's. I'll visit the town with him.

ROSA: ¿Dónde estarás el dos de julio?

Where will you be on July 2nd?

PABLO: Estaré en Culebra.

I'll be in Culebra.

ROSA: Deberías llamar a tu hermana Rosita. Es su cumpleaños.

You should call your sister Rosita. It's her birthday.

PABLO: Sí, por supuesto. Llamaré a Rosita.

Yes, of course. I'll call Rosita.

ROSA: ¿Y cuándo vas a estar en Vieques?

And when are you going to be in Vieques?

PABLO: Estaré en Vieques el diez de julio.

I'll be in Vieques on July 10th.

ROSA: Deberías visitar a tu tío Ernesto.

You should visit your uncle Ernesto.

PABLO: Sí, abuela, visitaré al tío Ernesto.

Yes, grandma, I'll visit Uncle Ernesto.

ROSA: Tienes que llamar todos los días, mi'hijo.

You have to call every day, son.

PABLO: Está bien, abuela. Llamaré todos los días, o escribiré un email.

O.K., grandma. I'll call every day, or I'll write an e-mail.

THE FUTURE WITH *IR* + *A*

Pablo and Rosa use **ir a** + (*infinitive*) to express future plans and intentions. This is similar to using *to be going to* when talking about the future in English. Look at these excerpts from the dialogue:

Voy a salir el veinticinco de junio.	*I'm going to leave on June 25th.*
¿Cómo vas a viajar?	*How are you going to travel?*
Voy a viajar en avión.	*I'm going to travel by plane.*
¿Qué vas a hacer en San Juan?	*What are you going to do in San Juan?*
¿Y cuándo vas a estar en Vieques?	*And when are you going to be in Vieques?*

As long as you remember how to conjugate the verb **ir** in the present, this is a very useful way to talk about the future because it's so easy! There are no verb endings and no different spellings to remember. Here's a quick reminder of the present tense of **ir**: **voy, vas, va, vamos, vais, van.**

You can use the future with **ir** with the following expressions of time:

Time Expressions

el lunes, el martes, etc.	*On Monday, on Tuesday, etc.*
en... días	*in . . . days*
el/este fin de semana	*over the weekend/this weekend*
mañana	*tomorrow*
pasado mañana	*the day after tomorrow*
el año que viene	*next year, this upcoming year*
el mes que viene	*next month, this upcoming month*
la semana que viene	*next week, this upcoming week*

You may also hear people use **la próxima semana**, **el próximo mes**, and **el próximo año** to say *next week*, *next month*, and *next year*.

Here are some example sentences using the future with **ir** and the above time expressions.

Nosotros vamos a viajar el año que viene.	*We are going to travel next year.*
Rosita va a venir el martes.	*Rosita is going to come on Tuesday.*
Ellas no van a necesitar esta maleta.	*They are not going to need this suitcase.*

To ask *yes/no* questions, simply add question marks in writing, and raise your vocal intonation at the end of the sentence. You can also form questions using question words.

¿Vas a ir a la fiesta este fin de semana?	*Are you going to the party this weekend?*
¿Qué vas a hacer mañana?	*What are you going to do tomorrow?*
¿Dónde van a comprar comida ustedes?	*Where are you going to buy food?*

When replying to *yes/no* questions, remember to begin your answer with **Sí** or **No**, even if it means having two **no**s in a row.

¿Usted va a ir a la fiesta el sábado?	*Are you going to the party on Saturday?*
Sí, voy a ir a la fiesta el sábado.	*Yes, I am going to go to the party on Saturday.*
No, no voy a ir a la fiesta el sábado.	*No, I am not going to go to the party on Saturday.*

Don't forget that you can also use these expressions with the simple present to refer to the future.

El año que viene viajamos a Chile.	*Next year we are traveling to Chile.*
Mañana llamo a Lourdes.	*Tomorrow I'll call Lourdes.*

The Many Meanings of *a*

The preposition **a** is used in a number of ways in Spanish. In this book you've seen several, including:

Before a destination to signal movement toward something:

Voy **a** la biblioteca.	*I am going **to** the library.*
Llegamos **a** casa.	*We arrived home.*

After **ir** to express the future with *going to*:

Voy **a** ir a la biblioteca.	*I am going **to** go to the library.*
Va **a** comer.	*He's going **to** eat.*

To connect a verb with the following infinitive:

Voy a ir a la biblioteca **a** estudiar.	*I am going to go to the library **to** study.*
Empiezan **a** hablar.	*They start **to** speak.*

You have also learned the personal **a**, which introduces a person if the person is a direct object.

Visito **a** Luisa.	*I visit Luisa.*

However, *don't* use the personal **a** when the direct object is a thing.

Visito la catedral.	*I visit the cathedral.*

Written Practice 8-2

Describe your friends' plans for the next couple of weeks. Translate the following sentences into Spanish using **ir a** to express the future. Use the following vocabulary words to help you:

| el apartamento | *apartment* | el parque | *the park* |
| buscar | *to look for* | ver | *to see* |

1. Saturday I'm going to go to a party.

   _____

2. Luisa is going to travel to Atlanta next week.

   _____

3. Julián and Regina are going to look for an apartment the day after tomorrow.

   _____

4. We are not going to see my mother next month.

   _____

5. Over the weekend you (*plural*) are going to visit the park.

   _____

Oral Practice 8-4

 TRACK 30

Listen to the following questions on the recording. After each question, press pause, and reply using the cue provided. Then listen to check your answers, and repeat what you hear. If you can't understand the questions, use the answer key in the back of the book to help you. Follow the example provided.

1. Cue: (no)

   You hear: ¿Vas a visitar a María? (*pause*)

   You answer: No, no voy a visitar a María.

2. (sí)
3. (no)
4. (sí)
5. (sí)
6. (no)
7. (en Chile)

8. (en avión)

9. (mi primo)

10. (visitar Santiago)

REPORTING FUTURE PLANS

The second way that Pablo and Rosa talk about the future is by using the simple future tense. Listen to the dialogue again, and pay attention to the excerpts shown below that use the simple future. What do you notice about the way the verbs **mandaré**, **estaré**, and **llamaré** are pronounced?

Te mandaré los detalles en un email.	*I'll send you the details in an e-mail.*
Estaré en casa del primo Juan.	*I'll be at cousin Juan's.*
Llamaré a Rosita.	*I'll call Rosita.*

Mandaré, **estaré**, and **llamaré** are all accented on the final syllable: **-é**. The tilde (´) tells you to accent this syllable in speech. To make the simple future, add the verb endings **-é**, **-ás**, **-á**, **-emos**, **-éis**, **-án** to the *infinitive* of the verb.

Simple Future (Regular Verbs)

	-ar: llamar *to call*	-er: comer *to eat*	-ir: vivir *to live*
yo	llamaré	comeré	viviré
tú	llamarás	comerás	vivirás
él/ella, usted	llamará	comerá	vivirá
nosotros(as)	llamaremos	comeremos	viviremos
vosotros(as)	llamaréis	comeréis	viviréis
ellos/ellas, ustedes	llamarán	comerán	vivirán

In general, you should use the simple future to talk about future plans when you would ordinarily use *will* in English.

El mes que viene hablaré con Rebeca.	*I'll speak with Rebeca next month.*
Héctor llamará mañana.	*Héctor will call tomorrow.*
En cinco días viviremos en la casa nueva.	*In five days we'll live in the new house.*
El fin de semana ustedes irán al parque.	*This weekend you'll go to the park.*

Unfortunately, the simplicity of the future tense forms doesn't save you from irregular verbs. With irregular verbs, you add the future endings to an irregular root (or stem), not to the infinitive. Here is a list of the most common irregular verbs in the future. The root has been provided in parentheses.

Simple Future (Irregular Verbs)

decir (dir-)	→	diré	saber (sabr-)	→	sabré
hacer (har-)	→	haré	salir (saldr-)	→	saldré
poder (podr-)	→	podré	tener (tendr-)	→	tendré
poner (pondr-)	→	pondré	venir (vendr-)	→	vendré

Here are some example sentences with irregular verbs in the future:

¿Harás tú la reservación hoy?	*Will you make the reservation today?*
¿Qué dirá usted?	*What will you say?*
Arturo no tendrá la paciencia.	*Arturo won't have the patience.*
¿Vendrás mañana?	*Will you come tomorrow?*

The future for **hay** (*there is/there are*) is **habrá**.

| ¿Habrá mucha gente en la fiesta? | *Will there be a lot of people at the party?* |
| ¿Habrá cajeros automáticos en Puerto Rico? | *Will there be ATMs in Puerto Rico?* |

Written Practice 8-3

Complete the following sentences with the simple future form of the verb in parentheses. After you finish, read the sentences aloud.

1. Cecilia _____ (viajar) a Perú el mes que viene.

2. Ustedes _____ (ir) en barco.

3. Esteban _____ (aprender) español el año que viene.

4. Nosotras _____ (necesitar) un mapa.

5. Tú _____ (pagar) con dólares.

6. Ellas _____ (comprar) muchas cosas en la tienda.

7. Yo _____ (hacer) una reservación para viajar en tren.

8. ¿Qué _____ (decir) tú si aprendo chino?

9. ¿_____ (haber) un mercado de artesanías en Cuzco?

10. ¿Dónde _____ (comprar) tú el libro?

Oral Practice 8-5

TRACK 31

Listen to the following dialogues, and indicate whether the statements are **cierto o falso** (*true or false*).

1. Ester gives Mario advice.

   ¿Cierto o falso? Mario va a viajar a México. *Mario is going to travel to México.* _____

2. Esteban and Ángela talk about an upcoming trip.

   ¿Cierto o falso? Esteban va a viajar a Argentina. *Esteban is going to travel to Argentina.* _____

3. Marta and Luis talk about a party.

   ¿Cierto o falso? Ambos Marta y Luis van a ir a la fiesta. *Both Marta and Luis are going to go to the party.* _____

4. Rebeca tells Antonio about her future move.

   ¿Cierto o falso? Rebeca y su esposo se van a mudar el mes que viene. *Rebeca and her husband are moving next month.* _____

Chapter Practice

 TRACK 32

Say the phrase or sentence that works best for each situation. Listen to the recording to hear the correct answer, and repeat what you hear.

1. You ask a friend's advice on what to do in Puerto Rico.

2. You ask a friend's advice on where to go.

3. A friend asks you **¿Dónde debería viajar?** You advise her to travel to Costa Rica.

4. A friend asks you **¿Qué necesito llevar?** You tell him he needs to take waterproof boots.

5. A friend asks you **¿Qué vas a hacer el fin de semana?** You are going to go to a party.

6. A friend asks you **¿Qué van a hacer ustedes el domingo?** You are going to go to the park.

7. You tell a friend he absolutely has to visit El Yunque.

8. You explain that if he goes to El Yunque, he has to take waterproof boots.

9. Someone asks you **¿Qué hará José en Londres?** He will learn English.

10. Someone asks you **¿Qué visitarán Mario y Ana en Honduras?** Tell him that they will visit Copán.

QUIZ

Circle the letter of the word or phrase that best completes each sentence.

1. Mañana _____ a mi prima Carmen.

    (a) visito

    (b) visité

    (c) visitaré

2. En dos días _____ a Ecuador.

   (a) voy a

   (b) iré

   (c) fui

3. El _____ empezaré clases de español.

   (a) semana pasada

   (b) mes pasado

   (c) mes que viene

4. Si necesitas ayuda, _____ llamar a Teresa.

   (a) llame

   (b) deberías

   (c) tienes

5. _____ ir a México. Es bellísimo.

   (a) Por qué

   (b) No deberías

   (c) Tienes que

 TRACK 33

Listen to the recording to hear a phrase or question. Press pause, and say your answer: a, b, or c. Then listen to the correct answer on the recording, and repeat what you hear. Go on to the next question, and repeat the process.

6. (a) No, no tienes que ir.

   (b) Sí, él siempre va.

   (c) No, no vamos a ir.

7. (a) Pasado mañana.

   (b) Anteayer.

   (c) La semana pasada.

8. (a) Estuve en México.

   (b) Estaré en México.

   (c) Estarán en México.

9. (a) Tienes que ir al cine.

   (b) Necesitas una computadora.

   (c) Van a usar una computadora.

10. (a) Voy a salir el quince de abril.

    (b) Voy a viajar en avión.

    (c) Viajaré a Cuzco.

CHAPTER 9

Arriving in a New Country

In this chapter you will learn:

How to report what you did

How to give the short version of a story using direct object pronouns

How to ask for something politely

How to describe pain

How to use indirect object pronouns

Sharing Experiences

 TRACK 34

Pablo has finally arrived in Puerto Rico. He calls Ana back home to report his first experiences on the island. Ana is very curious to find out what he's done while in Puerto Rico and asks lots of questions. Can you count how many questions she asks?

ANA: ¿Aló?

Hello?

PABLO: Hola, Ana. Soy Pablo. Llamo desde San Juan.

Hi, Ana. It's Pablo. I'm calling from San Juan.

ANA: ¡Hola! ¿Qué tal allí? ¿Qué te parece San Juan?

Hi! How are you doing over there? What do you think of San Juan?

PABLO: ¡Me encanta! Me gusta mucho estar aquí.

I love it! I really like being here.

ANA: ¿Visitaste a tu familia?

Did you visit your family?

PABLO: Sí, visité a mi primo y a mis tíos.

Yes, I visited my cousin and my uncles.

ANA: ¿Conociste a gente nueva?

Did you meet any new people?

PABLO: Sí. Conocí a varias personas de aquí. La gente es muy simpática.

Yes. I met several people from here. People are very nice.

ANA: ¿Tuviste algún problema?

Did you have any problems?

PABLO: Por ahora no. Todo fue muy bien. El vuelo estuvo muy bien y llegué a la hora. Encontré el hotel sin problemas y disfruté mucho de todo.

Not for now. Everything went really well. The flight was very good, and I arrived on time. I found the hotel without any problems, and I enjoyed it all a lot.

ANA: ¿Visitaste El Yunque?

Did you visit El Yunque?

PABLO: No, todavía no lo visité. Pero iré la semana que viene.

No, I haven't visited it yet. But I'm going next week.

ANA: ¿Probaste ya las piraguas? Son muy refrescantes.

Did you try the piraguas*? They're very refreshing.*

PABLO: No, todavía no las probé.   *No, I haven't tried them yet.*

ANA: ¿Comiste ya cuchifritos?   *Did you eat cuchifritos?*

PABLO: Sí, los probé.   *Yes, I did try them.*

ANA: ¿Y qué te parecieron?   *What do you think?*
   ¿Te gustaron?   *Did you like them?*

PABLO: La verdad, no me gustaron   *The truth is, I didn't really like them*
   mucho...   *that much . . .*

REPORTING WHAT YOU DID

Ana asks Pablo ten questions! Some of them are to find out what Pablo already did; others ask his opinion about things he's seen and experienced while in Puerto Rico. Among them she asks about **piraguas** (similar to snow cones), which he hasn't tried yet, and the **cuchifritos** (local fried food), which he was not too fond of.

   Ana asks Pablo a number of questions about what he has done already. Look at what she says:

¿Visitaste a tu familia?   *Did you visit your family?*

¿Conociste a gente nueva?   *Did you meet new people?*

¿Tuviste algún problema?   *Did you have any problems?*

¿Visitaste El Yunque?   *Did you visit El Yunque?*

Pablo tells Ana about several things he has done while in Puerto Rico:

Visité a mi primo y a mis tíos.   *I visited my cousin and my uncles.*

Conocí a varias personas.   *I met several people.*

Encontré el hotel sin problemas.   *I found the hotel without any problems.*

Disfruté mucho de todo.   *I really enjoyed everything.*

   Both Ana and Pablo use the *simple past*, also called the *preterite*, to talk about completed past actions.

   To conjugate the simple past, drop the **-ar**, **-er**, or **-ir** from the infinitive, and add endings to the root of the verb. Here are the simple past (preterite) conjugations for regular verbs:

Simple Past or Preterite (Regular Verbs)

	visitar	comer	escribir
yo	visité	comí	escribí
tú	visitaste	comiste	escribiste
usted	visitó	comió	escribió
él/ella	visitó	comió	escribió
nosotros(as)	visitamos	comimos	escribimos
vosotros(as)	visitasteis	comisteis	escribisteis
ustedes	visitaron	comieron	escribieron
ellos/ellas	visitaron	comieron	escribieron

Here are some examples of verbs that are *regular* in the simple past:

comer	*to eat*	pagar	*to pay*
comprar	*to buy*	perder	*to lose*
disfrutar	*to enjoy*	probar	*to taste*
encontrar	*to find*	vender	*to sell*
escribir	*to write*	viajar	*to travel*
llamar	*to call*	vivir	*to live*
llegar	*to arrive*		

The simple past is used to describe an action that is completed and not ongoing.

Compré un mapa.	*I bought a map.*
Ellos llegaron tarde.	*They arrived late.*
Nosotras visitamos las ruinas de Caparra.	*We visited the Caparra Ruins.*
Roberto vio a Ester en la calle.	*Roberto saw Ester in the street.*

Form negative statements and questions as you do with all other verb tenses. Here are some examples:

¿Encontraste el mapa?	*Did you find the map?*
¿Dónde encontraste el mapa?	*Where did you find the map?*

GRAMMAR DEMYSTIFIED

The Simple Past

In Spanish, the simple past is usually translated into English with the *-ed* form of the verb, such as: *we arrived* or *she called*, or, in the case of English irregular verbs, *they slept* or *I wrote*. However, in Latin America, you may often hear the simple past where you might use the present perfect (*he has gone*, *we have eaten*, etc.) in English. For instance, Ana asks Pablo, **¿Ya probaste las piraguas?** In English you would probably say, *Have you tried the* **piraguas** *yet?* So, don't let English equivalents confuse you! If you see a simple past ending on a Spanish verb, then it's the simple past.

No encontré el mapa.	*I did not find the map.*
Pablo no llamó.	*Pablo didn't call.*

Here are some Spanish expressions of time that indicate the speaker is talking about the past. These time expressions are usually paired with the simple past because they refer to completed actions in the past.

Past Time Expressions

ayer	*yesterday*
anteayer	*the day before yesterday*
anoche	*last night*
el lunes pasado	*last Monday*
el mes pasado	*last month*
hace dos días	*two days ago*
hace una semana	*a week ago*

You can use **... pasado(a)** and **hace...** with any time period to express concepts of *last* and *ago*. Remember that **pasado(a)** is an adjective and agrees with the time period it describes. For example:

hace un año	*a year ago*
hace un mes	*a month ago*
hace dos semanas	*two weeks ago*
el año pasado	*last year*
la semana pasada	*last week*
el fin de semana pasado	*last weekend*

Here are examples of the time expressions used in sentences with the simple past:

Hace una semana llamé a Teresa.	*I called Teresa a week ago.*
Anoche hablé con mi abuela.	*I talked to my grandmother last night.*
¿Vieron ustedes a Luisa ayer?	*Did you see Luisa yesterday?*
No disfrutamos de la fiesta anteayer.	*We did not enjoy the party the day before yesterday.*

Some of the verbs that Ana and Pablo use are irregular in the past: **estuvo** (from **estar**), **fue** (from **ser**), and **tuviste** (from **tener**) are some examples. Here are conjugations of some common irregular verbs in the simple past:

Simple Past (Irregular Verbs)

	tener	estar	ser	ir	ver	hacer
yo	tuve	estuve	fui	fui	vi	hice
tú	tuviste	estuviste	fuiste	fuiste	viste	hiciste
usted	tuvo	estuvo	fue	fue	vio	hizo
él/ella	tuvo	estuvo	fue	fue	vio	hizo
nosotros(as)	tuvimos	estuvimos	fuimos	fuimos	vimos	hicimos
vosotros(as)	tuvisteis	estuvisteis	fuisteis	fuisteis	visteis	hicisteis
ustedes	tuvieron	estuvieron	fueron	fueron	vieron	hicieron
ellos/ellas	tuvieron	estuvieron	fueron	fueron	vieron	hicieron

Did you notice how similar the past of **ser** and **ir** are? (O.K., they are the same!) You can usually use the context to differentiate them, and the good news is that you learn two verbs for the effort of one. Here are some example sentences with irregular verbs in the past:

El martes pasado tuvimos una reunión.   *We had a meeting last Tuesday.*

Nosotras fuimos en metro.   *We went by subway.*

¿Estuviste en El Yunque el mes   *Were you at El Yunque last month?*
  pasado?

Anoche fueron al cine.   *They went to the movies last night.*

Written Practice 9-1

Complete the following dialogue by writing the correct form of the verb in the simple past. Careful: The verbs with an asterisk (*) are irregular. Then read the whole dialogue out loud. If you want to challenge yourself, don't write the answers first. Do the entire exercise orally.

ANTONIO: Rebeca, ¿tú _____ (viajar) a Costa Rica?
  Rebeca, have you traveled to Costa Rica?

REBECA: Sí, lo _____ (visitar) hace un año. ¡Me encanta
  Costa Rica!
  Yes, I visited it a year ago. I love Costa Rica!

ANTONIO: ¿Con quién _____ (ir*)?
  Who(m) did you go with?

REBECA: _____ (viajar) con Luis.
  I traveled with Luis.

ANTONIO: ¿Cuánto tiempo _____ (estar*) ustedes allí?
  How long were you there?

REBECA: Nosotros _____ (estar*) allí dos semanas.
  _____ (disfrutar) mucho.
  We were there for two weeks. We enjoyed it a lot.

ANTONIO: ¿Y qué _____ (hacer*)?
  And what did you do?

REBECA: _____ (ir*) al Parque Nacional Manuel Antonio.
  We went to Manuel Antonio National Park.

ANTONIO: ¿_____ (ver*) ustedes muchos animales?
  Did you see a lot of animals?

REBECA: Sí, _____ (ver*) de todo. _____ (ver*) monos, cocodrilos, tortugas, aves...
Yeah, we saw all kinds of animals. We saw monkeys, crocodiles, turtles, birds . . .

ANTONIO: ¿_____ (tener*) ustedes un guía?
Did you have a guide?

REBECA: Sí, el guía _____ (ser*) muy bueno.
Yes, the guide was very good.

ANTONIO: ¿_____ (comer) ustedes comida típica costarricense?
Did you eat typical Costa Rican food?

REBECA: Yo _____ (probar) de todo, pero Luis no _____ (comer) mucho. Oye, si quieres más información mis amigos _____ (escribir) un artículo sobre su viaje. Te lo daré.
Yes, I tried all kinds, but Luis didn't eat much. Hey, if you'd like more information, my friends wrote an article about their trip. I'll give it to you.

ANTONIO: Muchas gracias.
Thanks a lot.

REBECA: De nada. Costa Rica me parece precioso. Deberías ir.
You're welcome. I think Costa Rica is beautiful. You should go.

Oral Practice 9-1

 TRACK 35

Imagine you're a food critic. A friend asks you about a restaurant. Listen to the following questions on the recording. Pause after each question, and reply using a complete sentence in the past. Then listen to check your answers, and repeat what you hear.

1. ¿Comiste en el Restaurante Coquí? (sí)

2. ¿Probaste el sopón de pollo? (no)

3. ¿Comieron ustedes arroz con pollo? (sí)

4. ¿Pagó Luisa? (sí)

5. ¿Escribiste un artículo sobre el restaurante? (sí)

GIVING THE SHORT VERSION WITH DIRECT OBJECT PRONOUNS

Using *direct object pronouns*, you won't need to constantly repeat information when answering questions (as you did in the above exercise). Direct object pronouns allow you to give a shorter answer. You saw this in the opening conversation, when Pablo answers some of Ana's questions. Look at the following excerpts from the dialogue. What do **las** and **los** refer to?

ELENA: ¿Probaste ya las piraguas? Son muy refrescantes.

Have you tried the piraguas yet? They're very refreshing.

PABLO: No, todavía no **las** probé.

*No, I haven't tried **them** yet.*

ELENA: ¿Comiste ya cuchifritos?

And did you eat cuchifritos?

PABLO: Sí, **los** probé.

*Yes, I tried **them**.*

In the previous examples, **las** refers to **las piraguas,** and **los** refers to **los cuchifritos**. Here, **las** and **los** are *direct object pronouns*. A direct object pronoun replaces a noun that behaves as the direct object in a sentence. The direct object is a person or thing that receives the action. Here are the Spanish direct object pronouns:

Direct Object Pronouns

me	*me*		
te	*you (informal)*		
lo	*him, it, you (masculine)*	la	*her, it, you (feminine)*
nos	*us*		
os	*you (informal plural)*		
los	*them, you (masculine)*	las	*them, you (feminine)*

The pronoun **lo** replaces a singular masculine noun; **la** replaces a singular feminine noun; **los** replaces a plural masculine noun; and **las** replaces a plural feminine noun.

Here are some examples that show how direct object pronouns replace nouns:

¿Viste **la película**?

*Did you see **the movie**?*

No, no **la** vi.

*No, I did not see **it**.*

¿Compraste ya **el libro**?	*Did you buy **the book** already?*
Sí, ya **lo** compré.	*Yes, I already bought **it**.*
¿Encontraron ustedes **los lentes**?	*Did you find **the eyeglasses**?*
No, no **los** encontramos.	*No, we did not find **them**.*
¿Comieron ellas **las galletas**?	*Did they eat **the cookies**?*
Sí, **las** comieron.	*Yes, they ate **them**.*

The pronoun **lo** can also replace an entire phrase. It acts as a neutral indicator of something that does not necessarily have a gender. For example:

¿Visitaste ya el museo Bacardí?	*Did you already visit the Bacardi Museum?*
No. **Lo** haré mañana.	*No. I'll do **it** tomorrow.*

In the previous example, **lo** (*it*) refers to **visitar el museo Bacardí**, a phrase that does not have a specific gender.

Direct object pronouns can be used to refer to people as well as to things. Remember, when talking about more than one person, **las** refers to a group made up entirely of women or girls; if there's even one male in the group, you have to use **los**.

¿Vieron ustedes a **Paco**?	*Did you see **Paco**?*
No, no **lo** vimos.	*No, we didn't see **him**.*
¿Encontraron ustedes a **las niñas**?	*Did you find **the girls**?*
Sí, **las** encontramos.	*Yes, we found **them**.*
¿Conociste a **Dilenia y Rubén**?	*Did you meet **Dilenia and Rubén**?*
Sí, **los** conocí.	*Yes, I met **them**.*

Me, te, os, and **nos** refer *only* to people.

¿**Te** conocí en San Juan?	*Did I meet **you** in San Juan?*
No, no **me** conociste en San Juan.	*No, you didn't meet **me** in San Juan.*
Sí, **nos** ayudó mucho.	*Yes, she helped **us** a lot.*

VOCABULARY DEMYSTIFIED

Leísmo

Note that in Spain, **le** often replaces **lo** when referring to people. This practice is called **leísmo**. If you were Spanish, you might say:

No **le** vimos.   *We didn't see **him**.*

Instead of:

No **lo** vimos.   *We didn't see **him**.*

This is considered acceptable, often correct, usage in Spain.

The object pronoun can go before the conjugated verb, as you see in the above examples. It can also be tacked on to the end of an infinitive. For example:

No quiere ayudar**me**. *or* No **me**   *He doesn't want to help **me**.*
   quiere ayudar.

¿Vamos a conocer**te** mañana? *or*   *Are we going to meet **you** tomorrow?*
   ¿**Te** vamos a conocer mañana?

Voy a hacer**lo** la semana que viene. *or*   *I'm going to do **it** next week.*
   Lo voy a hacer la semana que viene.

Written Practice 9-2

Look at the following questions, and answer using the appropriate direct object pronoun.

1. ¿Viste la película *Titanic*?   *Did you see the movie* Titanic?

   Sí, _____ vi.

2. ¿Compraste el teléfono celular?   *Did you buy the cell phone?*

   No, no _____ compré.

3. ¿Escribiste ya la carta?   *Did you already write the letter?*

     Sí, ya _____ escribí.

4. ¿Vendiste todos los CDs?   *Did you sell all of the CDs?*

     Sí, _____ vendí.

5. ¿Encontró usted los lentes?   *Did you find the eyeglasses?*

     No, _____.

6. ¿Viste a Rebeca y María?   *Did you see Rebeca and María?*

     Sí, _____.

7. ¿Compraron ellas las artesanías?   *Did they buy the craft items?*

     No, _____.

8. ¿Escribieron ustedes un email?   *Did you write an e-mail?*

     Sí, _____.

9. ¿Nos viste en el cine?   *Did you see us at the movies?*

     Sí, _____.

10. ¿Me vieron ustedes en la fiesta?   *Did you see me at the party?*

     No, _____.

Oral Practice 9-2

 TRACK 36

Listen to the dialogues, and indicate whether the statements following are **cierto o falso** (*true or false*).

1. Ana and Fidel discuss movies.

     ¿Cierto o falso? Fidel vio la película *Gladiador. Fidel has seen the movie Gladiator.* _____

2. Renata and Daniel talk about Daniel's trip to Spain.

     ¿Cierto o falso? Daniel fue a Barcelona. *Daniel went to Barcelona.*

     _____

     Daniel fue al Parque Güell. *Daniel went to Parque Güell.* _____

     Daniel visitó la Sagrada Familia. *Daniel visited la Sagrada Familia.*

     _____

3. Paco and Isabel discuss the food choices at a Mexican restaurant.

¿Cierto o falso? Isabel va a comer fajitas. *Isabel is going to eat fajitas.* ____

Paco no probó los burritos en este restaurante. *Paco hasn't tried the burritos at this restaurant.* _____

Paco no probó las quesadillas en este restaurante. *Paco hasn't tried the quesadillas at this restaurant.* _____

Asking and Offering Politely

 TRACK 37

Until now, everything has gone well on Pablo's trip. But as he is walking around Old San Juan, his tooth really starts to throb! He remembers seeing a hospital nearby and thinks maybe he can get something for it there. Pablo stops a man to ask for help. Listen to their conversation on the recording. How does Pablo get lucky?

PABLO: Disculpe, ¿me puede ayudar?   *Excuse me, can you help me?*

DAVID: Sí, claro que lo puedo ayudar. ¿Qué necesita?   *Yes, of course I can help you. What do you need?*

PABLO: Perdí el mapa. ¿Dónde está el hospital?   *I lost my map. Where's the hospital?*

DAVID: Está allí mismo. ¿Ve el cartel? Dice «Hospital Cruces».   *It's over there. Do you see the sign? It says "Cruces Hospital."*

PABLO: ¡Ah, sí! Gracias. Lo veo.   *Ah, yes. Thank you. I see it.*

DAVID: ¿Necesita usted un médico?   *Do you need a doctor?*

PABLO: Necesito un dentista. Tengo dolor de muelas.   *I need a dentist. I have a toothache.*

DAVID: Tiene usted mucha suerte. Mi hermana es dentista. Ella puede ayudarlo.   *You're very lucky. My sister is a dentist, and she can help you.*

PABLO: ¡Ah, qué bien!   *Oh, that's great!*

DAVID: Si usted me da su nombre,
le puedo hacer una cita para
esta tarde.

*If you give me your name, I can make
an appointment for you this
afternoon.*

PABLO: Se lo agradezco. Me llamo
Pablo Torres. ¿Dónde está
su consulta?

*I appreciate it. My name is Pablo
Torres. Where's her office?*

DAVID: En la calle Soles. Le doy la
dirección y el número de teléfono...
Ay, no tengo bolígrafo.

*It's on Soles Street. I'll give you the
address and the phone number . . .
Oh, I don't have a pen.*

PABLO: Espere, le doy el mío...
Aquí tiene.

*It's O.K., I'll give you mine . . .
Here you go.*

DAVID: Gracias. Es la calle Soles 43.
En frente de la oficina de correos.

*Thanks. It's Soles Street 43, across
from the post office.*

PABLO: ¿Está muy lejos? ¿Podría
indicarme el camino?

*Is it very far? Could you show me
the way?*

DAVID: Está a dos minutos de aquí a
pie. Vaya por esa calle. ¿Le duele
mucho la muela?

*It's two minutes from here on foot.
Go down that street. Does your
tooth hurt a lot?*

PABLO: Sí. La verdad es que sí...

Yes. The truth is it does . . .

DAVID: Pues mi hermana le puede
dar unas pastillas también.

*Then my sister can give you some
pills as well.*

PABLO: Muchas gracias.

Thanks a lot.

DAVID: No hay de qué.

It was nothing.

ASKING FOR SOMETHING POLITELY

Pablo is very lucky to meet someone whose sister is a dentist, just when he has a toothache! He asks two things of David. Look at what he says:

¿Me puede ayudar?   *Can you help me?*

¿Podría indicarme el camino?   *Could you show me the way?*

The Verb *poder*

The verb **poder** is a stem-changing verb. The stem, or root, **pod-**, changes to **pued-** for all forms of the present conjugation, except **nosotros** and **vosotros**.

poder (*to be able to*): **Simple Present** (*can*)

yo	puedo	*I can*	nosotros(as)	podemos	*we can*
tú	puedes	*you can (informal)*	vosotros(as)	podéis	*you can (informal plural, Spain)*
usted	puede	*you can*	ustedes	pueden	*you can (plural)*
él/ella	puede	*he/she can*	**ellos/ellas**	**pueden**	*they can*

Poder is commonly used to talk about ability and possibility. You saw this in the dialogue when David said, **Ella puede ayudarlo** (*She can help you.*). Here are some more examples:

¿Puedo ir a la fiesta?	*Can I go to the party?*
Tú puedes llamarme Lola.	*You can call me Lola.*
Ustedes pueden ir a la fiesta mañana.	*You can go to the party tomorrow.*

The verb **poder** (*to be able to*) is very useful for asking for things politely. When used in the present, **puede(s)**, it means *can*. Use **Puede(s)** + (*infinitive*) to make a request. Listen to these examples:

 TRACK 38

¿Puede abrir la ventana?	*Can you open the window? (formal)*
¿Puedes recomendar un buen restaurante?	*Can you recommend a good restaurant? (informal)*

To sound even more polite, use **podría(s)** (*could*) to ask someone to do something. This is the conditional form of the verb **poder**. Use **Podría(s)** + (*infinitive*) to make an even more polite request.

¿Podría explicar esto?	*Could you explain this?*
¿Podrías pasar la sal?	*Could you pass the salt?*

To politely ask someone to do something *for you*, you can add the object pronoun **me** to your request. **Me** can go before the conjugated form of **poder** or tacked on to the infinitive for both formal and informal requests.

¿Podría explicar**me** esto? (*formal*)	*Could you explain this to me?*
¿**Me** podrías pasar la sal? (*informal*)	*Could you pass me the salt?*

Note that even though **podría(s)** is more polite than **puede(s)**, you still have to take into account whether you're addressing someone as **tú** (less formal) or **usted** (more formal). This will depend on the tone you would like to use, as well as whom you are addressing.

Compare the levels of politeness of the three types of requests you've learned thus far. Note that the more direct you are, the less polite you may appear. Tone of voice also makes a difference in how polite you sound. Listen to the differences between these three requests:

command: Llámame desde San Juan.	*Call me from San Juan.*
puede: ¿Puedes llamarme desde San Juan?	*Can you call me from San Juan?*
podría: ¿Podrías llamarme desde San Juan?	*Could you call me from San Juan?*

Of course, adding **por favor** (*please*) always makes everything sound nicer.

Poder can also be used to offer help politely. If you see someone in need of help, you could ask:

¿Puedo ayudarla?	*Can I help you? (addressing a woman)*
¿Puedo ayudarlo?	*Can I help you? (addressing a man)*

CULTURE DEMYSTIFIED

Politeness Is in the Eye of the Beholder

The Spanish tend to be more direct than Latin Americans when speaking, especially when asking for things. Therefore, expectations in Spain are different than in Latin America when it comes to politeness. Whereas in Spain it may be considered polite to use the more direct imperative: **Trae la cuenta, por favor** (*Bring the check, please*), in Latin America one often makes similar requests with more indirect language, often considered more polite: **¿Podría traer la cuenta, por favor?** (*Could you bring the check, please?*) Similarly, in a restaurant in Spain you might order this way: **Quiero la sopa** (*I want the soup.*), whereas in Latin America you would probably say: **Quisiera la sopa** (*I'd like the soup.*). So remember that how polite you sound depends not only on the language and the personal pronoun you use (**tú** or **usted**), but also on where you are.

Written Practice 9-3

Indicate the level of politeness/directness in the following statements: + being the least polite (most direct), ++ the next level of politeness (somewhat direct) and +++ being the most polite (least direct).

1. ¿Podría repetir su nombre, por favor? _____

2. ¿Puedes ayudar a Lola? _____

3. Llama a Ronaldo. _____

4. ¿Podría llamar a Ronaldo? _____

5. ¿Puede repetir su nombre? _____

Oral Practice 9-3

 TRACK 39

Now use the cues to make polite requests using a command (+), **puede** (++) or **podría** (+++), always addressing the person with **usted**. Listen to the recording to check your answers, and repeat what you hear.

1. +++/hablar más despacio
2. +/hablar más despacio
3. ++/venir a mi casa
4. +++/visitar a Daniel en el hospital
5. ++/hablar más bajo

IT HURTS! DESCRIBING PAIN

To describe pain, you can use **Tengo dolor de** + (*body part*).

Tengo dolor de muelas.	*I have a toothache.*
Tengo dolor de cabeza.	*I have a headache.*
Tengo dolor de estómago.	*I have a stomachache.*

You can also say **Me duele** + (*singular body part*) or **Me duelen** + (*plural body part*).

Me duele la cabeza.	*My head hurts.*
Me duele la espalda.	*My back hurts.*
Me duelen los pies.	*My feet hurt.*

Remember that you can use a dictionary to look up any words you need. In the meantime, here is some basic vocabulary to describe parts of the body:

Body Parts

el cuello	*neck*
el dedo	*finger*

la espalda	*back*
el hombro	*shoulder*
la mano	*hand*
el oído	*inner ear*
el ojo	*eye*
el pie	*foot*
la rodilla	*knee*
el tobillo	*ankle*

INDIRECT OBJECT PRONOUNS

You may have noticed some unexplained pronouns in the two opening dialogues of this chapter, such as the **me** you used when making polite requests: **¿Podría indicarme el camino?** (*Could you show me the way?*), or when the man on the street tells Pablo: **... le puede dar unas pastillas** (*she can give you some pills*). The **me** and **le** in these sentences are *indirect object pronouns*. They replace indirect object nouns. For example, in the sentence **¿Podría indicarme el camino?**, **me** is the *indirect* object pronoun meaning *me* and **el camino** is the *direct* object noun. In **le puede dar unas pastillas**, the indirect object pronoun is **le** (*you, formal*) and **unas pastillas** is the direct object.

The dialogue between Pablo and David contains a number of indirect object pronouns:

Le doy la dirección.	*I'll give **you** the address.*
¿Podría indicar**me** el camino?	*Could you show **me** the way?*
¿**Le** duele mucho la muela?	*Does your tooth hurt a lot? (lit.: Does the tooth hurt **you** a lot?)*
Le puede dar unas pastillas.	*She can give **you** some pills.*
Le doy el mío.	*I'll give **you** mine.*

Here are the Spanish indirect object pronouns:

me	*(to) me*	nos	*(to) us*
te	*(to) you (familiar)*	os	*(to) you (plural, familiar)*
le	*(to) him, her, it, you (formal)*	les	*(to) them, you (plural)*

Knowing when to use direct and indirect object pronouns is complicated in Spanish—a complication compounded by the fact that usage varies according to country or region. This book will lay out the basic rules to help you use these pronouns and to understand them when other people are speaking.

You've learned that the verb acts *directly on* the direct object.

Enrique ayuda a Silvia.	*Enrique helps Silvia.*
Enrique **la** ayuda.	*Enrique helps **her**.*

It answers the question *Who(m)?* or *What?*

Who(m) did Enrique help?	*He helped Silvia.* or *He helped her.*

A verb affects the indirect object as well, but the indirect object does not directly receive the action of the verb.

Le doy mi bolígrafo.	*I give **him** my pen.*
Le doy mi bolígrafo **a Juan**.	*I give my pen **to Juan**.*

Sentences with an indirect object noun in Spanish commonly also use an indirect object pronoun, as in the example above.

The indirect object will answer the question *To whom?* or *To what?*

To whom did I give my pen?	*I gave my pen **to Juan**.* or *I gave my pen **to him**.*

In the previous example, **Le** refers to **Juan**, or **him**, the indirect object. **Bolígrafo** is the direct object.

To clarify whom the indirect object pronoun is referring to, use a prepositional phrase with **a**.

Yo **les** di el dinero.	*I gave **them** the money.*
Yo **les** di el dinero **a ellos**.	*I gave the money **to them**.*
Yo **les** di el dinero **a Claudio y Luis**.	*I gave the money **to Claudio and Luis**.*
Yo **les** di el dinero **a mis amigos**.	*I gave the money **to my friends**.*

Here are the pronouns you can use with **a** to clarify or emphasize who is receiving the action:

a mí	*to me*	a nosotros(as)	*to us*
a ti	*to you*	a vosotros(as)	*to you*
a él/a ella	*to him/to her*	a ellos/a ellas	*to them*
a usted	*to you*	a ustedes	*to you*

For example:

Ella **me** habló **a mí.**	*She spoke **to me**.*
Carlos **les** dio el regalo **a ustedes**.	*Carlos gave the present **to you**.*

Other verbs you have learned that often take indirect objects are **mandar** (*to send*), **hablar** (*to speak*), **comprar** (*to buy*), **decir** (*to tell, to say*), and **mostrar** (*to show*).

Mónica le dio dinero a su hermana.	*Mónica gave money to her sister.*
Felipe me mandó un email.	*Felipe sent me an e-mail.*
Nosotros les hablamos en español.	*We speak to them in Spanish.*
Nuestra abuela nos compra muchas cosas.	*Our grandmother buys us a lot of things.*
Julieta te manda muchos recuerdos.	*Julieta sends you many regards.*

The position of the indirect object pronoun is flexible and will vary according to the tense of the verb.

Before the verb:

With the present tense:	**Nos** habla.	*He talks **to us**.*
With the future tense:	**Nos** hablará.	*He will talk **to us**.*
With the simple past:	**Nos** habló.	*He talked **to us**.*

Before or after the verb:

With an infinitive:	Va a hablar**nos**./ **Nos** va a hablar.	*He/She is going to talk **to us**.*
	Quiere hablar**nos**./ **Nos** quiere hablar.	*He/She wants to talk **to us**.*

After the verb:

With commands:	Habla**nos**.	*Talk **to us**.*

Written Practice 9-4

Complete the sentences with the appropriate indirect object.

1. Mi primo ＿＿＿＿＿＿ mandó una carta. *My cousin sent me a letter.*

2. ¿＿＿＿＿＿ escribió José un email? *Did José write you an e-mail?* (informal)

3. Su padre ＿＿＿＿＿＿ compró muchos regalos. *Their dad bought them lots of presents.*

4. ¿＿＿＿＿＿ vas a dar un abrazo? *Are you going to give me a hug?*

5. ¿Usted ＿＿＿＿＿＿ compró flores a su esposa? *Did you buy your wife flowers?*

6. Nosotros ＿＿＿＿＿＿ hablamos a nuestros hijos en español. *We talk to our children in Spanish.*

Oral Practice 9-4

 TRACK 40

Listen to the dialogues, and indicate whether the statements following are **cierto o falso** (*true or false*).

1. Delia asks a man for help at a department store.

    ¿Cierto o falso? Delia quiere comprarle una corbata a su padre. *Delia wants to buy her father a tie.* _____

2. Sergio talks to Diego about how he feels.

    ¿Cierto o falso? Diego tiene dolor de cabeza. *Diego has a headache.* _____

    Sergio le da un vaso de agua a Diego. *Sergio gives Diego a glass of water.* _____

3. Ana talks to Arturo about her boyfriend.

    ¿Cierto o falso? El novio de Ana no le manda emails. *Ana's boyfriend doesn't send her e-mails.* _____

    El novio de Ana le compra flores el Día de San Valentín. *Ana's boyfriend buys her flowers on Valentine's Day.* _____

Chapter Practice

 TRACK 41

Imagine you are chatting with a nosy friend who asks all kinds of questions. Write down your answers. After you are done, practice your conversation with him by listening to the recording and filling in the empty spaces with your responses. At the end of the track, listen to the sample dialogue that gives you a possible version of the dialogue.

FRIEND: Hola. Oye, ¿tú viajaste a Latinoamérica? ¿Dónde?

YOU: _____

FRIEND: ¿Visitaste alguna ciudad grande?

YOU: _____

FRIEND: ¿Qué te pareció la comida?

YOU: _____

FRIEND: ¿Hablaste mucho español? ¿Con quién?

YOU: _____

FRIEND: ¿Qué te gustó más?

YOU: _____

FRIEND: Ay, ¡es tarde! Hasta luego.

YOU: _____

QUIZ

Circle the letter of the word or phrase that best completes each sentence.

1. Hace dos años nosotras _____ a Chile.
   - (a) viajas
   - (b) viajamos
   - (c) viajaremos

2. El viaje _____ muy bien.
   - (a) vimos
   - (b) viajó
   - (c) estuvo

3. En El Salvador Rebeca y Arturo _____ dieron un libro a nosotros.
   - (a) nos
   - (b) les
   - (c) me

4. Daniel vio un cocodrilo, pero yo no _____ vi.

   (a) los

   (b) la

   (c) lo

5. ¿Anita _____ mandó un email a ti?

   (a) nos

   (b) fue

   (c) te

 TRACK 42

Now listen to the recording to hear a phrase or question. Press pause, and say your answer: a, b, or c. Listen to the correct answer on the recording, and repeat what you hear. Then go to the next question, and repeat the process.

6. (a) La llamé anteayer.

   (b) Lo llamé mañana.

   (c) Las llamaré la semana pasada.

7. (a) No, no lo compré.

   (b) No, no la compré.

   (c) No, no las compré.

8. (a) Fueron allí.

   (b) Estuve en el cine.

   (c) Estoy aquí.

9. (a) No, no le escribí un email.

   (b) No, no nos escribí un email.

   (c) No, no me escribí un email.

10. (a) Las encontré ayer.

    (b) No, las tengo aquí.

    (c) ¡Ay, sí! Los perdí.

CHAPTER 10

Out on the Town

In this chapter you will learn:

How to talk about things that used to happen

How to connect ideas

How to use idiomatic expressions

Talking About the Past

 TRACK 43

In Old San Juan, Pablo is out on the town with his cousin Laura, trying out all sorts of new things: foods, music, even language! After a night of partying, they enjoy a big plate of **cuchifritos**.

PABLO: Estos cuchifritos están muy buenos. Antes no me gustaban los cuchifritos, pero ahora me encantan.

These cuchifritos are really good. I didn't like them before, but now I love them.

LAURA: ¿Qué más pediste?

What else did you order?

PABLO: Pedí una agua de coco. De pequeño bebía mucha agua de coco y me encantaba.

I ordered coconut water. As a child I used to drink lots of coconut water, and I loved it.

LAURA: ¿Qué más hacías tú de pequeño? ¿Hablaban ustedes español en casa?

What else did you do as a child? Did you speak Spanish at home?

PABLO: Sí, mi padre nos hablaba en español, mientras mi madre nos hablaba en inglés.

Yes, my father spoke to us in Spanish, while my mother would speak to us in English.

LAURA: ¿Por qué hablaban los dos idiomas?

Why did they speak both languages?

PABLO: Porque era importante que aprendiéramos los dos. Es importante mantener las dos culturas también. Por eso estoy aquí.

Because it was important that we learn both. It's important to maintain both cultures as well. That's why I'm here.

LAURA: Pues tú cada día estás más puertorriqueño.

Well, you're getting more Puerto Rican by the day.

PABLO: ¡Más boricua! Antes decía puertorriqueño, pero ahora digo «boricua».

More Boricua! Before I used to say Puerto Rican, but now I say "Boricua."

LAURA: Aquí llega la cuenta. ¡Ay, qué caro!

Here's the check. Oh, it's so expensive!

PABLO: ¡Te invito yo!

I am treating you!

LAURA: ¿Ya tienes chavos?

Do you have any chavos (money)?

PABLO: ¿Chavos?

Chavos?

LAURA: ¡Chavos! ¡Plata! ¡Guita! ¿Cómo dices tú en Estados Unidos?

Chavos! Plata! Guita! (money) What do you call it in the U.S.?

PABLO: Ah, dinero. Sí, ya tengo.   *Oh money. Yes, I have some.*

LAURA: Si vas a ser más boricua,   *If you are going to be more Boricua,*
tendrás que hablar como un   *then you'll have to speak like one.*
boricua. Muchas gracias por   *Thanks so much for treating me.*
la invitación.

PABLO: Gracias a ti por la compañía,   *Thanks to you for the company, and*
y ¡las lecciones de español!   *the Spanish lessons!*

REPORTING WHAT USED TO HAPPEN

Laura asks Pablo lots of questions about his childhood, and what it means to be bicultural. To talk about how things *used to be* and what Pablo *used to do* as a child, they use the *imperfect* tense. The imperfect describes repeated, ongoing, or habitual actions in the past. It is also used to talk about when you *used to* do something. Look at the following excerpts from the dialogue. Can you pick out the verbs in the imperfect?

Antes no me gustaban los cuchifritos,   *Before I didn't like cuchifritos, but*
pero ahora me encantan.   *now I love them.*

Antes decía puertorriqueño, pero   *Before I used to say Puerto Rican,*
ahora digo «boricua».   *but now I say "Boricua."*

Mi padre nos hablaba en español,   *My father spoke to us in Spanish,*
mientras mi madre nos hablaba   *while my mother would speak to us*
en inglés.   *in English.*

No me gustaban, **decía**, and **hablaba** are in the *imperfect*—each example sentence above shows a different use.

The imperfect can describe continuing, customary, or habitual actions in the past. This is often translated as *would* or *used to* in English.

Mi madre nos **hablaba** en inglés.   *My mother would speak to us in English.*

Antes **decía** puertorriqueño.   *I used to say Puerto Rican.*

Often you will see the imperfect describe a continuing action that gets interrupted. For example, **Antes no me gustaban los cuchifritos, pero ahora me encantan.** Pablo disliked **cuchifritos** during a continuous time in the past. But now

he likes them. The imperfect can also get interrupted by the simple past (preterite).

Andaba por la calle cuando empezó el dolor de muelas.	*I was walking down the street when my tooth began to ache.*

It is also used to give descriptions in the past.

Un día de verano hacía sol. Eran las seis de la mañana y corría en el parque.	*One summer day it was sunny. It was six in the morning, and I was jogging in the park.*

GRAMMAR DEMYSTIFIED

The Imperfect

To form the imperfect of regular verbs, drop the **-ar**, **-er**, or **-ir**, and add the endings shown in the table below. Note that there is no stem change for stem-changing verbs.

	hablar	**comer**	**decir**
yo	habl**aba**	com**ía**	dec**ía**
tú	habl**abas**	com**ías**	dec**ías**
usted	habl**aba**	com**ía**	dec**ía**
él/ella	habl**aba**	com**ía**	dec**ía**
nosotros(as)	habl**ábamos**	com**íamos**	dec**íamos**
vosotros(as)	habl**abais**	com**íais**	dec**íais**
ustedes	habl**aban**	com**ían**	dec**ían**
ellos/ellas	habl**aban**	com**ían**	dec**ían**

There are only three irregular verbs in the imperfect.

	ser	**ir**	**ver**
yo	era	iba	veía
tú	eras	ibas	veías
él/ella, usted	era	iba	veía
nosotros(as)	éramos	íbamos	veíamos
vosotros(as)	erais	ibais	veíais
ellos/ellas, ustedes	eran	iban	veían

Expressions of time indicating prolonged or repeated action in the past often accompany the imperfect.

Time Expressions

a menudo	*often*
antes	*before*
con frecuencia	*frequently*
siempre	*always*
todos los días	*every day*
todos los lunes, martes, etc.	*every Monday, Tuesday, etc.*

Written Practice 10-1

Complete the dialogue between Pablo and his mother by writing the imperfect form of the verb in parentheses.

PABLO: Mamá, ¿cómo _____ (ser) yo de pequeño?

MADRE: Ay, Pablito. Tú _____ (ser) muy movidito, pero también muy bueno.

PABLO: ¿A qué escuela _____ (ir) yo?

MADRE: De muy pequeñito, tu hermana y tú _____ (ir) a la Escuela Soles. Tú _____ (tener) muchos amigos. Los niños allí _____ (ser) muy amables.

PABLO: ¿Nosotros _____ (hablar) inglés o español en la escuela?

MADRE: Ustedes _____ (hablar) los dos. Las maestras _____ (ser) bilingües.

PABLO: ¿Y qué me _____ (gustar) hacer?

MADRE: Te _____ (gustar) mucho correr y jugar con pelotas. Tú _____ (jugar) mucho al fútbol. Tu hermana _____ (jugar) más con los rompecabezas y _____ (dibujar).

PABLO: ¿_____ (comer) yo bien?

MADRE: Sí, te _____ (encantar) comer. _____ (comer) de todo. Tu hermana _____ (ser) más problemática en este aspecto.

PABLO: ¿Dónde _____ (vivir) nosotros en esos tiempos?

MADRE: _____ (vivir) en la Avenida Central. La casa _____ (tener) un jardín muy lindo. Ustedes _____ (tener) una casita en el jardín y _____ (subir) a los árboles. En esa casita tu hermana _____ (leer) libritos y tú _____ (escuchar) con mucha atención. ¡Qué tiempos tan lindos _____ (ser) aquellos!

MAKING CONNECTIONS

In the opening dialogue and throughout the book you have seen many examples of conversations with words that connect phrases, such as **y** (*and*) and **o** (*or*) or **que** (*that*). As you learn more Spanish, you will need to use these connecting words to make complex sentences that join a number of ideas.

Connecting Words

además	*furthermore*	o sea	*in other words*
así que	*so*	pero	*but*
aunque	*although*	por eso	*because of this, that's why*
en vez de	*instead of*	porque	*because*
mientras	*while*	sin embargo	*however*
ni... ni	*neither . . . nor*	también	*also*
o	*or*	y	*and*

VOCABULARY DEMYSTIFIED

Multiple Meanings

As you have seen time and time again, different words can be used to express the same concept, depending on the country or region. Similarly, the same word can mean different things in different parts of the world. In México, **horchata** is a cold drink made from rice, flavored with sugar and cinnamon. In Spain, it is a cold drink made from tiger nuts (tubers, also called **chufa**), water, and sugar. Either way, both are **refrescantes y deliciosas**.

Sometimes these variations of meaning can get you into trouble. The word **coger**, which means *to take* in Spain and some Latin American countries, is considered vulgar in Argentina and much of Central America, where the verb **tomar** is used instead. In Spain, **parar** only means *to stop*. In Latin America, however, it also means *to stand up*. The list goes on. . . . You'll learn many of these multiple meanings by making a few humorous mistakes, but making a mistake is sometimes the best way to remember something.

🔘 TRACK 44

Listen to these example sentences:

Diana habla español, pero su
   hermana no lo habla.

*Diana speaks Spanish, but her
   sister doesn't.*

Aunque vivía en México, David no
   hablaba español de pequeño.

*Although he lived in México, David
   didn't speak Spanish when he was
   young.*

Nosotros vivíamos en Perú. Por eso
   aprendí español.

*We used to live in Peru. That's why I
   learned Spanish.*

Juan es puertorriqueño. O sea,
   es boricua.

*Juan is Puerto Rican. In other words,
   he's "Boricua."*

Belén no disfrutó en México.
   Sin embargo Juan disfrutó
   muchísimo.

*Belén didn't enjoy México. However,
   Juan enjoyed it a lot.*

En vez del pollo, voy a pedir un burrito de carne.	*Instead of chicken, I'm going to order a beef burrito.*
Me encantó Puerto Plata, así que decidí quedarme más tiempo allí.	*I loved Puerto Plata, so I decided to stay there longer.*
También me gustó mucho Santo Domingo.	*I also liked Santo Domingo a lot.*

Note that **o** (*or*) changes to **u** when the following word starts with an **o** sound, and **y** (*and*) changes to **e** when the word that follows starts with an **i** sound.

Rebeca **e** Inés quieren helado de fresa.	*Rebeca and Inés want strawberry ice cream.*
¿Quieres limonada **u** horchata?	*Do you want lemonade or* horchata *(a cold drink made from rice)?*

Finally, the word **porque** (*because* [one word]) answers a question beginning with **¿Por qué... ?** (*Why . . .* [two words]?).

¿Por qué no habla español Luisa?	*Why doesn't Luisa speak Spanish?*
Porque de pequeña no hablaban español en casa.	*Because when she was little they didn't speak Spanish at home.*

Oral Practice 10-1

 TRACK 45

Justo is telling Lidia about a past trip to Cartagena, Colombia. Complete the dialogue with the connecting words from the table below, using each word only once. Then say the complete dialogue out loud. Listen to the recording to check your answers, and repeat what you hear.

Además	Aunque	o	Por qué	Sin embargo
así que	en vez de	pero	Porque	y

JUSTO: En Cartagena hacía sol todos los días. El hotel estaba al lado de la playa, _____ pasábamos todo el día allí.

LIDIA: ¿_____ decidiste ir a Colombia, _____ México?

JUSTO: _____ tengo familia en Colombia _____ quería visitarlos.

LIDIA: Entonces, tu familia es de México. _____, viven en Colombia.

JUSTO: Sí, así es. De pequeño vivíamos en México, _____ ahora viven todos en Colombia. _____ yo vivo en Estados Unidos, voy a visitarlos a menudo.

LIDIA: ¡Qué complicado! ¿Qué te gusta más, México _____ Colombia?

JUSTO: A mí me gusta más Colombia. El país es precioso y tengo familia allí. _____, la gente es muy simpática.

Oral Practice 10-2

TRACK 46

Listen to the dialogues, and indicate whether the statements following are **cierto o falso** (*true or false*).

1. Carolina talks about her friend Luisa.

   ¿Cierto o falso? Antes Luisa era pesimista. *Luisa used to be a pessimist.*

   _____

   Antes Carolina y Luisa cenaban juntas todos los miércoles. *Before, Carolina and Luisa used to have dinner together every Wednesday.*

   _____

2. Juan and Ronaldo talk about being in the same class as children.

   ¿Cierto o falso? Ronaldo y Juan tenían una maestra que se llamaba Señora Monstruo. *Ronaldo and Juan had a teacher called Señora Monstruo (monster).* _____

   A la maestra le gustaba el nombre «Señora Monstruo». *The teacher liked the name "Ms. Monster."* _____

   Ronaldo y Juan no estaban en la clase juntos en segundo, porque la familia de Ronaldo se fue a México. *Ronaldo and Juan were not in the same class in second grade, because Ronaldo's family moved to Mexico.*

   _____

Written Practice 10-2

Write complete sentences using the cues provided. The first example is done for you.

1. Antes/a mí/gustar/el jugo de piña/pero/ahora/no/gustar

   Antes a mí me gustaba el jugo de piña, pero ahora no me gusta.

   _____

   I used to like pineapple juice, but now I don't like it.

2. Antes/Rebeca/Laura/ser buenas amigas/Sin embargo/ahora/no/lo/ser

   _____

   Before Rebeca and Laura were good friends. However, now they are not.

3. El sábado pasado/nosotras/querer/ver a Luisa/en vez de/a Gema

   _____

   Last Saturday we wanted to see Luisa instead of Gema.

4. Ayer/Roberto/hablar por teléfono/mientras/Rosa/escribir un email

   _____

   Yesterday Roberto was talking on the phone while Rosa was writing an e-mail.

5. De pequeña/Rosita/a menudo/jugar/con Ester/Pepita/Inés

   _____

   As a child Rosita often would play with Ester, Pepita, and Inés.

6. De pequeño/aunque/Carlitos/hablar español muy bien/no querer hablarlo

   _____

   As a child, although Carlitos spoke Spanish very well, he did not want to speak it.

Talking the Talk

At the end of his trip to Puerto Rico, Pablo finally visits El Yunque, which his friend Ana had recommended so enthusiastically. He toured the national park with a group, where he met a Mexican named Diego. Back in San Juan, they report to Laura about their weekend. Listen to their conversation. What happened to Diego on the trip?

TRACK 47

LAURA: ¿Qué hicieron ustedes el «finde»?

What did you do over the weekend?

PABLO: Fuimos al Yunque.

We went to El Yunque.

DIEGO: Sí, hicimos varias caminatas e hicimos camping allí.

Yes, we did several hikes, and we camped there.

LAURA: ¿Y qué les pareció?

And what did you think?

DIEGO: ¡Es padre! Y también un poco peligroso. Caminábamos bien tranquilos y de repente, ¡híjole! ¡Vimos una iguana grandísima enfrente de nosotros!

It's incredible. And also a bit dangerous. We were walking along, totally chill, when suddenly, oh my goodness! We saw a huge iguana in front of us!

LAURA: ¿Y vieron más animales?

And did you see more animals?

PABLO: Sí, y cuando estábamos en el camping vimos una ranita coquí muy chiquitita.

Yes, when we were at the camp we saw a tiny little coquí frog.

DIEGO: También hicimos excursiones por la zona. ¡Y yo tuve un accidente!

We also took day trips in the area. And I had an accident!

LAURA: ¿Qué pasó?

What happened?

DIEGO: Iba yo en bici bien tranquilo y de repente salió una tortuga gigante en medio de la carretera!

I was calmly riding my bike, and suddenly a gigantic turtle walked out into the middle of the road!

PABLO: No era gigante... Y caminaba muy despacio. ¡Qué exagerado eres!

It was not gigantic . . . and it was walking very slowly. You exaggerate so much!

DIEGO: ¡Era grandísima!

It was huge!

LAURA: ¿Y te atacó la tortuga?

And did the turtle attack you?

DIEGO: No, pero me caí de la bicicleta.

No, but I fell off my bike!

UNDERSTANDING IDIOMATIC AND COLLOQUIAL EXPRESSIONS

It looks like Diego almost ran into a turtle and fell off his bike. As you have seen throughout the book, Spanish has idiomatic and colloquial expressions that vary immensely depending on country, region—even **barrio**. Colloquial language is language that is informal, and generally spoken, not written, as when Laura said **finde** instead of **fin de semana** for *weekend*, or when Diego says **bien tranquilo** instead of **muy tranquilo**.

Idioms (which can be colloquial, but are not, by definition) are expressions whose parts do not make up the whole. In other words, the meaning of the expression is not necessarily related to the words that make it up. For example: **tener algo en la punta de la lengua** (*to have something on the tip of your tongue*) is a figurative way of saying that you are about to remember something but can't quite. Often, Spanish idioms can use parts of the body, such as **tomarle el pelo a uno** (*lit.: to pull someone's hair*), which is the same as saying *to pull someone's leg,* which actually means *to tease.* There is no logic to a lot of these expressions, so just try them out, and you will slowly build a repertoire of favorite idioms. If you don't understand something, use the context to help. Ask yourself, what makes sense in the context of this conversation? And if you still don't get it, ask: **¿Qué quiere decir... ?**

Here are some example colloquial and idiomatic expressions to get you started:

- To express surprise or disbelief:

  ¡Híjole! ¡Qué iguana tan grande! (*Mexico*) — *Oh my!* *What a huge iguana!*

  Puchis la próxima vez no grites. (*Guatemala*) — *Ay, next time, don't scream!*

  Ana y Juan se van a divorciar. **¡Adió!** Y eran tan felices antes. (*Costa Rica*) — *Ana and Juan are going to get divorced.* **Oh my!** *And they were so happy before.*

  ¿Qué se van a divorciar? **¡Anda ya!** (*Spain*) — *They are going to get divorced?* **Yeah, right!**

- To say something is **grande** (*big*), **enorme** (*huge*), or **gigante** (*gigantic*):

  Arturo tiene un problema **de la leche**. (*Spain*) — *Arturo has a **huge** problem.*

VOCABULARY DEMYSTIFIED

Money

At the beginning of this chapter, Laura uses the word **chavos** to talk about money (not to be confused with the same word used to mean *boys* in Mexico). As in English (think *dough, bread, loot, moola*), Spanish speakers have a number of colloquial expressions to refer to money: **plata** (means *silver*, *South America*), **pasta** (*Spain*), **cushqui** (*Ecuador, from Quechua*), **pesos** (used to describe dollars, *U.S.*), **guita** (*Argentina, Uruguay, Peru, Ecuador*), **lana** (*Panama*), or **real** (*Venezuela*).

Spanish speakers also have a lot of expressions to talk about money. Here are just a few:

estar forrado (*Spain*) *to be loaded (really rich)*
echarse la papa (*Nicaragua*) *to earn a lot of money*
estar ajustado(a) (*Dominican Republic*), **estar limpio(a)** (*Costa Rica*), **andar liso(a)**
    (*Honduras*), or **estar pelado(a)** (*Spain*) *to be broke*

Arturo tiene un problema **supergrande**. (*Spain*)	*Arturo has a **huge** problem.*
Arturo tiene **un tronco** de problema. (*Venezuela*)	*Arturo has a **huge** problem.*

- To say something is very small: **minúsculo** (*tiny*), **chiquito**, **chiquitito**, **chiquitico**, **chiquitín**:

El carro es **chiquitito**.	*The car is **tiny**.*
Pedrito es **un chiquitín**.	*Pedrito is **a little one**.*

- To talk about *a bit* or *a little*: **un poquito**, **un poquitín**, **un chin** (*Dominican Republic*):

Sólo quiero **un poquito**.	*I just want **a little**.*
Dame **un chin** de café.	*Give me just **a bit** of coffee.*

- To talk about *a lot* or *a ton*: **un montón** (*Spain*), **un mogollón** (*Spain*), or **harto/harta** (*Mexico, Perú, Chile*):

Tengo **harto** trabajo.	*I have **tons of** work.*
Había **un montón de** gente.	*There were **tons of** people.*

EXAGGERATING

In Spanish you can add suffixes to adjectives to exaggerate. Add **-ísimo** (for masculine) and **-ísima** (for feminine) to an adjective to say that something is the extreme of its category.

pequeño(a)	→	pequeñísimo(a)	*tiny*
grande	→	grandísimo(a)	*gigantic*
guapo(a)	→	guapísimo(a)	*gorgeous*
exagerado(a)	→	exageradísimo(a)	*totally exaggerated*

VOCABULARY DEMYSTIFIED

Shortened Words

A lot of Spanish slang consists of shortening words. For example:

la bici: short for **bicicleta** (*bicycle*)

el finde: short for **fin de semana** (*weekend*)

la moto: short for **motocicleta** (*motorbike*)

la peli: short for **película** (*movie*)

porfa: short for **por favor** (*please*)

⊙ TRACK 48

Listen to some examples:

Felipe es graciosísimo.	*Felipe is hilarious.*
Andrea is lindísima.	*Andrea is gorgeous.*
Teo e Isabel están contentísimos con su bebé.	*Teo and Isabel are thrilled with their baby.*
Nosotras estamos hartísimas de esta canción.	*We are totally fed up with this song.*

If you hear someone who exaggerates all the time, there are a number of ways to respond. Listen to a few examples:

¡Qué exagerado eres! (*general*)	*You are such an exaggerator!*
¡Qué azotado eres! (*Mexico*)	*You are such an exaggerator!*
Su relato era muy jalado. (*Guatemala*)	*His story was very exaggerated.*
¡Qué pasada! (*Spain*)	*What an exaggeration!*

Written Practice 10-3

Imagine that you exaggerate all the time. Complete the second sentence by adding -**ísimo(a)** to the adjective used in the first sentence.

1. David es muy gracioso. O sea, es _____.
2. Julián está muy enojado con su hermano. O sea, está _____.
3. Alicia está muy emocionada por la fiesta. O sea, está _____.
4. Rebeca es muy tímida. O sea, es _____.
5. Rubén nos ayuda a todos y es muy generoso. O sea, es _____.
6. Estefanía exagera todo el día. O sea, es _____.

Chapter Practice

 TRACK 49

Read along as you listen to the following short dialogues that use colloquialisms you may not know. Use the context to help you guess the meaning of each phrase in bold.

1. Margarita and Beto talk about a party they went to.

   MARGARITA: Hola, Beto. ¿Qué tal la fiesta anoche?

   BETO: ¡Chévere! Había **un mundo de gente** y mucho ambiente.

    a. fast, in a jiffy

    b. delicious

    c. a lot of people

    d. there was something fishy

    e. to speak nonstop

2. Sergio and Oscar talk about their friend Juan and his skills fixing computers.

   SERGIO: ¿Resolviste el problema con tu computadora?

   OSCAR: Yo no. Lo resolvió Juan. Vino y **en un dos por tres**, ya funcionaba.

3. Juan asks Lidia about an inexpensive car she was going to buy from an ad.

   JUAN: Lidia, ¿compraste el carro del anuncio?

   LIDIA: No, **había gato encerrado**. El precio no era $1.000, era $10.000.

4. Rebeca and Fidel gossip about their friend Julia.

   REBECA: Oye, ¿qué te parece Julia?

   FIDEL: Es simpática, pero **habla hasta por los codos**.

5. Luisa and Gerardo are eating cuchifritos.

   GERARDO: Están buenísimos.

   LUISA: Sí, están **para chuparse los dedos**.

QUIZ

Circle the letter of the word or phrase that best completes each sentence.

1. De pequeñas, Lisa y Ángela _____ español.
   (a) hablaban
   (b) viajan
   (c) hablarán

2. Antes nosotros escribíamos cartas _____ no había email.
   (a) también
   (b) por qué
   (c) porque

3. Voy a viajar a Chile _____ México.
   (a) en vez de
   (b) pero
   (c) sin embargo

4. «Grandísimo» quiere decir _____.
   (a) muy divertido
   (b) pequeño
   (c) muy grande

5. «Boricua» quiere decir _____.
   (a) fin de semana
   (b) chévere
   (c) puertorriqueño

🔘 **TRACK 50**

Now listen to the recording to hear a phrase or question. Press pause, and say your answer: a, b, or c. Listen to the correct answer on the recording, and repeat what you hear. Then go to the next question, and repeat the process.

6. (a) Habla inglés.

   (b) Hablaré inglés.

   (c) Hablaba inglés.

7. (a) Porque vivo en México.

   (b) Vivíamos en México.

   (c) Viviremos en México.

8. (a) De nada.

   (b) Gracias.

   (c) Por favor.

9. (a) Porque es aburrido.

   (b) Así que es aburrido.

   (c) O sea, es graciosísimo.

10. (a) Muy exagerado.

   (b) bastante pesimista.

   (c) Un poco aburrido.

Circle the letter of txhe word or phrase that best completes each sentence.

1. Hable más _____, por favor.
    (a) noches
    (b) despacio
    (c) fenomenal

2. _____, ¿dónde está la calle Solares?
    (a) Plaza
    (b) De nada
    (c) Disculpe

3. ¿_____ repetirlo, por favor?
    (a) Perdón
    (b) Puede
    (c) Hable

4. Sonia y Mónica _____ mis hermanas.
    (a) es
    (b) está
    (c) son

5. El Señor Cruz es el abuelo _____ David.
    (a) es
    (b) de
    (c) el

6. Adiós. _____ el fin de semana.
    (a) Hasta
    (b) Para
    (c) Lo siento

7. ¿Ustedes _____ de Canadá?
    (a) están
    (b) son
    (c) trabajan

8. Ellas son _____ .

   (a) sudafricana

   (b) norteamericanos

   (c) canadienses

9. Chicago _____ en Estados Unidos.

   (a) estoy

   (b) eres

   (c) está

10. Rosa es alta y _____ el cabello rizado.

   (a) está

   (b) quieren

   (c) tiene

11. Ronaldo es bajito y tiene los ojos _____ .

   (a) verdes

   (b) rojas

   (c) dos

12. Silvia y Delia son _____ y delgadas.

   (a) altas

   (b) más

   (c) bajos

13. Julia, David y Andrea son _____ .

   (a) estudiante

   (b) abogadas

   (c) maestros

14. Rebeca y Mónica son _____ generosas.

   (a) muy

   (b) pocos

   (c) simpáticas

15. _____ es la Señora Jiménez.

   (a) Éstas

   (b) Éste

   (c) Ésta

16. Roberto nunca _____ el periódico.

   (a) leemos

   (b) leo

   (c) lee

17. Susana le _____ emails a José todos los días.

   (a) escriben

   (b) escribes

   (c) escribe

18. ¿Dónde _____ usted?

   (a) trabajan

   (b) trabaja

   (c) trabajas

19. No me _____ trabajar.

   (a) gustaron

   (b) gusta

   (c) gustan

20. Me _____ las arepas de carne.

   (a) encantan

   (b) gusta

   (c) quiero

21. Ricardo me _____ muy divertido.

   (a) gusta

   (b) parece

   (c) quiere

22. ¿Qué te _____ las quesadillas?

    (a) encanta

    (b) gustan

    (c) parecen

23. El Señor Castillo _____ clases de español.

    (a) tienen

    (b) llega

    (c) da

24. Nosotras _____ veinte primos.

    (a) tienen

    (b) tenemos

    (c) damos

25. ¿A qué hora _____ Pablo?

    (a) viene

    (b) tiene

    (c) salen

26. Leticia y María _____ español ahora.

    (a) hablando

    (b) están hablando

    (c) estoy escribiendo

27. La hermana de mamá es _____ tía.

    (a) sus

    (b) mis

    (c) nuestra

28. ¿_____ usted como se llama la hermana de Ana?

    (a) Conoce

    (b) Sabe

    (c) Eres

29. ¿_____ tú a Luisa?

    (a) Conoces

    (b) Sabes

    (c) Eres

30. ¿Qué _____ a hacer ustedes el fin de semana?

    (a) van

    (b) vas

    (c) irás

31. ¿Cómo _____ nosotras a México?

    (a) viaja

    (b) vamos a viajar

    (c) viajarán

32. ¿Dónde _____ tú el martes que viene?

    (a) estarás

    (b) eres

    (c) estuvo

33. _____ estaremos de vacaciones en Puerto Rico.

    (a) Anteayer

    (b) La semana pasada

    (c) En dos días

34. Ayer Rosa y Ana _____ en un restaurante español y _____ mucho de la comida.

    (a) comió/disfrutó

    (b) comen/disfrutan

    (c) comieron/disfrutaron

35. ¿_____ tú a Luisa en la fiesta ayer?

    (a) Verás

    (b) Viste

    (c) Ves

36. Si viajas a Colombia, _____ Cartagena.

    (a) visitaré

    (b) visita

    (c) visitaste

37. _____ visitar Perú. ¡Es bellísimo!

    (a) No debería

    (b) Fueron

    (c) Tienen que

38. Si Luis viaja a Florida, _____ visitar a su abuela.

    (a) tenemos que

    (b) debería

    (c) porque

39. Yo _____ mucho chocolate y ahora me duele el estómago.

    (a) comí

    (b) comeré

    (c) comiste

40. Compré un carro nuevo. _____ ya no voy a trabajar en autobús.

    (a) En vez de

    (b) Por qué

    (c) Por eso

41. Por favor, _____ usted su nombre aquí.

    (a) escribe

    (b) escriba

    (c) escribió

42. _____ las instrucciones antes de usarlo.

    (a) No lean

    (b) Lee

    (c) Escribirás

43. _____ en autobús, en vez de en avión. Es más barato.

   (a) Haz

   (b) Tenemos

   (c) Vaya

44. ¿Dónde _____ la fiesta ayer?

   (a) veremos

   (b) fue

   (c) será

45. Andrea vio la película, pero yo no _____ vi.

   (a) lo

   (b) la

   (c) nos

46. Delia no _____ vio a nosotros en la fiesta, pero vio a Rita.

   (a) se

   (b) nos

   (c) fue

47. Antes yo _____ francés muy bien, pero ahora no lo hablo.

   (a) habla

   (b) hablaba

   (c) hablaré

48. ¿Dónde _____ ustedes de pequeños?

   (a) vivía

   (b) vivían

   (c) viven

49. Rebeca me parece atractiva. Es _____.

   (a) feísima

   (b) muy tímido

   (c) lindísima

50. Caminé muchísimo hoy. _____ no me duelen los pies.

    (a) Aunque

    (b) Sin embargo

    (c) Por eso

 TRACK 51

Now listen to the recording to hear a question. Press pause, and say your answer: a, b, or c. Listen to the correct answer on the recording, and repeat what you hear when appropriate. Then go to the next question, and repeat the process.

51. (a) *"student"*

    (b) e-s-t-u-d-i-a-n-t-e

    (c) estudiante

52. (a) La «h» no se pronuncia.

    (b) *Hi.*

    (c) h-o-l-a

53. (a) 5

    (b) 50

    (c) 15

54. (a) veintidós

    (b) treinta y dos

    (c) doce

55. (a) dos mil diez

    (b) el diez de octubre

    (c) diciembre dos

56. (a) A la una y veinte.

    (b) Son las dos y diez.

    (c) Es sábado.

57. (a) Las quince horas de la tarde.

    (b) Las once y cuarto de la noche.

    (c) Las once de la mañana.

58. (a) Es en casa de Daniel.

    (b) Él está en Chicago.

    (c) A las diez de la noche.

59. (a) Voy a la ciudad.

    (b) Voy en metro.

    (c) Voy a las ocho de la mañana.

60. (a) Comienza a las cinco.

    (b) Termina a las seis.

    (c) Sale en dos horas.

61. (a) Es la hermana de David.

    (b) Es cocinera.

    (c) Es un anciano.

62. (a) Tiene el cabello rubio.

    (b) Es muy generosa.

    (c) Es estudiante.

63. (a) Es bastante simpático.

    (b) Es bajita y delgada.

    (c) Son asiáticas.

64. (a) Es nuestro abuelo.

    (b) Está a la derecha.

    (c) Sí, es la hermana de Ana.

65. (a) Sí, hay una en la calle Mayor.

    (b) No hay tiendas en esta calle.

    (c) Sale en cinco minutos.

66. (a) Sí, hay una detrás de la librería.

    (b) Sí, hay ninguno allí.

    (c) No, no hay ningún baño.

67. (a) Hablé español.

    (b) Van a clase de español.

    (c) Voy a estudiar español.

68. (a) Estará en casa.

    (b) Está viendo al TV.

    (c) Estuvo en casa de Delia.

69. (a) No, me duele la cabeza.

    (b) El dos de enero.

    (c) Están caminando.

70. (a) Hace siglos.

    (b) Sí, claro. Es por allí.

    (c) No, nunca manejo.

71. (a) Está lloviendo.

    (b) En febrero.

    (c) Llueve mucho en enero.

72. (a) Nunca hace viento.

    (b) No está lloviendo.

    (c) Sí, en invierno nieva mucho.

73. (a) Hace sol.

    (b) Hace setenta grados.

    (c) Hace viento.

74. (a) Les dio dinero.

    (b) Te dará un regalo.

    (c) Me dio un libro.

75. (a) Sí, ella conoce a Luisa.

    (b) No, no nos mandó ningún email.

    (c) Te escribirá pronto.

76. (a) Nunca hablamos.

    (b) Nos habla en español.

    (c) Le habla en inglés.

77. (a) No, no lo vimos.

    (b) No la vimos.

    (c) Sí les vimos.

78. (a) Sí, ya lo compré.

    (b) No, no los compré.

    (c) No nos tengo.

79. (a) No estoy leyendo ningún libro.

    (b) Estoy en el supermercado.

    (c) Están leyendo un email.

80. (a) No, gracias.

    (b) No bebí agua.

    (c) Me duelen los pies.

81. (a) Visitaba a mis amigas.

    (b) Fui al cine.

    (c) Comeré gazpacho.

82. (a) Estuve en casa de Ángela.

    (b) Llamé a Rosita.

    (c) Vendremos a las cinco.

83. (a) Me gustaron bastante.

    (b) Sí, me pareció muy interesante.

    (c) No será buena.

84. (a) Es una película romántica.

    (b) Empieza a las seis.

    (c) ¡Me encanta esa película!

85. (a) Me parece simpática.

    (b) Está a cinco minutos.

    (c) Es muy malo. No vaya allí.

86. (a) No, no está. ¿Quiere dejar un mensaje?

    (b) ¿Está cerca?

    (c) Estamos lejos.

87. (a) Un momento, por favor.

    (b) ¿Quién le llama, por favor?

    (c) Sí, dígale que llamó Pedro.

88. (a) No vendré mañana.

    (b) Llamaré a las ocho.

    (c) ¿Aló?

89. (a) Salimos el lunes.

    (b) Llega en dos minutos.

    (c) Sale a las cinco.

90. (a) Visite el Parque Manuel Antonio.

    (b) Tendré frío.

    (c) No hablas español.

91. (a) Fueron al mercado.

    (b) Tenía dos hermanas.

    (c) Estaba con su abuela.

92. (a) Es puertorriqueño. O sea, es boricua.

    (b) Es puertorriqueño, aunque no es boricua.

    (c) Es puertorriqueño. Sin embargo, es boricua.

93. (a) Te gustará.

    (b) Me gustaba dibujar.

    (c) Me encanta escribir emails.

94. (a) enorme

    (b) muy pequeño

    (c) muy grande

95. (a) «muy grande»

    (b) «exagera mucho»

    (c) «muy tímido»

96. (a) «muy bueno»

    (b) «horrible»

    (c) «puertorriqueño»

97. (a) Fue en la playa.

    (b) No, fui a una fiesta en vez del concierto.

    (c) O sea, era muy divertido.

98. (a) Además, me gusta bailar.

    (b) Me pareció divertida.

    (c) Porque no tuve tiempo.

99. (a) Tenga paciencia.

    (b) No tienes dinero.

    (c) Tendremos muchos primos.

100. (a) No digan sus nombres.

    (b) Vaya por la derecha.

    (c) Practica mucho.

ANSWER KEY

CHAPTER 1

Written Practice 1-1
1. a   2. c   3. c   4. b   5. a

Oral Practice 1-1
1. g-i-r-a-s-o-l   2. o-t-o-ñ-o   3. ll-u-v-i-a   4. c-h-a-n-c-l-e-t-a   5. H-e-r-n-á-n-d-e-z con tilde en la «a»   6. t-e-rr (doble erre)-e-m-o-t-o

Oral Practice 1-2
1. Juan j-u-a-n   2. Marta m-a-r-t-a   3. Laura l-a-u-r-a   4. Pablo p-a-b-l-o
5. Jorge j-o-r-g-e   6. Gilda g-i-l-d-a   7. Roberto r-o-b-e-r-t-o   8. Mercedes m-e-r-c-e-d-e-s   9. Señor Herrero s-e-ñ-o-r h-e-rr-e-r-o   10. Señora Castillo s-e-ñ-o-r-a c-a-s-t-i-ll-o   11. Mauro m-a-u-r-o   12. Leo l-e-o

Written Practice 1-2
1. la   2. la   3. los   4. el   5. las   6. el   7. un   8. unas   9. una   10. una
11. un   12. una

Oral Practice 1-3
1. yo   2. *female teacher*   3. los hijos   4. *actors*   5. nosotros *or* nosotras
6. *the man*   7. las mujeres   8. la mesa   9. la película buena   10. la comunicación

QUIZ
1. a   2. b   3. c   4. c   5. a   6. c, ¿Puede repetirlo, por favor?   7. b, Hable más despacio, por favor.   8. c, ¿Cómo es, «el CD» o «la CD»?   9. a, ¿Cómo se escribe «Eugenia»?   10. b, ¿Cómo se pronuncia esta palabra?

CHAPTER 2

Oral Practice 2-1
1. Buenos días, Susana.   2. Buenas noches, Pablo.   3. Buenas tardes, Señor Moreno.   4. Hola, David.

Written Practice 2-1
1. b   2. c   3. a   4. b   5. b

Oral Practice 2-2
a. Conversation 2

Miguel: Hola, Marta. *Hi, Marta. What's up?* / Marta: Hola, ¡cuánto tiempo! *Hi, it's been a long time!* / Miguel: Sí, hace siglos. ¡Qué alegría verte! *Yes, it's been ages. I'm happy to see you.*

b. Conversation 1

Señor Torres: Buenos días, Señor Rosado. *Good morning, Mr. Rosado.* / Señor Rosado: Buenos días, Señor Torres. Que pase un buen día. *Good morning, Mr. Torres. Have a nice day.* / Señor Torres: Gracias, usted también. *Thanks, you too.*

c. Conversation 4

Julián: Hasta luego, Mónica. *See you later, Mónica.* / Mónica: Adiós, Julián. Hasta el martes, ¿no? *Bye, Julián. See you Tuesday, right?* / Julián: ¡No! Hasta el jueves. Nos vemos el jueves. *No! See you on Thursday. We will see each other on Thursday.* / Mónica: ¡Ah, sí! Hasta el jueves. Chau. *Ah, yes! See you Thursday. Ciao.*

d. Conversation 3

Señor Juárez: Me voy. Señor Ponce. Hasta mañana. *I'm leaving, Mr. Ponce. See you tomorrow.* / Señor Ponce: Adiós, Señor Juárez. Hasta mañana. *Bye, Mr. Juárez. See you tomorrow.*

Oral Practice 2-3
1. ésta   2. Ésta   3. Éste   4. Éstos   5. ésta   6. éste   7. éstos   8. éstas
9. éste, ésta   10. éstos

Oral Practice 2-4
1. Cómo te llamas; Me llamo   2. él es; Soy   3. mi nombre es; Mi nombre es; Ella es; él es

Oral Practice 2-5
(*Possible answers*) 1. Hola.   2. Hasta luego.   3. ¿Cómo te llamas?   4. Soy Pablo; Me llamo Pablo; Mi nombre es Pablo.   5. Mucho gusto; encantado.
6. Hasta el sábado.   7. Éste es mi amigo Carlos; Él es mi amigo Carlos.
8. Hola, somos Sonia y Pablo.   9. Buenos días, Señora Márquez.   10. Buenas noches.

Written Practice 2-2

1. Yo estoy feliz. 2. Oscar está sorprendido. 3. Isabel y Guillermo están tristes. 4. Mi amiga está deprimida. 5. Ester está muy cansada. 6. David no está contento. 7. Los chicos están un poco hartos. 8. ¿Tu hermana está nerviosa?

Chapter Practice

1. falso (*Julián is doing fantastically.*)
Mauricio: Hola Julián. ¿Qué tal? *Hi, Julián. How are you doing?* / Julián: ¡Fantástico! ¿Y tú? ¿Cómo estás? *Fantastic! And you? How are you?* / Mauricio: Genial, gracias. ¿Qué tal tu familia? *Great, thanks. How's your family?* / Julián: Muy bien, también, gracias. *Very well, also, thanks.*

2. cierto, falso (*Manuel is tired too.*)
Manuel: Buenos días. ¿Cómo está, Rosa? *Good morning. How are you, Rosa?* / Rosa: La verdad, un poco cansada… *The truth is, a bit tired . . .* / Manuel: Yo también. Estoy muy cansado. *Me too. I'm really tired.* / Rosa: ¡Qué bien que es viernes! *Thank goodness it's Friday.*

3. falso (*Gerardo is disappointed.*)
M: Gerardo, ¿cómo estás? *Gerardo, how are you?* / G: Estoy bien… *I'm well . . .* / M: ¿Estás enfadado? *Are you angry?* / G: No, no estoy enfadado. Estoy un poco desilusionado. *No, I'm not angry. I'm just a bit disappointed.*

QUIZ

1. b 2. c 3. c 4. c 5. a 6. c, ¿Cómo se llama? 7. b, ¿Qué tal? 8. a, ¿Cómo estás? 9. c, ¿Cómo está Susana? 10. b, ¿Cómo están ustedes?

CHAPTER 3

Oral Practice 3-1

1. Ecuador
Rita: Hola, ¿de dónde es usted? / David: Soy ecuatoriano. ¿Y usted? / Rita: Yo también soy ecuatoriana. / David: ¿De qué parte es? / Rita: Soy de Quito, ¿y usted? / David: Yo soy de Portoviejo.

2. Chile, Argentina
Mónica: Oye, Mauricio. ¿De dónde eres tú? / Mauricio: Soy argentino. / Mónica: ¿De qué parte? / Mauricio: De Buenos Aires. ¿Y tú de dónde eres? / Mónica: Yo soy chilena. Toni y yo somos de Santiago.

3. Bolivia, Canadá
Juan: Ester, ¿de dónde eres tú? / Ester: Soy canadiense. / Juan: ¿Eres de Montreal? / Ester: No, soy de Quebec. ¿De dónde eres tú? / Juan: Yo soy boliviano.

4. Colombia, Venezuela

José: ¿De dónde eres? ¿Eres colombiana? / Elena: No, no soy colombiana. / José: ¿Eres panameña? / Elena: No, no soy de Panamá. / José: ¿Eres Nicaragüense? / Elena: No, tampoco soy de Nicaragua. / José: ¿De dónde eres, entonces? / Elena: Soy venezolana. ¿Y tú? / José: Adivina. / Elena: ¿Eres colombiano? / José: Sí, soy de Medellín.

Written Practice 3-1

1. Mario tiene los ojos azules.   2. Sofía tiene el cabello largo y rizado.
3. Mónica es afroperuana.   4. Lola y Marisa son aburridas.   5. Luis es tranquilo y honesto.   6. Mari Carmen es generosa y un poco tímida.   7. Yoko es asiática y bastante alta.   8. Amelia tiene el cabello pelirrojo y corto. / Amelia es pelirroja y tiene el cabello corto.   9. Ester y Pedro son latinos.   10. Vicente tiene los ojos negros y el cabello canoso.

Oral Practice 3-2

uruguaya, uruguayo, soy, cabello, muy, dónde, parte

Oral Practice 3-3

1. Es la nieta de María.   2. Es la suegra de Arturo.   3. Es el tío de Sonia.
4. Es el novio/prometido de Estela.   5. Son las sobrinas de Andrea.   6. Es el abuelo de Linda.

Written Practice 3-2

1. Es mi sobrino.   2. Es nuestra abuela.   3. Es tu hermano.   4. Es su padrastro.   5. Son mis sobrinas.   6. Son sus primos.

Written Practice 3-3

1. Olivia es más generosa que Jaime.   2. Rebeca es más interesante que Laura.
3. Samuel es menos pesado que Alberto.   4. Marta es más tranquila que José.
5. Rosita es la niña más tímida de la clase.   6. ¡Tu tío es el más gracioso!
7. *Gladiador* es la mejor película.   8. Mi hermana es menos atractiva que mi prima.   9. Nuestro padre no es tan fuerte como nuestro tío.   10. La hermana de Diana es la muchacha más honesta que conozco.

Oral Practice 3-4

1. cierto, falso (*She's red-haired.*)

Esteban: Andrea, ¿quién es esa muchacha? / Andrea: ¿Quién? / Esteban: La muchacha alta. Tiene el cabello pelirrojo. / Andrea: Es Rebeca. Es mi prima.

2. falso (*He's her father.*)

David: ¿Quién es ese hombre hispano? / Susana: ¿Tiene el cabello castaño y ojos negros? / David: Sí, ese hombre. / Susana: Es mi padre. Se llama Alberto.

3. falso (*She thinks Renata is a little annoying.*)
Daniela: En mi opinión, Luisa es muy simpática. / Jorge: ¿Quién es Luisa? / Daniela: Es la prima de Renata. / Jorge: ¡Ah, sí! Es muy simpática, pero la más simpática es Renata. / Daniela: ¿Tú crees? En mi opinión, Renata es un poco pesada.
4. falso (*Antonio's father is less tall [shorter].*)
Roberto: Antonio, ¿cómo es tu padre? / Antonio: Es tranquilo y muy generoso. / Roberto: ¿Es tan alto como tú? / Antonio: No, mi padre es menos alto que yo. / Roberto: ¿Y tu madre? ¿Cómo es? / Antonio: Es muy simpática. Es más divertida que mi padre.

Chapter Practice
1. ¿De dónde es usted?   2. ¿De qué parte de México es usted?   3. Soy norteamericano(a) *or* Soy estadounidense *or* Soy de los Estados Unidos.
4. ¿Quién es ese hombre alto?   5. ¿Quién es esa muchacha hispana?   6. Mi hermana es muy generosa.   7. Su abuela es bastante fuerte.   8. Mi tío Miguel es más divertido que mi tío José.   9. Fernando es bajo y tiene los ojos verdes.
10. Mi prima es latina y tiene el cabello largo.

QUIZ
1. c   2. c   3. a   4. b   5. b   6. b, ¿De dónde es usted?   7. a, ¿De qué parte de Australia?   8. b, ¿Cómo es Diana?   9. b, ¿Cómo es Miguel?   10. b, ¿Quién es esa muchacha alta?

CHAPTER 4

Written Practice 4-1
1. b   2. c   3. a   4. c   5. b   6. a

Oral Practice 4-1
1. ¿Hay un banco cerca?   2. ¿Hay una plaza por aquí?   3. ¿Hay una estación de tren en este barrio?   4. No hay mercados cerca.   5. Hay una librería en esta calle.   6. ¿Hay un bar cerca?   7. Hay un parque grande en Chicago.   8. ¿Hay un museo en esta calle?   9. No hay tiendas cerca.   10. Hay supermercados por aquí.

Written Practice 4-2
1. b   2. c   3. a   4. b   5. c   6. a   7. d   8. c

Written Practice 4-3
1. Qué tipo de tienda   2. Qué tipo de restaurante   3. Qué tipo de bar   4. Qué tipo de tienda   5. Qué tipo de persona

Oral Practice 4-2
1. un mercado

Dora: Perdone, ¿hay un mercado en este barrio? / Simón: No, lo siento. No hay ningún mercado. / Dora: Gracias. / Simón: No hay de qué.

2. una parada de autobús

Teo: Disculpa, ¿hay una parada de autobús en esta calle? / S: Sí, hay una allí. / Teo: Muchas gracias. / S: De nada.

3. un supermercado

Gilda: Perdone, señor. ¿Hay un supermercado cerca? / Toni: No, no hay ninguno. Lo siento. / Gilda: ¿Qué tipo de tienda es Soles? / Toni: Es una tienda de ropa. / Gilda: Gracias. / Toni: No hay de qué.

4. un gimnasio

Diana: Perdone, ¿hay un gimnasio en esta calle? / Señor: Sí, el gimnasio Músculo. Está allí. / Diana: ¿Y qué es Aldi? / Señor: Es un supermercado. / Diana: ¡Ah, sí! Muchísimas gracias. / Señor: No hay de qué.

Oral Practice 4-3

1. Con permiso.   2. Muchas gracias.   3. De nada./No hay de qué.   4. ¿Hay una cafetería por aquí?   5. ¿Hay un estacionamiento en la Calle Sol?   6. ¿Qué es Fallabella?   7. ¿Qué tipo de restaurante es el Restaurante Callao?   8. No, no hay ninguna oficina de correos cerca.   9. No, no hay ninguna por aquí.   10. Sí, hay uno en Calle Central.

Oral Practice 4-4

1. ¿Dónde está el parque?   2. ¿Dónde está la biblioteca?   3. ¿Dónde están las tiendas baratas?   4. ¿Dónde está la parada de metro?   5. ¿Dónde están Andrés y Sergio?   6. ¿Dónde están los buses?   7. ¿Dónde está el supermercado natural? 8. ¿Dónde está la oficina de correos?

Written Practice 4-4

1. El supermercado está al lado del estacionamiento.   2. La plaza está a la izquierda del museo.   3. El gimnasio está a la derecha de la tienda de ropa. 4. El museo de arte está cerca de la Avenida Central.   5. El Bar Sol está lejos. 6. La biblioteca está detrás del parque.   7. La cafetería está a cinco minutos a pie. 8. La librería está a diez minutos en bus.

Written Practice 4-5

1. Sabe   2. Conoce   3. Sabe   4. Conoce   5. Conoce   6. Sabe

Written Practice 4-6

1. Do you know where there is a spacious (big) parking lot?   2. Do you know the neighborhood of San Juan?   3. Do you know where Atocha Station is?   4. Do you know where there is a subway station?   5. Do you know where Dolores Street is?   6. Do you know Ana, Eduardo's friend?

Oral Practice 4-5

1. falso (*It is to the right of the restaurant.*)

F: Disculpe, ¿sabe dónde está la librería Alcón? / D: La librería Alcón… Ah sí. Mire. Está allí. / F: ¿Dónde? / D: Allí. Está a la derecha del restaurante. / F: Ah, sí. A la derecha del restaurante. Gracias.

2. cierto

J: Perdone. ¿Conoce usted el restaurante Olla? / L: Sí, es un restaurante muy bueno. / J: ¿Está lejos? / L: No, está allí. Al lado del Bar Copa. / J: ¿Dónde? / L: Allí. En la plaza. Al lado del Bar Copa. / J: Ah sí. Ya lo veo. Muchas gracias. / L: De nada.

3. falso (*It's thirty minutes by car.*)

T: Perdón. ¿Dónde está la calle Mayor? / N: Está en el barrio Soledad. / T: ¿Está lejos? / N: Sí, está a treinta minutos en carro. / T: Ya veo. Muchas gracias. / N: De nada.

4. cierto

R: Perdone. Busco la cafetería. / T: Está a cinco minutos a pie, por allí. / R: ¿Está dentro o fuera del centro comercial? / T: Está dentro. Pero no está cerca. / R: Gracias. / T: No hay de que. Adiós.

Chapter Practice

Sample conversation: Pablo: Disculpe. ¿Hay un restaurante mexicano cerca? / You: Sí, hay uno en la Calle Mayor. / Pablo: Qué bien. ¿Está lejos la calle Mayor? / You: Sí, está a veinte minutos en metro. / Pablo: ¿Hay una parada de metro cerca? / You: Sí, hay una allí, a dos bloques. / Pablo: Muchas gracias. / You: De nada. / Pablo: Hasta luego. / You: Adiós.

QUIZ

1. b   2. c   3. b   4. b   5. c   6. a, ¿Dónde está la librería Castillo?   7. b, Muchas gracias.   8. b, ¿Qué tipo de tienda es GAP?   9. c, ¿Sabe dónde hay un bar romántico?   10. a, ¿Conoce usted el Barrio Solares?

CHAPTER 5

Oral Practice 5-1

1. Son las dos.   2. Son las tres y media./Son las tres y treinta.   3. Es la una y diez.   4. Son las siete y cuarto./Son las siete y quince.   5. Son las ocho menos cuarto./Son las siete y cuarenta y cinco.   6. Son las once y trece.   7. Son las diez menos veinte./Son las nueve y cuarenta.   8. Son las cinco y veintisiete de la mañana.   9. Son las cuatro y cuarto de la tarde./Son las cuatro y quince de la tarde.   10. Es la una menos diez./Son las doce y cincuenta.

Oral Practice 5-2

1. a, A: ¿Qué hora es? / B: Son las once de la noche.

2. c, A: ¿Qué hora es? / B: Son las diez de la mañana.

3. a, A: Disculpe. ¿Qué hora es? / B: Es la una y cuarto de la tarde.

4. b, A: Perdona. ¿Qué hora es? / B: Son las ocho y veinte.

5. a, A: ¿Qué hora es? / B: Son las seis y media de la mañana.

6. c, A: ¿Qué hora es? / B: Son las dos menos diez de la tarde.

Written Practice 5-1

1. el cinco de noviembre   2. el veinte de julio   3. el nueve de febrero   4. el veintisiete de mayo   5. el siete de junio   6. el veintidós de septiembre/setiembre del dos mil once   7. el trece de marzo del mil novecientos cincuenta y tres   8. el treinta de agosto del dos mil nueve   9. el uno de enero del mil novecientos noventa y seis   10. el veinticinco de diciembre del dos mil uno

Oral Practice 5-3

1. falso (*It's 10:30.*)

A: Disculpe, ¿qué hora es? / B: Son las diez y media. / A: Muchas gracias. / B: No hay de qué.

2. falso (*It's 11:15.*)

A: ¿Tienes hora? / B: Sí, son las once y cuarto. / A: ¡Ay, qué tarde! Adiós. / B: Hasta luego.

3. cierto, falso (*It's 1:00 P.M.*)

A: ¿Sabe qué día es hoy? / B: Sí, hoy es... sábado. / A: Muy bien. ¿Y qué fecha es? / B: El veinte de junio. / A: ¿Sabe qué hora es? / B: Es la una de la tarde. / A: Perfecto. Está usted bien.

4. falso (*It's April 30.*), cierto

A: Hoy es mi cumpleaños. / B: ¿Ah sí? ¿Qué fecha es hoy? / A: Es el treinta de abril. / B: ¡Feliz cumpleaños! / A: ¿Qué hora es ahora? / B: Las cinco y media de la tarde. / A: Hora de ir a casa. ¡Vamos!

Written Practice 5-2

1. por   2. a las   3. a qué hora   4. tarde   5. los   6. los

Written Practice 5-3

1. h   2. c   3. e   4. g   5. i   6. a   7. j   8. f   9. b   10. l   11. k   12. d

Oral Practice 5-4

1. aprendo   2. corre   3. discuten   4. Comen   5. limpia   6. trabajan   7. compramos   8. vive, vivo   9. Comprende   10. pronuncias

Written Practice 5-4

1. van   2. voy   3. va   4. van   5. vamos   6. vas

Written Practice 5-5

1. falso (*It leaves every half hour.*)   2. falso (*It leaves every ten minutes.*)   3. cierto   4. falso (*It's at 9:14.*)   5. cierto   6. Sale a las nueve de la mañana.   7. Sale a las nueve menos diez/a las ocho cincuenta.   8. Sale a las nueve menos doce/a las ocho cuarenta y ocho.   9. No, no hay un tren a las ocho y treinta y dos.   10. No, no hay un tren. Hay un autobús y un metro.

Oral Practice 5-5

1. falso (*It's at 2:10.*)
A: Perdone, ¿a qué hora es el siguiente autobús? / B: Sale a las dos y diez. / A: Muchas gracias. / B: De nada.

2. cierto; falso (*It opens at 6:00 P.M.*)
A: Ana, ¿vas a la fiesta hoy? / B: Sí, voy en autobús. / A: ¿A qué hora comienza la fiesta? / B: Comienza a las nueve de la noche. / A: ¿Y dónde es? / B: En el bar Copas. / A: ¿Y a qué hora abre el bar? / B: Abre a las seis de la tarde.

3. cierto
A: Perdón, ¿a qué hora es el metro? / B: El metro… El metro viene cada diez minutos. / A: Ay, ¿qué día es hoy? / B: Es sábado. El sábado el metro viene cada media hora. / A: Muy bien. Gracias. / B: No hay de qué.

4. cierto
A: ¿Cómo vas a trabajar? / B: En tren. / A: ¿Y a qué hora sale el tren? / B: Sale a las quince y cuarenta. / A: Muchas gracias. / B: De nada.

Chapter Practice

Sample conversation: Friend: Hola. Oye, ¿cuándo es tu cumpleaños? / You: Es el veinte de julio. / Friend: ¿Celebras tu cumpleaños? / You: Sí, generalmente salgo con amigos. / Friend: ¿Cómo vas a trabajar? / You: Voy en autobús. / Friend: ¿A qué hora vas a trabajar? / You: Voy a las ocho y media de la mañana. / Friend: ¿Y a qué hora vas a casa? / You: Voy a las seis de la tarde. / Friend: ¿Qué hora es? / You: Son las nueve. / Friend: Ay, ¡es tarde! Adiós. / You: Adiós. Hasta mañana.

QUIZ

1. a, ¿Qué hora es?   2. c, ¿Qué día es hoy?   3. c, ¿A qué hora sale el tren?
4. b, ¿Qué fecha es?   5. c, ¿Cómo vas a trabajar?   6. a, ¿Dónde vives?   7. b, ¿Miguel viaja mucho?   8. c, ¿Aprendes tú español?   9. a, ¿Comprenden ustedes?   10. c, ¿A qué hora sale el siguiente autobús?

CHAPTER 6

Oral Practice 6-1

1. ¿Qué haces (tú)?   2. ¿Qué hace usted?   3. ¿Qué hacen Héctor y José?
4. ¿Qué hacen ustedes?   5. ¿Qué hacen ellas?   6. ¿Qué hace Rebeca?

Written Practice 6-1

1. Gerardo es cocinero.   2. David es estudiante.   3. Irma y Manuela son enfermeras.   4. Soy maestra.   5. Alicia es vendedora.   6. Javier es periodista.
7. Julia y Debora son abogadas.

Written Practice 6-2

1. tiene: *Petra has a temporary job.*   2. dan: *Do you give information?*   3. doy: *I give instructions to clients.*   4. tienes: *Do you have work/a job?*   5. damos: *We don't give loans.*   6. tenemos: *We have a lot of work.*

Oral Practice 6-2

1. cierto

A: Oye, ¿qué hace Manuel? / B: Es médico. / A: ¿Dónde trabaja? / B: Trabaja en el Hospital Cruces.

2. falso (*Rocío is a lawyer.*)

A: ¿Qué hacen tus hermanas? / B: Rocío es abogada. / A: ¿Y Ester? ¿Qué hace? / B: Ester es consultora en un banco.

3. cierto

A: ¿Qué hace usted? / B: Trabajo para caritas. / A: ¿Y qué hace allí? / B: Soy recepcionista. Contesto el teléfono y doy la bienvenida.

4. falso (*Rubén has a part-time job.*)

A: ¿Tienes trabajo? / B: Sí, tengo un trabajo de tiempo parcial. / A: ¿Cuándo trabajas? / B: Trabajo de nueve a una.

Oral Practice 6-3

1. ¿Qué hace usted?   2. Soy estudiante.   3. Es vendedora.   4. Son todos médicos.   5. ¿Tienes trabajo?   6. Tengo un trabajo de tiempo parcial.   7. Enseño computadoras.   8. Nosotros ayudamos a otros estudiantes.   9. Inés da clases de español.   10. El Señor Ruiz tiene un equipo de cinco personas.

Oral Practice 6-4

1. Bernardo está comiendo chocolate.   2. Susana está hablando con su hermana.
3. Ana está viviendo con su novio.   4. Nosotros estamos escribiendo emails.
5. Ustedes están hablando español.   6. Tú estás organizando fiestas.

Oral Practice 6-5

1. Me encanta el chocolate.   2. Me gusta la música clásica.   3. No me gusta viajar en avión.   4. Me gusta mucho visitar a mi familia.   5. Me encantan las novelas de misterio.   6. No me gustan las pupusas de queso.

Oral Practice 6-6

1. ¿Te gusta leer?   2. ¿Le gusta la música rock?   3. ¿Qué te parece la fiesta?
4. ¿Qué te parecen los cuchifritos?   5. ¿Qué le parece la novela?   6. ¿Te gusta comer en restaurantes?   7. ¿Le gustan las películas?   8. ¿Qué le parece el trabajo?   9. ¿Qué te parece la nueva profesora?   10. ¿Qué te parece el hermano de Javier?

Oral Practice 6-7

1. ¿Qué te parece Pablo?   2. Me parece atractivo.   3. Me parece interesante.
4. ¡Me encanta bailar!   5. ¿Qué está haciendo Luisa?   6. Luisa está viviendo en

Paris. 7. Estoy trabajando en una oficina. 8. Está hablando español. 9. Estoy haciendo tamales. 10. Estamos comiendo tamales.

Chapter Practice

1. cierto

Mario: Ester, ¿dónde trabajas? / Ester: Trabajo en el Restaurante Olla. / Mario: ¿Y qué haces allí? / Ester: Soy camarera. / Mario: ¿Te gusta trabajar allí? / Ester: Sí, me gusta mucho.

2. falso (*She thinks he's boring and arrogant.*)

Luis: ¿Qué te parece Pablo, Ángela? / Ángela: La verdad, me parece bastante aburrido. / Luis: Pero es bastante atractivo, ¿no? / Ángela: No me parece atractivo. Me parece bastante arrogante.

3. cierto

Marta: Rosa tiene un novio nuevo. Se llama Miguel. / Gerardo: ¿Ah, sí? ¿Y qué hace? / Marta: Da clases de español. Es maestro. / Gerardo: ¿Dónde enseña? / Marta: En una escuela privada. Es peruano. / Gerardo: ¿Y qué te parece Miguel?

4. falso (*She's living and working in Mexico.*)

Alberto: ¿Qué está haciendo Ariana? / Elena: Está trabajando en un supermercado. / Alberto: ¿Y qué hace? / Elena: Es cajera. / Alberto: ¿Dónde está viviendo? / Elena: Está viviendo con su novio, en México. / Alberto: ¿Qué te parece su novio? / Elena: Me parece interesante.

QUIZ

1. b, ¿Qué hace Luis? 2. c, ¿Qué hacen María y Linda? 3. a, ¿Dónde trabaja el Señor Morán? 4. b, ¿Qué hace Luis en la editorial? 5. a, ¿Qué tipo de trabajo tiene Ana? 6. c, ¿Qué está haciendo Oscar en México? 7. a, ¿Te gusta viajar? 8. a, ¿Qué están haciendo Lola y Pedro? 9. b, ¿Qué le parece la película? 10. c, ¿Qué te parece este libro?

CHAPTER 7

Oral Practice 7-1

1. Quisiera información sobre Puerto Plata. 2. Queremos un folleto sobre Brasil. 3. Quisiera hablar con Roberto. 4. Quiero hablar español. 5. Quisiera hacer una reservación. 6. No quiere ir a Argentina. 7. Quiero información sobre Portugal. 8. ¿Ustedes quieren hablar con un médico?

Oral Practice 7-2

Dialogue 1: Está, soy; *Dialogue 2*: Está Isabel, un mensaje, que llamó Rosa, Llamaré otra vez; *Dialogue 3*: Quisiera, de quién, Soy, Un momento, disponible, un mensaje

Written Practice 7-1

1. b   2. c   3. a   4. c   5. c   6. a   7. b   8. a

Oral Practice 7-3

1. b

Man: ¿Aló? / Rosa: Quisiera hablar con Ernesto, por favor. / Man: Lo siento. No está. / Rosa: Gracias. Llamaré más tarde.

2. a

Pedro: ¿Sí? / Ana: Hola, soy Ana. ¿Cómo estás? / Pedro: Bien, pero aquí está lloviendo. ¿Qué tiempo hace allí? / Ana: Hace calor y está despejado ¡Hace setenta grados! / Pedro: Qué bien. Aquí hace cuarenta grados…

3. a

Fernando: Hola. Quisiera información sobre Puerto Rico, por favor. / Man: ¿Quiere un DVD o un folleto? / Fernando: Un folleto, por favor. / Man: De acuerdo. Le podemos enviar uno.

4. c

Rafa: ¿Aló? / Alicia: Hola Rubén. Soy Alicia. Quiero información sobre… / Rafa: Lo siento. Rubén no está. Soy Rafa. / Alicia: Ah, lo siento. / Rafa: ¿Quieres dejar un mensaje? / Alicia: Sí. ¿Puede decirle que llamó Alicia? Quiero información sobre su escuela. / Rafa: De acuerdo. / Alicia: Muchas gracias.

Oral Practice 7-4

1. Hable en español.   2. Repita su nombre, por favor.   3. Escriban un email. 4. Lean el libro.   5. Coma una empanadilla.   6. No hagan ruido.   7. No mande el paquete por correo.   8. Diga la verdad.   9. Espere un minuto, por favor. 10. No digan su nombre.

Oral Practice 7-5

comas, Come, bebas, Bebe, vayas, Ve, haz, compra, aprende, hables

Oral Practice 7-6

1. falso (*Daniel is Eva's sister's friend.*)   2. cierto   3. cierto   4. falso (*She says it's about fifty degrees.*)   5. falso (*She offers tips about restaurants.*)   6. cierto Eva: ¿Aló? / Daniel: Buenas tardes. Quisiera hablar con Eva Gómez. / Eva: Sí, soy yo. / Daniel: Hola, Eva. Soy Daniel. Soy amigo de tu hermana. / Eva: Sí, hola. Dime, ¿qué quieres? / Daniel: Quisiera tu opinión. Viajo a España. Tú conoces España, ¿verdad? / Eva: Sí, muy bien. / Daniel: ¿Qué tiempo hace en Madrid en invierno? / Eva: Hace mucho frío. No vayas en invierno. Ve en verano. / Daniel: ¿Y en Sevilla? ¿Nieva allí? / Eva: No, allí no nieva. Hace aproximadamente cincuenta grados Fahrenheit en invierno. / Daniel: Está bien. Quiero ir en invierno, entonces. / Eva: Oye, no comas en restaurantes para turistas. Llama a mi amiga Lupe. Ella conoce los restaurantes buenos. / Daniel: Gracias. / Eva: Escribe su número de teléfono. Es el 9-555-6783. Habla español con ella. Ella no habla inglés. / Daniel: Está bien. Muchas gracias.

Chapter Practice
1. Quisiera información sobre Costa Rica.   2. ¿Qué tiempo hace en Costa Rica?
3. Hace frío.   4. Hace ochenta grados.   5. Hable más despacio, por favor.
6. Habla español.   7. No vayas al Restaurante Cortés.   8. Digan sus nombres.

QUIZ
1. b   2. a   3. c   4. a   5. c   6. a, ¿Qué tiempo hace?   7. a, ¿Qué tiempo
hace en verano?   8. b, ¿Qué temperatura hace?   9. c, ¿Está María, por favor?
10. b, ¿Me puede comunicar con la Señora Torres, por favor?

CHAPTER 8

Oral Practice 8-1
1. ¿Dónde debería ir?   2. ¿Qué debería llevar?   3. ¿Qué debería visitar?
4. ¿Dónde debería comer?   5. ¿Qué debería comprar?   6. ¿Cuánto debería
pagar?   7. ¿Por qué debería ir?   8. ¿Cómo debería viajar?

Oral Practice 8-2
1. Si vas a México, deberías llevar pesos.   2. Si vas a Costa Rica, deberías ir al
Volcán Poás.   3. Si vas a Colombia, deberías ir a Cartagena.   4. Si vas a Argentina, no deberías viajar en tren.   5. Si vas a Chile, deberías llamar a Marta.
6. Si va a México, debería llevar pesos.   7. Si va al Restaurante Cuzco, debería
hacer una reservación.   8. Si compra artesanías en el mercado, debería regatear.
9. Si necesita información, no debería mandar un email.   10. Si hace una reservación, debería repetir su nombre.

Written Practice 8-1
1. Yo necesito unas botas de caminar.   2. Nosotros necesitamos unas gorras.
3. Ustedes necesitan una guía turística del bosque tropical.   4. Tú no necesitas
una computadora.   5. Ellas necesitan un mapa del bosque.   6. Usted no necesita
una corbata.

Oral Practice 8-3
1. cierto
Marta: ¿Qué debería visitar en Perú? / José: Deberías ir a Cuzco y hacer el Camino
Inca. / Marta: ¿Qué debería llevar? / José: Deberías llevar unas buenas botas y
mucha agua.
2. falso (*He needs to make a reservation.*)
Gilberto: ¿Qué debería comer? / Aurora: Deberías comer las arepas. Son deliciosas.
/ Gilberto: ¿Y qué debería beber? / Aurora: Tienes que beber un mojito. ¡Están
buenísimos! / Gilberto: ¿Algo más? / Aurora: Deberías hacer una reservación. Es un
restaurante muy popular.
3. falso (*She needs pesos.*)

Mónica: ¿Qué debería hacer? / Ramón: Deberías regatear. / Mónica: ¿Necesito pesos? / Ramón: Sí, necesitas pesos. No aceptan dólares en el mercado. / Mónica: ¿Qué debería comprar? / Ramón: Deberías comprar unos platos.

4. falso (*Her car has a GPS.*)

Rocío: ¿Qué carro debería alquilar? / Julio: Deberías alquilar un carro pequeño. Necesita menos gasolina. / Rocío: ¿Necesito un mapa? / Julio: No, no necesitas un mapa. El carro tiene GPS.

Written Practice 8-2

1. El sábado voy a ir a una fiesta.   2. Luisa va a viajar a Atlanta la semana que viene.   3. Julián y Regina van a buscar un apartamento pasado mañana.
4. Nosotras no vamos a ver a mi madre el mes que viene.   5. El fin de semana ustedes van a visitar al parque.

Oral Practice 8-4

2. *¿Vas a hablar con Luis mañana?* Sí, voy a hablar con Luis mañana.   3. *¿Vas a comer tamales?* No, no voy a comer tamales.   4. *¿Vas a beber agua?* Sí, voy a beber agua.   5. *¿Va a bailar Elena?* Sí, va a bailar Elena.   6. *¿Van a bailar Isabel y Ana el sábado?* No, no van a bailar el sábado. 7. *¿Dónde vas a aprender español?* Voy a aprender español en Chile.   8. *¿Cómo vas a viajar a Chile?* Voy a viajar en avión.   9. *¿A quién vas a visitar en Chile?* Voy a visitar a mi primo.
10. *¿Qué vas a hacer en Chile?* Voy a visitar Santiago.

Written Practice 8-3

1. viajará   2. irán   3. aprenderá   4. necesitaremos   5. pagarás   6. comprarán   7. haré   8. dirás   9. Habrá   10. comprarás

Oral Practice 8-5

1. cierto

Mario: Ester, ¿dónde debería viajar? / Ester: Deberías viajar a Chile. Es muy bonito. / Mario: Chile está lejos. Quiero viajar en carro. / Ester: Entonces deberías viajar a México. / Mario: Sí, México está cerca. Viajaré a México.

2. falso (*It's Ángela who's going.*)

Esteban: Ángela, ¿cuándo vas a ir a Argentina? / Ángela: El mes que viene. Voy a salir el día diez. / Esteban: ¿Necesitas contactos allí? / Ángela: No, gracias. Voy a viajar con un grupo. / Esteban: ¿Vas a ir a la Patagonia? / Ángela: No. Voy a estar solamente en Buenos Aires.

3. cierto

Marta: Luis, ¿van a ir a la fiesta este fin de semana? / Luis: No, mi esposa estará en España. Va a visitar a su familia. ¿Y tú? / Marta: Sí, yo voy a ir con mi novio. / Luis: Si ustedes van, iré yo también. ¿Qué día será la fiesta, el sábado o el domingo? / Marta: Es el sábado. / Luis: ¿Irá Susana? / Marta: No, no va a ir. Estará en España también.

4. falso (*It's next week.*)

Antonio: ¿Y dónde vivirán? / Rebeca: Viviremos en San Francisco. Al principio viviremos con mis padres. / Antonio: ¿Cuándo viajarán allí? / Rebeca: La semana que viene. / Antonio: ¡Tan pronto! ¿Y dónde trabajarán? / Rebeca: Yo no sé. Mi esposo trabajará con mi padre. / Antonio: ¿Estarás en contacto? / Rebeca: Claro que sí, estaré en contacto. / Antonio: Buena suerte a los dos.

Chapter Practice
1. ¿Qué debería hacer en Puerto Rico?   2. ¿Dónde debería ir?   3. Deberías viajar a Costa Rica.   4. Necesitas llevar unas botas impermeables.   5. Voy a ir a una fiesta.   6. Vamos a ir al parque.   7. Tienes que visitar El Yunque.
8. Si vas al Yunque, tienes que llevar unas botas impermeables.   9. Aprenderá inglés.   10. Visitarán Copán.

QUIZ
1. c   2. b   3. c   4. b   5. c   6. c, Ustedes van a ir a la fiesta?   7. a, ¿Cuándo vas a visitar a tu abuela?   8. b, ¿Dónde estarás el año que viene?   9. b, ¿Qué necesito si quiero mandar un email?   10. b, ¿Cómo vas a viajar a Perú?

CHAPTER 9

Written Practice 9-1
viajaste, visité, fuiste, Viajé, estuvieron, estuvimos, Disfrutamos, hicieron, Fuimos, Vieron, vimos, Vimos, Tuvieron, fue, Comieron, probé, comió, escribieron

Oral Practice 9-1
1. Sí, comí en el Restaurante Coquí.   2. No, no probé el sopón de pollo.   3. Sí, comimos arroz con pollo.   4. Sí, pagó Luisa.   5. Sí, escribí un artículo sobre el restaurante.

Written Practice 9-2
1. la   2. lo   3. la   4. los   5. no los encontré   6. las vi   7. no las compraron
8. lo escribimos   9. los vi   10. no te vimos

Oral Practice 9-2
1. falso (*Ana saw it.*)
Ana: Fidel, ¿viste la película *Gladiador*? / Fidel: No, no la vi. ¿Qué te pareció? / Ana: Fue muy buena. Me encanta Russell Crowe. / Fidel: A mí no me gusta mucho. / Ana: ¿Viste *Gángster Americano*? / Fidel: Sí la vi y me gustó mucho.
2. cierto, falso (*No, he did not have enough time.*), cierto
Renata: ¿Dónde fuiste? / Daniel: Fui a Barcelona. / Renata: ¿Qué visitaste? / Daniel: Fui al Barrio Gótico. También vi edificios de Gaudí y la Sagrada Familia. / Renata: ¿Visitaste el Parque Güell, de Gaudí? / Daniel: No, no lo visité. No tuve tiempo. / Renata: ¿Qué te parece La Sagrada Familia? / Daniel: Me parece preciosa. Es increíble.

3. falso (*She's going to eat a vegetarian burrito.*), falso (*Paco has tried the burritos.*), cierto

Isabel: ¿Ya probaste las fajitas de aquí? / Paco: Sí, las probé. Están deliciosas. Hay fajitas de carne y de pollo. Las fajitas de carne son mejores que las fajitas de pollo. / Isabel: No sé… No me gusta la carne. ¿Probaste los burritos? / Paco: Sí los probé. Los burritos están muy buenos. / Isabel: ¿Comiste tú las quesadillas? / Paco: No, las quesadillas no las probé. / Isabel: Voy a probar un burrito vegetariano. / Paco: Me parece genial. Te gustará.

Written Practice 9-3

1. +++ 2. ++ 3. + 4. +++ 5. ++

Oral Practice 9-3

1. ¿Podría hablar más despacio? 2. Hable más despacio. 3. ¿Puede venir a mi casa? 4. ¿Podría visitar a Daniel en el hospital? 5. ¿Puede hablar más bajo?

Written Practice 9-4

1. me 2. Te 3. les 4. Me 5. le 6. les

Oral Practice 9-4

1. falso (*It's for her husband.*)

Delia: Disculpe, ¿puede ayudarme, por favor? / Antonio: Sí, ¿qué necesita? / Delia: No puedo decidir… Quiero comprarle una corbata a mi esposo. ¿Cuál le gusta? / Antonio: La corbata azul es más bonita que la roja. / Delia: Ay, no sé… / Antonio: ¿Va usted a comprarla? / Delia: Mmmm, ¡sí! La voy a comprar.

2. falso (*It's a stomachache.*), cierto

Sergio: ¿Cómo estás, Diego? / Diego: No muy bien… Tengo dolor de estómago. / Sergio: Lo siento. ¿Necesitas algo? / Diego: No puedo comer nada. / Sergio: ¿Puedes beber agua? / Diego: Sí, un poco. Dame un vaso de agua, por favor. / Sergio: Sí, claro. Aquí lo tienes. / Diego: Gracias.

3. falso (*He doesn't call her every day.*), cierto

Ana: Arturo, tengo un problema con mi novio. / Arturo: ¿Cuál es el problema? / Ana: Mi novio Romeo no me llama todos los días. / Arturo: ¿Hace otras cosas, como mandarte mensajes de texto? / Ana: Sí, me escribe textos y me manda emails, pero no hablamos todos los días. / Arturo: ¿Te compra flores el Día de San Valentín? / Ana: Sí y también me escribe cartas románticas. / Arturo: Entonces no te puedo ayudar. No tienes ningún problema.

Chapter Practice

Sample conversation: Friend: Hola. Oye, ¿tú viajaste a Latinoamérica? ¿Dónde? / You: Sí, el año pasado viajé a Argentina. Visité la Patagonia. / Friend: ¿Visitaste alguna ciudad grande? / You: Sí, visité Buenos Aires. / Friend: ¿Qué te pareció la comida? / You: Me pareció deliciosa. / Friend: ¿Hablaste mucho español? ¿Con quién? / You: Sí, conocí a mucha gente nueva en el viaje y practiqué mi español

con ellos. / Friend: ¿Qué te gustó más? / You: Me encantó la Patagonia. / Friend: Ay, ¡es tarde! Hasta luego. / You: Adiós.

QUIZ

1. b   2. c   3. a   4. c   5. c   6. a, ¿Cuándo la llamó usted a Ana?   7. b, ¿Compraste ya la comida?   8. b, ¿Dónde estuvo usted ayer?   9. a, ¿Le escribiste un email a María?   10. c, ¿Perdió usted los lentes?

CHAPTER 10

Written Practice 10-1

era, eras, iba, iban, tenías, eran, hablábamos, hablaban, eran, gustaba, gustaba, jugabas, jugaba, dibujaba, Comía, encantaba, Comías, era, vivíamos, Vivíamos, tenía, tenían, subían, leía, escuchabas, eran

Oral Practice 10-1

Por qué; en vez de; Porque; y; Sin embargo; pero; Aunque; o; Además

Oral Practice 10-2

1. falso (*She used to be optimistic.*), cierto

Carolina: Ay, no entiendo a Luisa. Ella antes era muy optimista, ahora no lo es. / David: ¿Por qué? / Carolina: No lo sé. Antes todo le parecía bien, pero ahora todo le parece mal. Antes siempre disfrutaba de todo, pero ahora no le gusta nada. / David: Qué extraño… / Carolina: Antes hacíamos cosas juntas a menudo. Íbamos al cine, y hablábamos mucho. Además, siempre cenábamos juntas todos los miércoles. Ahora ella no quiere hacer nada. / David: Luisa necesita tu ayuda. Habla con ella. / Carolina: Sí, tienes razón. Voy a hablar con ella.

2. falso (*Her name was Ms. Monroe.*), falso (*She disliked the name.*), cierto

Ronaldo: Nosotros íbamos a la misma escuela, ¿no? / Juan: Sí, la Escuela Chávez. En primero estábamos en la misma clase. / Ronaldo: Ay, sí. ¿Cómo le decíamos a la maestra? ¿Cuál era su nombre? / Juan: Se llamaba Señora Monroe, pero nosotros en vez de «Monroe» le decíamos Señora «Monstruo». / Ronaldo: Sí, y ella se enojaba siempre, ja, ja. Aunque no éramos muy buenos, ella era muy buena maestra. / Juan: Sí, la verdad sí. Tú no estabas en esa escuela en segundo. ¿Por qué? / Ronaldo: Porque mi familia se fue a México ese año. De pequeño vivíamos en Arizona. Sin embargo, ese año nos mudamos a México.

Written Practice 10-2

2. Antes Rebeca y Laura eran buenas amigas. Sin embargo, ahora no lo son.
3. El sábado pasado nosotras queríamos ver a Luisa en vez de a Gema.   4. Ayer Roberto hablaba por teléfono mientras Rosa escribía un email.   5. De pequeña Rosita a menudo jugaba con Ester, Pepita e Inés.   6. De pequeño, aunque Carlitos hablaba español muy bien, no quería hablarlo.

Written Practice 10-3

1. graciosísimo   2. enojadísimo   3. emocionadísima   4. timidísima
5. generosísimo   6. exageradísima

Chapter Practice

1. c   2. a   3. d   4. e   5. b

QUIZ

1. a   2. c   3. a   4. c   5. c   6. c, ¿Qué idioma hablabas tú de pequeño?
7. b, ¿Dónde vivían ustedes antes?   8. c, ¿ Qué quiere decir "porfa"?
9. a, ¿Por qué no te gusta Juan?   10. a, ¿Qué quiere decir "exageradísimo"?

Final Exam

1. b   2. c   3. b   4. c   5. b   6. a   7. b   8. c   9. c   10. c   11. a   12. a
13. c   14. a   15. c   16. c   17. c   18. b   19. b   20. a   21. b   22. c
23. c   24. b   25. a   26. b   27. c   28. b   29. a   30. a   31. b   32. a
33. c   34. c   35. b   36. b   37. c   38. b   39. a   40. c   41. b   42. b
43. c   44. b   45. b   46. b   47. b   48. b   49. c   50. b   51. c, ¿Cómo se
dice "student" en español?   52. c, ¿Cómo se escribe "hola"?   53. c, ¿Qué quiere
decir "quince"?   54. a, ¿Cómo se dice "twenty-two" en español?   55. b, ¿Qué
fecha es hoy?   56. b, ¿Qué hora es?   57. b, ¿Cómo se dice *"11:15 P.M."* en español?   58. a, ¿Dónde es la fiesta?   59. c, ¿A qué hora vas a trabajar?   60. b, ¿A
qué hora termina la clase?   61. a, ¿Quién es Ana?   62. c, ¿Qué hace Ana?
63. b, ¿Cómo es Ana?   64. c, ¿Conoces a Marta?   65. a, Perdón, ¿sabe usted
dónde hay una parada de autobús?   66. c, ¿Hay un baño cerca?   67. c, ¿Qué vas
a hacer hoy?   68. a, ¿Dónde estará Julia mañana?   69. a, ¿Estás bien?   70. b,
¿Podría indicarme el camino a la Calle Mayor?   71. a, ¿Qué tiempo hace allí
ahora?   72. c, ¿Nieva mucho en Chicago?   73. b, ¿Qué temperatura hace?
74. c, ¿Qué regalo te dio el abuelo a ti?   75. b, ¿Les mandó Ramón un email a
ustedes?   76. c, ¿En qué idioma le habla Ana a su hija?   77. a, ¿Vieron ustedes a
Miguel ayer?   78. a, ¿Compraste el libro ya?   79. a, ¿Qué libro estás leyendo
ahora?   80. a, ¿Quiere usted beber algo?   81. b, ¿Qué hiciste anoche?   82. a,
¿Dónde estuviste ayer?   83. b, ¿Te gustó la película?   84. a, ¿Qué tipo de
película es?   85. c, ¿Qué le parece ese restaurante chino?   86. a, ¿Está Luisa,
por favor?   87. c, ¿Quiere dejar un mensaje?   88. b, ¿A qué hora llamará usted?
89. c, Disculpe, ¿a qué hora sale el siguiente tren?   90. a, Voy a viajar a Costa
Rica. ¿Qué debería hacer?   91. c, ¿Qué hacía el bebé mientras la mamá traba-
jaba?   92. a, De dónde es José?   93. b, ¿Qué te gustaba hacer de pequeño?
94. b, ¿Qué quiere decir "chiquitito"?   95. b, ¿Qué quiere decir "exageradísimo"?
96. a, Pablo dijo "chévere." ¿Qué quiere decir?   97. b, ¿Fuiste al concierto?
98. c, ¿Por qué no viniste a la fiesta?   99. a, ¿Me da usted un buen consejo?
100. c, ¿Qué consejo le das a un estudiante de español?

INDEX

a (personal), 90, 170
a (preposition), 170
Accent marks, 15–16
Adjectives
  algunos, 79
  cognates, 8
  describing people, 55
  describing places, 89
  expressing opinion, 132
  gender, 21–22
  mood, 43–44
  muchos, 79
  number, 21–22
  personal adjectives, 63
  pocos, 79
  race and ethnicity, 57
  ser vs. **estar**, 56
  varios, 79
Adverbs
  acá, 77
  allá, 77
  allí, 77
  aquí, 77
  bastante, 56
  cerca, 77
  muy, 56
  of place, 77
  un poco, 56
  used with **hay**, 77

Advice, 159–65
  asking for, 160–62
  conditional advice, 163–65
  giving, 162–63
Agreement
  gender, 17–18, 21–22
  number, 17–18, 21–22
¿Aló?, 144
Alphabet, 10
Anglicized words, 7
Appearance, 54–60
  ser vs. **estar**, 54
-ar verbs, 25–26, 107–8, 152, 172, 182, 208
Articles, 17
  gender and, 17–18, 20–21
  indefinite with **hay**, 76, 79
  number, 20–21
Assistance, asking for, 72, 191
  polite expression, 73–75

Body parts, 196–97
Borrowed words, 7
  anglicized, 7
  geographic features, 7
  place names, 7
bueno, 89

Calendar, 104–6
coger, 211

Cognates, 7–8
  adjectives, 8
  false, 8
  nouns, 8
  verbs, 8
Colloquial expressions, 216–18
Commands
  formal, 152–53
  informal, 154–55
Comparisons
  describing people, 64–67
  superlatives, 66–67
Connecting words, 210–11
conocer vs. **saber**, 87–89, 173
Countries, 50–54
Culture notes, 52, 58, 195
Cyber Spanish, 23

Daily life, 95–116
  calendar, 104–6
  habits, 104–6
  quizzes, 115–16
  schedules, 104
  time and date, 95–103
  timetables, 111–14
  transportation, 110–11
dar, 127
Dates
  asking, 101–3
  months, 101
  telling, 101–3
Days of the week, 33
debería, 162–65
decir, 173
Describing people. *See* People,
  describing
Describing places, 75–78
  adjectives, 89
  hay, 75–78
  place names, 75–76

  quiz, 93–94
  stores, 76
Describing things, 75–78
  hay, 75–78
Diphthongs, 13, 14–15
Directions, 83–86
  how far away, 86
  locations, 84–85
¿Dónde está?, 84–85

Entertainment, 205–22
  colloquial expressions, 216–18
  money, 217
  quiz, 221–22
-er verbs, 25–26, 107–8, 152, 172, 182, 208
esta/estas/este/estos, 77–78
ésta/éste, 36–38
estar, 184
  with directions, 84–85
  estar + a, 86
  mood, 42–43
estar vs. **ser**. *See* **ser** vs. **estar**
Euphemisms, 55
Exaggerating, 218
Exam, 223–35
Eye color, 58–59

Family members, 62–64
Future plans, 166–74

Gender, 17–18
  -a ending, 17–18
  adjectives, 21–22
  agreement, 17–18
  articles, 18–19, 20–21
  exceptions to rule, 18–19
  nouns, 19
  -o ending, 17–18
Geographic features, 7
Gossiping, 128–36

granizar, 148
Greetings, 31–35
  goodbye, 32
  hello, 31–32
  pauses, 32
gustar, 133–36

Habits, 104–6
habrá, 173
hacer, 121–22, 147–48, 173, 184
Hair color and types, 57
hay, 75–79, 173
  describing places, 75–78
  describing things, 75–78
  giving information with, 78–81
¿Hola?, 144

Idiomatic expressions, 216–18
Information gathering, 140–41
Introductions, 29–31, 35–40
  ésta, 36–38
  éste, 36–38
  llamarse, 38–39
  responding to, 39–40
  ser, 35
  su/s, 38
ir, 109, 184, 208
ir + a, 168–69
-ir verbs, 25–26, 107–8, 172, 182, 208
-ísimo, 218–19

Jobs. *See* Occupations

leísmo, 189
llamarse, 38–39
llover, 148

Making friends, 29–31
  introductions, 35–40
malo, 89

Money, 217
Months, 101
Mood, 42–44
  estar, 42–43

Names, 15, 38
Nationality, 50–54
  ¿De dónde... ?, 53
  "American," 52
necesitar, 165–66
Needs, 165–66
Negatives, 44
  double, 80
nevar, 148
ninguno, 80
Nouns
  cognates, 8
  gender, 18, 19
  number, 19
Number, 19–22
  adjectives, 21–22
  articles, 20–21
  nouns, 19
Numbers, 86, 97–98

Occupations, 119–28
  professions, 122–24
  workplaces, 124–26
Offers
  asking and offering politely, 191–95
Opinions, expressing, 132–36
  adjectives for, 132
  with **gustar**, 133–36
  with **parecer**, 132–33, 136

Pain, 196–97
parar, 211
parecer, 132–33
Past, talking about, 205–10. *See also* Verb
  tense

Pauses
  bueno, 32
  pues, 32
People, describing, 50–51
  adjectives, 55
  appearance, 54–60
  comparisons, 64–67
  eye color, 58–59
  family members, 62–64
  hair color and types, 57
  nationality, 50–54
  quiz, 69–70
  race and ethnicity, 57, 58
  talking about different people, 60–70
People, getting in touch with, 139–58
  commands, 152–57
  information gathering, 140–41
  quiz, 157–58
  requests, 143, 151–57
  telephone, 143–47
People, talking about, 119–38
  gossiping, 128–36
  occupations, 119–28
  quiz, 137–38
Personal **a**, 90, 170
Personal adjectives, 63
Phrases
  basic, 5–7
  conversational, 5
  meaning of words, 5
  pronunciation, 6
  quiz, 26–27
  repetition of words, 5
  spelling, 6
  thank you, 5
Place names, 7
Places, asking about, 81. *See also*
    Directions
Places, describing. *See* Describing places
poder, 173, 193–94

Polite expression, 73–75
  asking and offering politely, 191–95
  con permiso, 74
  culture note, 195
  disculpe, 74–75
  perdonar, 73–74
poner, 173
Prepositions
  a, 170
  de, 82
  en, 77
  list, 85
Present participles, 130–31
Professions, 122–24
Pronouns
  direct object, 187–88
  indirect object pronouns, 197–200
  leísmo, 189
  subject, 23–25
Pronunciation, 9–10
  b, 12
  c, hard, 12
  c, soft, 11, 12
  comerse las eses, 11
  cu, 13
  d, hard, 13
  d, soft, 13
  diphthong, 13
  g, 10
  g, hard, 12
  g, soft, 12
  gue, 12
  gui, 12
  h, silent, 10
  j, 10, 13
  ll, 11, 13
  ñ, 10, 13
  qu, 13
  que, 12
  qui, 12

r, double, 14
r, rolled, 10, 14
regional variation, 11
s, 11, 14
u, 12, 13
ü, 13
umlaut, 13
v, 12
word stress, 15–16
x, 14
y, 11, 14
z, 9–10, 11, 14

¿Qué es?, 83–84
querer, 142
Questions
  yes/no questions, 44, 53
quisiera, 142
Quizzes
  daily life, 115–16
  describing people, 69–70
  describing places, 93–94
  entertainment, 221–22
  getting in touch with people, 157–58
  meeting people, 46–47
  phrases, 26–27
  talking about people, 137–38
  travel (arriving in new country), 202–3
  trip planning, 176–77

Race and ethnicity, 57, 58
  in Latin America, 58
  ser, 57
Reporting actions, 181–86
Requests
  asking and offering politely, 143, 191–95
  asking people to do things, 151–57

saber. *See* **conocer** vs. **saber**
salir, 173

Schedules, 104
ser, 184, 208
  race and ethnicity, 57
ser vs. **estar**, 43
  adjectives, 56
  appearance, 54
Sharing experiences, 180–81
¿Sí?, 144
si (conditional), 163–65
Small talk, 40–41
Spanish
  cyber, 23
  English influence on, 9
Spelling, 9–10
  alphabet and, 10
Subject pronouns, 23–25
  omission with verb, 25
  tú vs. **usted**, 24–25
  vosotros vs. **ustedes**, 25
Superlatives, 66–67
Symbols
  @, 23

Telephone, 143–47
tener, 127, 173, 184
tener que, 162–64
Time, telling, 97–100
Time expressions, 168, 209
  past, 183–84
Timetables, 111–14
Titles
  Señor, 31
  Señora, 31
  Señorita, 31
tomar, 211
Translations, 87
Transportation, 110–11
Travel
  arriving in a new country, 179–203
  asking and offering politely, 191–95

quiz, 202–3
    sharing experiences, 180–81
    trip planning, 159–77
Trip planning, 159–77
    advice for, 159–65
    future plans, 166–74
    needs and, 165–66
    quiz, 176–77
tú vs. **usted**, 24–25

Umlaut, 13
usted vs. **tú**, 24–25
ustedes vs. **vosotros**, 25

venir, 173
ver, 184, 208
Verb tense
    conditional, 194
    imperative, 152–57, 194
    imperfect, 207–10
    present, 106–10, 112, 121, 127, 142
    present progressive, 130–36
    preterite, 182–86
    simple future, 172–74
Verbs, 25–26
    -ar, 25–26, 107–8, 152, 172, 182, 208
    cognates, 8
    endings, 25–26
    -er, 25–26, 107–8, 152, 172, 182, 208

-ir, 25–26, 107–8, 172, 182, 208
    irregular, 109, 112, 121, 127, 153, 173,
        184–86, 208
    mood, 25
    stem-changing, 193
    tense, 25 (*See also* Verb tense)
Vocabulary
    computer Spanish, 154
    excuse me, 74
    expressing "types of," 82
    hello, 144
    leísmo, 189
    meanings of **a**, 170
    money, 217
    multiple meanings, 211
    pauses, 32
    shortened words, 218
    what's up, 42
vosotros vs. **ustedes**, 25
Vowels
    diphthongs, 13, 14–15
    pronunciation, 12

Weather, 147–50
Word stress, 15–16
Workplaces, 124–26

Yes/no answers, 78–79
Yes/no questions, 44